A HANDBOOK
on
THE LETTER FROM JUDE
and
THE SECOND LETTER FROM PETER

The Handbooks in the **UBS Handbook Series** are detailed commentaries providing valuable exegetical, historical, cultural, and linguistic information on the books of the Bible. They are prepared primarily to assist practicing Bible translators as they carry out the important task of putting God's Word into the many languages spoken in the world today. The text is discussed verse by verse and is accompanied by running text in at least one modern English translation.

Over the years church leaders and Bible readers have found the UBS Handbooks to be useful for their own study of the Scriptures. Many of the issues Bible translators must address when trying to communicate the Bible's message to modern readers are the ones Bible students must address when approaching the Bible text as part of their own private study and devotions.

The Handbooks will continue to be prepared primarily for translators, but we are confident that they will be useful to a wider audience, helping all who use them to gain a better understanding of the Bible message.

Helps for Translators

UBS Handbook Series:

A Handbook on . . .

Guides:

A Translator's Guide to . . .

Technical Helps:

The Letter from Jude and The Second Letter from Peter

by Daniel C. Arichea
and Howard A. Hatton

UBS Handbook Series

United Bible Societies
New York

Books in the series of **Helps for Translators** may be ordered from a national Bible Society or from either of the following centers:

United Bible Societies
European Production Fund
D-70520 Stuttgart 80
Postfach 81 03 40
Germany

United Bible Societies
1865 Broadway
New York, NY 10023
U. S. A.

L. C. Cataloging-in-Publication Data:

Arichea, Daniel C.
    A handbook on the letter from Jude and the second letter from Peter / by Daniel C. Arichea and Howard A. Hatton.
        p.   cm. — (UBS handbook series) (Helps for translators)
    Includes bibliographical references.
    ISBN 0-8267-0172-8
    1. Bible. N.T. Jude—Commentaries. 2. Bible. N.T. Jude—Translating. 3. Bible. N.T. Peter, 2nd—Commentaries. 4. Bible. N.T. Peter, 2nd—Translating. I. Hatton, Howard, 1929-   .
    II. Title. III. Title: Letter from Jude and the second letter from Peter. IV. Series. V. Series: Helps for translators.
    BS2815.3.A85   1993
    227'.93077—dc20   93-18768
                                                                        CIP

ABS-1993-750-CM-1-105035

Contents

CONTENTS

Preface

This Handbook, like others in the series, concentrates on exegetical information important for translators, and it attempts to indicate possible solutions for translational problems related to language or culture. The authors do not consciously attempt to provide help that other theologians and scholars may seek but which is not directly related to the translation task. Such information is normally sought elsewhere. However, many church leaders and interested Bible readers have found these Handbooks useful and informative, and we hope that this volume will be no exception.

The format of *A Handbook on The Letter from Jude and The Second Letter from Peter* follows the general pattern of earlier volumes in the series. The RSV and TEV texts are presented in parallel columns, first in larger segments that will make possible an overview of each section of discourse, and then in bold print, normally verse by verse, followed by detailed comments and discussion. RSV serves as the base upon which the discussion takes place, and quotations from the verse under discussion are printed in **boldface**. Quotations from other verses of RSV and from other versions are printed between quotation marks and in normal typeface. TEV serves as a primary model of how a translation may take shape; however, many other versions are provided as well, especially where they offer models that may be more satisfactory than those of TEV.

A limited Bibliography is included for the benefit of those interested in further study. The Glossary explains technical terms according to their usage in this volume. The translator may find it useful to read through the Glossary in order to become aware of the specialized way in which certain terms are used. An Index gives the location by page number of some of the important words and subjects discussed in the Handbook, especially where the Handbook provides the translator with help in rendering these concepts into the receptor language.

The editor of the UBS Handbook Series continues to seek comments from translators and others who use these books, so that future volumes may benefit and may better serve the needs of the readers.

Abbreviations Used

Translating Jude and 2 Peter

The Occasions for These Letters

The Second letter from Peter and *The Letter from Jude* have similar purposes. They are written to believers who are besieged by people who teach false doctrines among them.

The Second letter from Peter is addressed to Christians in general. The recipients are referred to as people "who have obtained a faith of equal standing with ours" (1.1). There is no other description found in the letter nor is there any mention of any geographical location.

From the letter itself it is clear that these Christians were troubled by the activities of teachers who "bring in destructive heresies" and who deny "the Master who bought them" (2.1). An example of the teaching of these false teachers is the denial of the second coming of Jesus Christ (chapter 3). The letter was therefore written to warn these Christians about the false teachers and to disprove some of their false doctrines.

Jude is also a general letter. The recipients of the letter are described as "those who have been called, beloved in God the Father and kept for Jesus Christ" (verse 1). Unlike 2 Peter, the deceivers are not exactly identified as false teachers but as "ungodly persons who pervert the grace of our God into licentiousness" (verse 4), who "defile the flesh," and who "reject authority" (verse 8). They are grumblers and use flattery to get their own way (verse 16).

As in 2 Peter, there is no geographical location found in Jude.

Authorship

The letter of 2 Peter makes clear that it is written by the same person who wrote 1 Peter; in fact it refers to a first letter (see 2 Peter 3.1). Furthermore, the letter includes material to show that the author of the letter is the apostle Peter: there is a reference to the transfiguration (1.16-18, which echoes Mark 9.2-7 and parallels) as well as to Jesus' statement about Peter's death (1.14), which seems to refer to John 21.17b-19. The authors of this Handbook are of course aware of current scholarly discussions on the authorship of 2 Peter, particularly the scholarly consensus that 2 Peter is a pseudonymous letter that was written after Peter was martyred. Any respectable commentary will give a good discussion on this issue. For the sake of convenience as well as respect for the tradition of the church, the author of 2 Peter will be simply referred to as Peter.

Jude on the other hand is the only letter in the New Testament that bears that name. The author identifies himself as a "servant of Jesus Christ and brother of James" (verse 1). Other than the brief autobiographical description of the author, there is no clue as to his identity. This has led scholars to suggest various theories as to who this Jude really was. Among the noteworthy suggestions are the following:

1. Jude is identified with the brother of Jesus who is mentioned in the Gospels (Matt 13.55; Mark 6.3). If this is the case, then the James who is Jude's brother should be identified with James the brother of Jesus, who is also mentioned in the above references. This position is held by many scholars both past and present, although not all of them necessarily hold the view that it was this same Jude who wrote the letter. Some in fact believe that the letter could have been written by a disciple of Jude who wrote under Jude's name.

It should be noted that Jude identifies himself, not as the brother of Jesus, but as his servant. However, according to some scholars, the brothers of Jesus probably avoided identifying themselves as his brothers in order that their authority would not be based on blood relationships.

2. Jude is identified with the apostle who in the Greek is called literally "Judas of James" and who is mentioned in Luke 6.16 and Acts 1.13. It should be noted, however, that the author of this letter does not call himself an apostle.

3. Other possibilities mentioned are:
   (a) the apostle Thomas, who in Syrian tradition is known as Judas Thomas or Judas the Twin;
   (b) Judas Barsabbas, who is mentioned in Acts 15.22,27,32;
   (c) "Judas of James," who was the third bishop of Jerusalem.

Of these positions the first remains the most probable, although it does not necessarily follow that Jude the brother of Jesus wrote the present letter. More likely it was written by a Christian leader who wrote under Jude's name. It was fairly common at that time to write under the name of a well-known figure who had recently passed away.

Any good commentary on Jude will have a long discussion on the whole question of authorship, and it is worthwhile for translators to consult such commentaries so that they may know the reasons for the various theories put forward by scholars. Fortunately, however, it is not necessary for translators to come to a definite conclusion as to the identity of the author of this letter before they can translate it meaningfully.

In this Handbook the author will simply be referred to as Jude, following the long tradition of the church.

The Literary Relationship between Jude and 2 Peter

One question that may be asked is, why put Jude and 2 Peter together in one Handbook? The answer is that there is an obvious connection between these two letters, as shown when the following parts are compared:

Jude	2 Peter
verse 2	1.2
verse 3	1.4
verse 5a	1.12
verses 5b-19	2.1–3.3
verse 24	3.14

Translators will do well to translate the parallel parts together in order to do justice to the similarities. At the same time translators should guard against possibilities of copying the text of one into the other and should therefore be careful to preserve the differences between the two materials.

A further implication of the above relationship is how to arrange the order of the books in the Handbook. The most obvious choice is to follow the biblical order, which of course has 2 Peter before Jude. However, an in-depth study of the relationships of these two letters has led many scholars to conclude that 2 Peter is in fact influenced by Jude, and that therefore Jude is prior to 2 Peter. Therefore there is value in translating Jude before 2 Peter, so that translators can then refer back to Jude when they are working with 2 Peter. This latter position has been adopted for this Handbook. However, it should be stressed that the two books should appear in their usual order when translated and included in a printing of the New Testament.

Special Features of the Letters and the Translation Task

A particular feature of 2 Peter is that it is a testament, that is, a statement of some kind made by a person who expects to die soon. Parts of the Bible that may be classified under this type of literature are Deuteronomy (which is the farewell speech of Moses), Paul's farewell speech to the Ephesians (Acts 20.17-38), and Jesus' farewell speech in John 13–17. Translators will do well to pay attention to this in order to determine whether in fact there are similar types of literature in their own languages, and whether such types can influence their translation of this letter.

As to style, scholars have noticed that 2 Peter is characterized by long sentences and elaborate constructions. These are all attributed to Greek influences, which have also somewhat influenced the contents of the letter. But in contrast to 2 Peter, Jude seems to use simpler constructions, although not lacking in eloquence and in figurative language (see especially verses 12-13, where the figures of clouds, wind, fruitless trees, waves, and stars are used quite effectively to describe the state of the godless people). Translators will need to pay close attention to these stylistic features in order to treat them adequately in the translation task.

Like many of the other New Testament letters, these two letters contain many theological terms and expressions as well. Examples from the first chapter of 2 Peter are "righteousness of our God and Savior Jesus Christ" 1.1), "knowledge of God and of Jesus our Lord" (1.2), "divine power" (1.3), "called us to his own glory and excellence" (1.3), "become partakers of the divine nature" (1.4), "eternal kingdom of our Lord and Savior Jesus Christ" (1.11), and "the Majestic Glory" (1.17). The Handbook analyses these terms and suggests possible actors and goals where these are left implicit in the text.

It is the hope of the authors that this Handbook will help in making the task of understanding and translating these letters much easier and more enjoyable.

The Letter from Jude

Authorship

For a discussion of the problem of identifying the author, see pages 1 and following.

Contents and Section Headings

There are many ways of outlining this letter. The outline suggested below is followed in this Handbook:

1-2 Salutation
3-23 Body of the letter
    3-4 Purpose of the letter: to warn them about godless people
    5-7 Three Old Testament examples of how God deals with rebellious people
    8-16 The godlessness of the people emphasized through the use of Old Testament examples
    17-23 Ethical guidance for the recipients of the letter
24-25 Doxology

As far as section headings are concerned, translators may want to consult several versions that make use of this feature. If the TEV section headings are used as both an outline of the letter and as a model, translators may wish to use alternative ways of rendering the sections headings, and some suggestions will be made at the appropriate places in the Handbook.

Salutation
1-2

REVISED STANDARD VERSION	TODAY'S ENGLISH VERSION

1 Jude, a servant of Jesus Christ and brother of James,
  To those who are called, beloved in God the Father and kept for Jesus Christ:
  2 May mercy, peace, and love be multiplied to you.
	1 From Jude, servant of Jesus Christ, and brother of James—
	  To those who have been called by God, who live in the love of God the Father and the protection of Jesus Christ:
	  2 May mercy, peace, and love be yours in full measure.

Jude is a letter; it conforms to the literary structure of a letter of that time. The opening usually consisted of the following parts:

(1) the name of the author, which is in the third person;

(2) a description of the author, including his qualifications;

(3) the name or description of those who receive the letter;

(4) words of greeting.

These elements are clearly marked in this short letter. The author identifies himself as **Jude** and then describes himself as **a servant of Jesus Christ** and also as the **brother of James**. The recipients of the letter are then identified as **those who are called, beloved in God the Father and kept for Jesus Christ**. And finally verse 2 contains the greeting, **May mercy, peace, and love be multiplied to you.**

SECTION HEADING. TEV has no section heading. Translators may wish to use "Salutation" as in the outline of Jude, or "Greetings"; a full clause may be "Jude greets his readers."

1	RSV	TEV
	Jude, a servant of Jesus Christ and brother of James,	From Jude, servant of Jesus Christ, and brother of James—
	To those who are called, beloved in God the Father and kept for Jesus Christ:	To those who have been called by God, who live in the love of God the Father and the protection of Jesus Christ:

For a discussion of the identity of **Jude**, see the introduction, "Translating Jude and 2 Peter," page 1.

The expression **servant of Jesus Christ** is a popular formula in the opening parts of letters in the New Testament (see Rom 1.1; Phil 1.1; James 1.1; 2 Peter 1.1; also Gal 1.10; 2 Tim 2.24; 1 Cor 7.22; Eph 6.6). Many Old Testament characters are identified as "servants of God," which means that they understand their calling to be that of serving God and doing his will. In the New Testament this term is also used of Christians in general, suggesting that Christians have been freed by Christ from the slavery of sin and now belong to Jesus Christ as his slaves (1 Cor 7.23). In a special way the term is used of those who are called to a special task, indicating that the Christian leaders are an example in their life of the servant role that all of God's people are supposed to play. The term therefore includes the components of service, obedience, and complete surrender to Jesus Christ and recognition of his authority. Those who use this title for themselves are recognized as having some kind of authority in the Christian community, but this authority is based primarily on their call to serve Christ rather than on their personal qualities. Certain languages maintain a clear distinction between a person who works for a fixed salary and one who is a personal servant or attendant supported by his master, but who does not have a fixed salary. It is this latter term that should be used in this context, if it is necessary to make such a distinction. There are also languages where people will say "I am Jesus Christ's man," meaning "I work for Jesus Christ." In many languages it is impossible to maintain the structure **Jude, a servant of Jesus Christ and brother of James**, in which the descriptive expressions are simply placed alongside the name. In such a case we may translate this first section of the verse as "I, Jude, who am a servant of Jesus Christ, and a (younger) brother of James . . . ."

Some translators will find it helpful to begin this epistle in a way that is natural to letter writing in their own languages. So it may be necessary to start this letter in a different way from the English or Greek. In particular it may be desirable to adjust the third person reference to the writer to a first person reference, and the third person reference to his readers to second person reference. Examples are: "I, Jude, who am a servant of Jesus Christ and brother of James, write this letter to you . . ." or "This letter comes from Jude, who is a servant . . . ." It may also be necessary in certain languages to combine the opening clause with what follows and say, for example, "I, Jude, who am . . . write this letter to those people who . . ." or "to you who . . . ."

Jesus Christ is the usual Greek form of the name of Jesus. The word **Christ** comes from the word "Messiah," meaning God's promised King, but when it follows the name **Jesus**, it can be treated simply as a name and not as a title. The term **Christ** is a title if it is used with the definite article ("the Christ" or "the Messiah"). In some cases "Christ" may also function as a title when it comes before "Jesus." However, this doesn't seem to be the case in this letter.

The word **brother** is understood by some to mean "co-worker"; most probably, however, it is used here in its natural biological sense, "blood-brother." For identifying **James** see page 2. Since James is not described or identified in any way except by his name, this indicates that the readers of the letter had a very clear idea as to who he was, and that he was a famous personality at that time.

In some languages it is necessary to state whether Jude is the older or younger brother of James. This is not so with Greek, and therefore the text does not clearly give us this information. One clue is sometimes the order in which names are mentioned, and since in Matt 13.55 James is mentioned ahead of Jude, then perhaps Jude is the younger brother of James.

The intended readers of Jude's letter are not identified, either in terms of who they are or where they come from. This is one reason why it has been suggested that this letter is a "general" letter, addressed to the whole church and to Christians everywhere. However, the letter deals with certain particular problems, as we shall see; and this seems to indicate that Jude had a particular audience in mind.

Although Jude does not identify his readers, he describes them in three ways: they are **called**, they are **beloved in God the Father**, and they are **kept for Jesus Christ**. It should be noted that these three expressions are influenced by and perhaps derived from the passages in Isaiah known as the Servant Songs, where Israel is described in the same manner, that is, called, loved, and kept by God (for "called," see Isa 41.9; 42.6; 48.12; for "loved," see 42.1; 43.4; for "kept," see 42.6; 49.8). It is a common practice among New Testament writers to take descriptions of Israel as the people of God and apply these to Christians. They could do this because of the understanding that the Old

Testament promises are fulfilled in Christ, and that those who believe in Christ are in a real sense God's people.

In the Greek text, **called** comes last in the series, after **beloved** and **kept**. However, it is clear that **called** is intended both in grammar and in meaning to be primary in the series, and most translations therefore reflect this understanding (for instance, Phillips [Phps] "to those who have obeyed the call, who are loved by God the Father and kept in the faith . . .").

The word translated **called** is a technical term that in the New Testament is almost identical in meaning with "Christians." In much the same way that the Israelites were called by God to become his people, and were called out of slavery in Egypt in order to possess the promised land, so also Christians are called by God from a life of sin and evil to a new life of godliness. The use of this term for Christians puts a focus on the fact that it is God who takes the initiative in calling people to trust in him, and that when people respond in faith to this call of God, then they become God's children. In the New Testament God calls people primarily to trust in Christ and become Christ's followers. In languages that do not use the passive, translators will need to restructure this event word and say ". . . whom God has called" or "God has called you."

The expression **beloved in God the Father** is difficult to understand and has been the subject of much discussion. In the New Testament the expression "in God" is rarely used. A literal translation of the whole expression can give rise to the false meaning "loved (by Jude) in God the Father." Jude of course was not referring to his love for his readers but to God's love for them. The preposition "in" can be understood to mean either "by" (as the RSV footnote indicates), hence "loved by God the Father" (Phps), or else "in the sphere of." This latter meaning seems to be reflected in TEV "who live in the love of God," which means that they live in the consciousness of God's love for them, and as a result they experience God's love and presence with them. A similar expression appears in verse 21 of this same letter. Another way to render this expression is "who live knowing that God loves them (you)" or "who live with the certainty that God loves them (you)."

It should be noted further that **beloved** is a perfect participle in Greek, which includes as an element of its meaning the continuing effect of God's love for these people.

The expression **kept for Jesus Christ** translates an expression in which the name Jesus Christ is in the dative case and no preposition is used. Since there are several prepositions that can go with the dative case when translated, this has resulted in various interpretations of this phrase:

1. RSV represents one interpretation. In this case, **kept** has God as the unstated agent, and the whole expression can be understood as "kept safe by God until the coming of Jesus Christ," during which time they will have full fellowship with him (Christ). A less likely sense is "kept safe by God for the sake of Jesus Christ."

2. TEV represents a second interpretation, where the dative is understood as instrumental: "kept by Jesus Christ," hence "live . . . in the protection of Jesus Christ" or "whom Jesus Christ protects (or keeps safe)." In this case

the expression can mean that Christ keeps them safe from the influence of the godless people who threaten their faith (which Jude will discuss later in the letter). If we take the phrase as having a future sense, then it means that Christ keeps them safe in the present so that they can be with him when he comes again. This is probably the more likely interpretation.

3. A third interpretation takes "in" to be the preposition for the dative form. "In Christ" is a favorite expression in the letters of Paul and indicates the Christian's close relationship with Christ; hence "living in union with (or united to) Christ." Some translations have echoed this position, as, for example, Goodspeed's *American Translation* (AT) "kept through union with Jesus Christ."

Like **beloved** referred to above, **kept** is a perfect participle which carries the meaning that those addressed continue to be the object of Christ's (or God's) care and protection.

One further note: in the Greek text verses 1 and 2 form one rather long sentence; and it may be necessary to divide this into two or more sentences in order to achieve better communication with the audience. How this is done will depend on the requirements of the translator's language.

Two translation models for the whole verse are:

(1) I, Jude, who am a servant of Jesus Christ and a (younger) brother of James, write this letter to you whom God has called. You live with the sure knowledge that God the Father loves you, and that you are protected by Jesus Christ (Jesus Christ protects you.)

(2) I, Jude, who am a servant of Jesus Christ and a (younger) brother of James, write this letter to all of you fellow believers in Christ, who are loved by God the Father and are protected by Jesus Christ.

An example of the way the whole verse is handled in one major Asian language is:

Dear brothers and sisters, whom God the Father has called and loves very much, and whom Jesus Christ protects. I, Jude, write this letter to you and pray that God bestows his blessings, mercy, and peace on you bountifully.

It is also possible for the three elements ("God has called," "live with the sure knowledge that God the Father loves you," and "protected by Jesus Christ") to be arranged in a different sequence in order to arrive at a more smooth and natural rendering in the translator's language.

2   RSV   TEV

> May mercy, peace, and love be   May mercy, peace, and love be
> multiplied to you.   yours in full measure.

After the brief description of his readers, Jude now conveys his greetings
to them. The greeting formula that he uses varies somewhat from the
traditional greeting in the New Testament; instead of the usual three elements
of grace, mercy, and peace, Jude has **mercy, peace, and love**. **Mercy** is God's
compassion and kindness, of which his saving action through Jesus Christ is
the best example. **Peace** is a popular word of greeting among Jews and denotes
the total well-being that results from a close relationship with God. In many
languages **peace** will be rendered idiomatically; for example, "have coolness
and peacefulness." **Love** may be interpreted as God's love for all people which
is made known through Jesus Christ, or as the love and concern of Christians
for one another. It is quite tempting to take these terms in their fullest
theological meaning; it must be remembered, however, that they are used here
as elements of a greeting formula and must be translated to fit their function
within such a formula.

Be multiplied to you is similar to the expression found in 1 Peter 1.2 and
is a distinctive feature of Jewish prayers (compare Dan 4.1; 6.25). It conveys
the hope that mercy, peace, and love will be bestowed to them continually and
in abundance. (Note Phps "May you ever experience more and more of mercy,
peace and love!")

Alternative translation models for this verse are as follows:

(1) May you ever experience more and more mercy, peace, and
love from God.

(2) I pray that God will continue to be good to you, so that your
well-being will increase, and that your love for one another
will continue to grow.

Body of the letter
(3-23)

Purpose of the letter: to warn them about godless people
3-4

                RSV   TEV

                                                      False Teachers

3 Beloved, being very eager to write to   3 My dear friends, I was doing my best to
you of our common salvation, I found it neces- write to you about the salvation we share in
sary to write appealing to you to contend for common, when I felt the need of writing at
the faith which was once for all delivered to   once to encourage you to fight on for the faith
the saints. 4 For admission has been secretly   which once and for all God has given to his

gained by some who long ago were designated for this condemnation, ungodly persons who pervert the grace of our God into licentiousness and deny our only Master and Lord, Jesus Christ.

people. 4 For some godless people have slipped in unnoticed among us, persons who distort the message about the grace of our God in order to excuse their immoral ways, and who reject Jesus Christ, our only Master and Lord. Long ago the Scriptures predicted the condemnation they have received.

The body of the letter begins with verse 3 and ends at verse 23. Here again Jude follows the usual letter structure, and at the outset he informs his readers of the occasion for the letter and his purpose in writing to them.

SECTION HEADING. The major heading, "Body of the letter," may have to be revised if it is used. For example, "The things Jude wants to tell (write to) the people" or "The material (substance, juice) of the letter." The section heading for verses 3-4 should be limited as on the outline; one can also say "Jude warns Christians about godless people" or simply "Godless people." If the heading is to cover verses 3-16 as in TEV, the heading "False Teachers" may also be rendered as "People who teach false (untrue) doctrines." See also the heading at 2 Peter 2.1.

3	RSV	TEV

Beloved, being very eager to write to you of our common salvation, I found it necessary to write appealing to you to contend for the faith which was once for all delivered to the saints.

My dear friends, I was doing my best to write to you about the salvation we share in common, when I felt the need of writing at once to encourage you to fight on for the faith which once and for all God has given to his people.

This verse can be interpreted in at least two ways:
1. Jude was engaged in writing a general letter about **our common salvation**, when something happened that made him abandon this project and write at once in order to deal with the emergency situation. TEV leans toward this interpretation, and so also does the New English Bible (NEB) "I was fully engaged in writing to you about our salvation . . . when it became urgently necessary to write at once . . . ." This means that the letter that we have is not the letter that Jude originally planned to write; and there is no way of knowing whether such a letter was ever written.

Arguments for this interpretation include the following: Firstly, there is a difference of tense between the two infinitives "to write"; the first is present, which can mean that the action was not completed, while the second is aorist, which can refer to a completed act. This seems to make a distinction between an intention and an action that was carried through. Secondly, the structure of the verse seems to suggest a sharp contrast between a general letter or essay on the Christian faith and a letter written for the particular purpose of encouraging people to defend their faith. Thirdly, the shortness of the letter and the problems that it deals with tend to favor the position that this is indeed a letter dealing with particular problems rather than a general letter.

2. Jude had planned to write, and in fact was in the process of writing, when an emergency situation arose in the Christian communities to whom he was writing. Because of this he was compelled to carry out his plan much more quickly. This seems to be the position taken by RSV. (So also the translation by Knox, "As one who is ever ready to write to you . . . I am compelled to send you this letter . . . .") This means that the letter we have is identical with the general letter that Jude initially wanted to write.

Arguments put forward in support of this position include the following: Firstly, the expression **our common salvation** in the first part of the verse seems to mean the same thing as **the faith which was once for all delivered to the saints** in the second part. If this is so, then the two parts of the verse are parallel to each other. Then secondly, the second part of the verse can be understood simply as an action to carry out the intention expressed in the first part. Jude had a real desire to write to his readers, and because of special circumstances he has written faster than he originally intended.

Both interpretations are equally valid, and translators may choose either one. But in either case, adjustments will have to be made in the translation to give clear expression to that interpretation. As noted above, TEV as it now stands leans toward the first interpretation, although it can still be taken as agreeing with the second. On the other hand, RSV leans toward the second interpretation, but again it can also be taken as agreeing with the first.

Beloved is a word that is frequently used by New Testament writers to address their readers. As a form of address it expresses the writer's feeling of endearment toward his readers, hence TEV "My dear friends." Jude also uses it here as a signal to his readers that this is the beginning of the body of his letter. In some languages **Beloved** will be rendered "My dear fellow Christians." In other languages this word will be expressed idiomatically; for example, "My dear elders and youngers."

Being very eager is a Greek expression that can mean either "to be very eager to" or "to make every effort to," that is, "to try as hard as one can." The first of these focuses on Jude's intention, while the second makes it possible to understand that Jude was already engaged in writing. Here again, the choice out of the two possibilities discussed above will determine the meaning that is chosen for this expression.

As noted above, **to write** is a present infinitive and suggests a more leisurely style, as contrasted with the aorist in the second part of the verse, which suggests urgency.

Our common salvation (TEV "we share in common") means the salvation that is held in common by both Jude and his readers, or the salvation that is experienced by all Christians, including Jude and his readers. **Our** should therefore be taken as inclusive in languages that make a distinction between the exclusive and the inclusive first person plural pronoun—that is, Jude together with his readers, as contrasted to exclusive, which would be Jude only and not including his readers.

The term **salvation** has both its negative and positive aspects. Negatively it refers to being rescued from a bad or disadvantageous situation. Positively it is the gift of new life or new possibilities.

In the Gospels "salvation" primarily means being rescued from sickness and being given new health and wholeness. (The word for "heal" is the same word as that for "save.") In the rest of the New Testament, however, "salvation" refers to being rescued from the power of sin and being given new life, that is, a life that is in accord with what God has promised. This new life is something Christians experience at present, although they do not yet experience it in its completeness. It is in the end time when this experience of the new life will be full and complete through Jesus Christ. Theologically speaking, this **salvation** or new life has both a present and a future reference: it is a present experience, but it remains to be completed in the future, at the end of time. This latter interpretation may be a possibility in this letter, and especially in 2 Peter, considering its focus on the end times. However, considering the situation of the intended readers of these letters, who have to contend with a pagan environment, and who are clearly a very small segment of the population, it is perhaps better to understand the positive aspect of salvation as the power to live in accordance with God's will in the midst of all the temptations and trials arising out of a pagan or non-Christian environment.

Another possibility is to understand **salvation** as a technical term referring to the Christian faith or the Christian religion. This is the position of some commentaries and is reflected in some translations; for example, Barclay (Brc) has "the faith which we all share." It is much more likely, however, that **salvation** here refers to the gift of new life through Jesus Christ. If this is so, other translation models for the phrase **our common salvation** are "the new life God has given to all of us through Jesus Christ" or "the new life we all share that comes from God through Jesus Christ."

The word for **necessary** includes the components of necessity and compulsion. Jude seems to suggest that he is rather hesitant to write, but because of necessity he must now write at once. This understanding is echoed in some translations; for example, Moffatt (Mft) "I am forced to write." The verb here is in the aorist tense, which contrasts with the present participle "being very eager." This tends to favor the interpretation that Jude had a change of plans. (See discussion at the beginning of this verse.)

The purpose of Jude writing immediately is to **appeal** to them **to contend for the faith**. The word translated **appeal** can also mean "exhort," "encourage," "admonish," or in a stronger sense, "urge." This may be expressed idiomatically as, for example, "give strength to your hearts." **To contend** translates a word that also means "to fight," "to defend," "to strive urgently," "to struggle for," "to uphold." The verb is found only here in the New Testament and comes originally from the athletic arena. Whether it is used as a metaphor here cannot now be determined. What is clear though is that it is used here not in a passive but in a very active sense: Jude is exhorting his readers not simply to defend the faith, but to fight for it and to actively promote it, not only with words but also in action. In the latter part of his letter he will give particular ways in which his readers should fight for the faith (verses 20-23).

What does **faith** mean in this case? This word is rich in meaning and is used in a variety of ways in the New Testament. Among its meanings are the following:

1. trust in and commitment to someone (usually a person's trust in Christ or in God);
2. believing something as true or valid;
3. a body of teaching, or doctrine;
4. a religious movement (such as the Christian faith, which is essentially the same as "the Christian religion");
5. a Christian virtue, that is, a trait or ability that a Christian receives as a result of his trust in Christ; and
6. conviction or certainty.

It seems that of the above, meanings 1, 3, and 4 fit the context best. If **faith** refers to "the Christian faith" or "the Christian religion," it may mean the same as "salvation" in the first part of the verse. On the other hand, it may refer to a body of doctrine that is understood as embodying the main tenets of Christian teaching and is therefore regarded by the Christian community as authoritative. Most commentaries favor this second interpretation.

It is very important that in translating **faith** here, it must be distinguished from "faith" that means trust in and commitment to God or Jesus Christ. **Faith** as Jude uses it here refers not to a person's response, but primarily to the content of what is believed, that is, Christian doctrine or teaching, or to the Christian faith as a religious movement. If we follow this interpretation, in many languages the phrase **contend for the faith** may be translated as "defend the Christian religion" or "strive hard to uphold the Christian doctrine (teaching)."

This faith is described as **once for all delivered to the saints**. The word for **delivered** means to "hand down," "pass on," "transmit," and is used in the handing down or transmitting of tradition or religious teaching from one generation to the next. The subject or doer is not named in the text; it is suggested that the agent here is either God or the apostles. **Once for all** emphasizes that this faith was given only once, and that when it was handed down, it was complete, and therefore it should be handed down to future generations without any change whatsoever. Another way of saying this is "one time for all times."

The saints is literally "the holy ones." The focus here is not on moral holiness, but on relationship with God; people are described as "holy" because they are called by God and are consecrated, or dedicated, to him. It is in this sense that "holy ones" is used as a term for God's people. In Jude, as well as in other parts of the New Testament, the term **saints** has become another name for Christians, that is, people who are called to trust in Christ and are dedicated to him. (See, for example, Acts 9.13,32,42; Rom 12.13; Heb 6.10.) That is why in TEV **saints** when used in this way is usually translated as "God's people."

As is the case in verses 1 and 2, it may be necessary in some cases to divide this long sentence into two or more sentences. Alternative translation models for this verse are:

(1) My dear fellow believers, I was making every effort (doing my best) to write to you about the new life we all share which comes from God through Jesus Christ, when I felt the urgent need to write to you at once. I wanted to encourage you to try even harder to uphold the things we believe as Christians. It is this faith which, once and for all (one time for all times), God has given to his people, and which cannot be changed.

(2) My dear fellow believers, I have been always ready to write to you about the new life we all share that comes from God through Jesus Christ. But now I feel compelled to write to you and encourage . . . .

(3) My dear fellow believers, I was making every effort to write to you about the new life we all share that comes from God through Jesus Christ. But now I feel urged to encourage you through this letter, so that you will try even harder to uphold the Christian faith. God has given this faith once and for all to his people, and it cannot be changed.

4   RSV   TEV

For admission has been secretly gained by some who long ago were designated for this condemnation, ungodly persons who pervert the grace of our God into licentiousness and deny our only Master and Lord, Jesus Christ.^a

^a Or *the only Master and our Lord Jesus Christ*

For some godless people have slipped in unnoticed among us, persons who distort the message about the grace of our God in order to excuse their immoral ways, and who reject Jesus Christ, our only Master and Lord. Long ago the Scriptures predicted the condemnation they have received.

The reason for the strong and urgent call to contend for the faith in verse 3 is now given in this verse. It is signaled by the connective **For**, which in this context means one of three things:
1. "I am writing you because . . .";
2. "I am doing this (that is, asking you to contend for the faith) because . . .";
3. "It (the faith) is in danger because . . ." (see NEB).
The faith is in danger because some people have been causing problems within the Christian community. Jude does not identify who these people are; however, the context suggests that these **ungodly persons** are somehow

distorting the Christian message, both in their teachings and in their actions. TEV understands these people to be primarily teachers, hence its heading for this section is "**False Teachers.**" It is possible to make the application more general than this, referring to "ungodly people" (the New International Version [NIV] has the heading "godless men").

There are two possible ways of handling this lack of identification in translation: The translator can leave all possibilities open, for example, by retaining "some ungodly people" in the translation, but then identify these people as teachers in the section heading. Or the translator can identify these people as teachers in the translation itself as, for example, "some godless teachers." As always, the decision will depend on the intended audience; sufficient information should be included in the translation to make it understandable to those who will read it.

Even though Jude does not directly identify these godless people, he does mention four accusations against them.

1. First of all, they are intruders who have **secretly gained admission** to the church. The Greek verb here means "to sneak in under false pretenses," "to slip in unnoticed," "to slip in stealthily," "to infiltrate." This does not mean that these people are not members of the church; they probably are members, but they have become so by sinister means, not by legitimate means. It is as if they have smuggled themselves into the Christian community. The meaning and impact of the Greek verb is captured in some translations such as NEB "wormed their way in," and Phps "surreptitiously entered the Church." The verb is in the aorist tense but with a perfect force; that is, while it is aorist in form, it is perfect in meaning. This means that, while these people sneaked in at some time in the past, the effect of their action is still felt very strongly in the church.

2. Secondly, these people were long ago **designated for . . . condemnation**. This clause is difficult to analyze and presents many potential problems for translators. **Long ago** refers to a period of time in the distant past, although the text offers no clear clue as to when this actually occurred. This word may also be expressed as "in older times," "years that are gone," or "many generations ago." The word translated **designated** is literally "wrote beforehand," hence TEV "predicted." The text does not say from whom or from where this prediction comes, but there are at least three possibilities. (a) This may be an allusion to the book of 1 Enoch (see the description in the comments on verse 6). (b) This may refer to the predictions of the apostles (see verses 17-18 and comments). (c) The reference here may be to the Old Testament in general, which contains many statements regarding the punishment of false prophets. This also fits the use of **long ago**, which, as we have seen, usually denotes a long interval of time. This seems to be the most likely interpretation and is reflected in TEV, which identifies the source of the predictions as "the Scriptures." (So also NEB, "the very men whom Scripture long ago marked down for the doom they have incurred.") The **Scriptures** may also be expressed as "the holy writings."

The expression **this condemnation** is strange, since **this** marks the **condemnation** as old information, whereas Jude has just begun his letter and

16

has not as yet mentioned anything about condemnation. Here again, there are three possibilities: (a) This may be a reference to verse 3b, where Jude mentions fighting for the faith, and where he perhaps assumes the certain and imminent defeat of the godless. This is reading too much into verse 3b, however. (b) **This** may look forward to the condemnation of the people mentioned in verse 15; however, this seems to be too remote to establish any clear connections. (c) **This condemnation** may refer to the punishment that is mentioned in verses 5-7.

In view of the difficulty of determining what **this** refers to, it is possible and even advisable to restructure the clause and introduce **condemnation** as new information; for example, "the condemnation they will receive," or "the punishment that God will bestow on them," or "that God will punish them." (See TEV "the condemnation they have received," Knox "destined thus to incur condemnation.")

3. Thirdly, these people are **ungodly persons who pervert the grace of . . . God**. The word **ungodly** means "impious," "godless." It is a favorite word of Jude; he uses it six times, in various forms but always with the same meaning. It should, however, be noted that the Book of Enoch from which Jude quotes also uses this same word, and perhaps Jude's use of the word is directly influenced by the Greek translation of the Book of Enoch.

In wisdom literature (for example, in the Book of Proverbs) "ungodliness" has two basic elements: irreverence toward God and unrighteous or evil conduct as a result of such an attitude. It is related to lawlessness, or utter disregard for the law, which results in a person doing anything he or she wants to do. This word then is a very appropriate description of the people whose wickedness and lawless actions are mentioned by Jude in the latter part of his letter (see verses 15 and 18). Some ways of translating **ungodly persons** are: "people who disobey God," "people who have no use for God," or "people who are not faithful to God."

It should be noted that in TEV "godless" has been moved to the first part of the verse, and it thus functions as a general description of these people. (So also Knox "Godless men.") This adjustment makes it possible to identify immediately who these people are, and eliminates the translation problem created by the indefinite **some**.

The ungodliness of these people is manifested in the fact that they **pervert the grace of our God**. The word translated **pervert** also means "change," "alter" (TEV "distort,"), that is, make something into what it is not. **Licentiousness**, on the other hand, translates a word that stands generally for sensuality or immorality but which refers in particular to sexual indulgence, hence "immoral ways (TEV)," "evil sexual practices," or "indecent conduct."

But what does the whole expression **pervert the grace of our God into licentiousness** mean? There are two ways to understand the preposition **into**. First, it can express purpose or intention. This makes possible a translation such as "who pervert the grace of our God, in order that they can do immoral things," or as in TEV "distort the message about the grace of our God in order to excuse their immoral ways." Secondly, it can express result. This means that their perversion of the grace of God results in their engaging in immoral acts.

17

Of these two possibilities the first seems more likely, and it is echoed in TEV and in some other translations.

This leads us to a discussion of the meaning of the expression **the grace of God**. "Grace" is one of those biblical words that has a variety of meanings. In the New Testament one of its primary meanings is the undeserved love of God, that is, God's love for people even though they don't deserve to be loved. Taken in this sense it means that the godless people are using God's gracious love as an excuse for engaging in sinful and immoral actions. They seem to think that, since God loves people so much that he forgives them of their sins, people can commit as many sins as they like, for the more they sin the more God loves them. The clause can then be translated thus: "who distort the message about God's love and use it as an excuse for their immoral behavior." Another possibility is to interpret **grace** as referring to the Christian message, or to the Christian faith in general, and therefore having the same meaning as **faith** in verse 3. By their words and deeds these people have distorted the Christian message and have used it as an excuse for their utter disregard of acceptable Christian conduct. The clause can then be restructured as follows: "who distort the message of the Christian faith so that they can do evil sexual things." Either one is possible, but the first alternative seems more appropriate.

4. Finally, these people are indicted for denying Jesus Christ himself. While it is possible to take this as a further description of ungodliness, it is more likely that this is another characteristic of the people themselves. The word **deny** also means "disown," "repudiate," "reject." The text does not say how this denial is brought about; it is clear from the whole letter, however, that this denial is in both word and deed.

The word translated **Master** is a term used for the owner of household slaves (see for example 2 Peter 2.1; also Matt 10.25; Mark 13.27; Luke 13.25). In the present context **Master** indicates that Christians are owned by Christ and submit to his rule. The word **only** emphasizes the fact that Christians know only one Master, and that this Master tolerates no rival. The intimate relationship between Christians and their Master is indicated by the pronoun **our**, which here should be understood as inclusive, referring to both Jude and his readers.

Lord is one of the prominent titles used of Jesus in the New Testament. In the Greek translation of the Old Testament (the Septuagint, usually abbreviated LXX), "Lord" is the word used to translate the personal name of God (YHWH or Yahweh). In addressing Jesus as "Lord" Christians are elevating him to the level of God and indicating that they can give to Jesus the same loyalty that they give to God. It is also possible that the term **Lord** is used here with the Greek background in mind (that is, "Master," "owner," or "one who commands"). Since it can be assumed that many of Jude's readers are non-Jews, then they would understand the term "Lord" in this manner. The terms **Master** and **Lord** here seem to be almost synonymous in meaning. Translators should look for two synonyms in the receptor language. For example, alternative translation models in English for **our only Master and Lord** are "our only Leader and Commander" or "our only Chief and Ruler."

For **Jesus Christ** see comments on verse 1.

As indicated by the footnote of RSV, there are two ways of reading this part of verse 4. This is due to the order of words in the Greek text, which is translated literally in the RSV footnote: "the only Master and our Lord Jesus Christ." The question is, does this expression refer to two entities or to one? In other words, is **Master** different from **Lord**, or do both titles refer to **Jesus Christ**? Some commentaries take the first of these alternatives, with **Master** referring to God, and **Lord** referring to Jesus Christ. They justify this by the following reasons:

1. The order of the Greek text favors such an interpretation.
2. The word "only" is used in the Old Testament to refer to God, and this usage is also found in Jude 25. It is therefore probable that this is the usage here also.
3. The word for "Master" is used of God in the Bible rather than of Jesus Christ (for example, Luke 2.29; Acts 4.24; Rev 6.10).
4. In similar formulas in Jude, both God and Jesus Christ are normally included (see for example verses 1, 21, 25).

Arguments for the other alternative include the following:

1. The Greek definite article is present only before **Master**, which seems to suggest that both **Master** and **Lord** refer to the same person. It must be noted, however, that this argument is not really decisive, since the article is often omitted before "God" or "Lord," and its omission before **Lord** here may be simply a formal feature of the Greek and nothing else.
2. In 2 Peter 2.1, where Jude 4 is quoted, "Master" clearly refers to Jesus Christ. While this is not decisive in the sense that 2 Peter cannot be used to determine the meaning in Jude, it nevertheless does show that an early reader of Jude understood the term **Master** as referring to Christ.
3. Considering the structure of the whole expression, it seems much more natural to take both **Master** and **Lord** as parallels and therefore as titles referring to the only person mentioned, namely **Jesus Christ**.

A careful consideration of the evidence leads to the conclusion that the second of these alternatives is preferable, that is, that **Master** and **Lord** both refer to one person, namely, **Jesus Christ**.

Two other things need to be mentioned that are of relevance to translation. First, we should notice the difference between RSV and TEV in the ordering of events. RSV retains the order of the Greek text, whereas TEV restructures the Greek text in order to achieve a more natural translation into English. In much the same way translators should try to come up with the most natural translation in their language, even though this means changing the order of the Greek text. Secondly, the whole verse is one complicated sentence in the Greek; this is retained in RSV, whereas TEV has broken it into two sentences. Here again, for many languages translators should divide the sentence into two or more sentences, depending on the requirements of their language and the needs of the intended audience.

Taking into consideration the whole discussion of this verse, here are three possible translation models:

> (1) I am writing to you because certain godless people (people who disobey God) who teach false doctrines have slipped in among us without our noticing them. These are people whom God said many generations ago in the holy scriptures (writings) that he would punish. They distort the Christian message (about God's love, or favor) in order to have an excuse for doing evil sexual practices. They also reject Jesus Christ, our only Master and Lord (or, Chief and Ruler).
>
> (2) I am asking you to defend the Christian faith because certain godless people who teach false doctrines have . . . .
>
> (3) The Christian faith is in danger because certain godless people . . . .

Three Old Testament examples of how God deals with rebellious people
5-7

RSV	TEV
5 Now I desire to remind you, though you were once for all fully informed, that he who saved people out of the land of Egypt, afterward destroyed those who did not believe. 6 And the angels that did not keep their own position but left their proper dwelling have been kept by him in eternal chains in the nether gloom until the judgment of the great day; 7 just as Sodom and Gomorrah and the surrounding cities, which likewise acted immorally and indulged in unnatural lust, serve as an example by undergoing a punishment of eternal fire.	5 For even though you know all this, I want to remind you of how the Lord once rescued the people of Israel from Egypt, but afterward destroyed those who did not believe. 6 Remember the angels who did not stay within the limits of their proper authority, but abandoned their own dwelling place: they are bound with eternal chains in the darkness below, where God is keeping them for that great Day on which they will be condemned. 7 Remember Sodom and Gomorrah, and the nearby towns, whose people acted as those angels did and indulged in sexual immorality and perversion: they suffer the punishment of eternal fire as a plain warning to all.

After stating the problem regarding the godless people, Jude proceeds to give three examples from the Old Testament of how God deals with those who turn away from him in rebellion and indulge in wickedness. These examples are: the unbelieving Israelites in the desert (verse 5), the rebellious angels (verse 6), and the cities of Sodom and Gomorrah (verse 7). Jude's aim is twofold: he wants to affirm again that the godless people will incur punishment from God, and he wants to warn his readers that they will also receive the same punishment if they follow their bad example.

These verses, together with verses 8-16, form a single unit that is known in Greek letters as "the fuller disclosure formula," that is, a formula for introducing more details of information than that already known by the hearers. It usually starts with the expression "I wish you to know that." Jude, in his desire to be polite to his readers, revises the formula to **I desire to remind you**.

Of concern to translators is the fact that verses 5-7 form one long sentence in the Greek, with **the Lord** in verse 5 as the subject of the whole sentence. It is advisable and even necessary to divide this into shorter sentences in order to achieve a translation that is both easy to understand and appropriate to the stylistic and formal requirements of the language of the translation.

SECTION HEADING. The long heading in the outline may be reduced; for example, "Three groups of ungodly people," "How God deals with rebellious people," "These people behaved wrongly," or "God punished these evil people."

5	RSV	TEV

RSV

Now I desire to remind you, though you were once for all fully informed, that he[b] who saved people out of the land of Egypt, afterward destroyed those who did not believe.

[b] Ancient authorities read *Jesus* or *the Lord* or *God*

TEV

For even though you know all this, I want to remind you of how the Lord[a] once rescued the people of Israel from Egypt, but afterward destroyed those who did not believe.

[a] the Lord; *some manuscripts have* Jesus, *which in Greek is the same as* Joshua.

As noted above, **Now I desire to remind you** is a revision of a traditional formula that would open this part of the Greek letter. **Desire** can be "wish," or "want" (TEV). **Remind** can also be "cause you to remember," "bring again to your attention," "bring to your mind," or "cause you to think about again." It is a popular term in New Testament letters (as for example Rom 15.15; 1 Cor 11.2; 2 Thes 2.5; 2 Tim 2.8,14; Titus 3.1; 2 Peter 1.12; Rev 3.3), where the readers are reminded of the content of the Christian message; in much the same way, Old Testament writers reminded their readers to keep on remembering God's mighty acts and his commandments (as for example Num 15.39-40; Mal 4.4; and the whole book of Deuteronomy, which consists primarily of reminders).

The expression **Now I desire to remind you** is related not only to verse 5 but also to verses 6 and 7. This is the reason why TEV starts verses 6 and 7 with the word "Remember."

Jude appears to be apologizing to his readers when he acknowledges that they are already **fully informed** of, or "know all about," what he was going to tell them. The records of the past are fully known to them, and they only need to be reminded of these things. It is of course possible that this is a further case of politeness on the part of Jude, and what he is doing here is similar to a modern speaker who says "I am sure you know," although he is not at all certain that his audience in fact knows what he is going to tell them.

A comparison between RSV and TEV indicates a textual problem involving the Greek word *hapax* (RSV **once for all**, TEV "once"). RSV translates a Greek text that takes *hapax* with "fully informed," hence "once for all fully informed." In this case *hapax* would have the same meaning as it has in verse 3 (see "once for all" in verse 3 and comments). TEV, however, translates a text that reads *hapax* with "saved," hence "the Lord once rescued . . . ." This is the text preferred by the United Bible Societies (UBS) Greek New Testament, although the decision for this is rated "D," which means that there is very much doubt and uncertainty as to what really was written in the original text. Taken in this manner *hapax* simply has the meaning "once," or "in the first instance," as contrasted with **afterward** (literally "the second time"), during which time God did not save but destroyed. Most modern translations prefer the text that is reflected in TEV (for example, the New Revised Standard Version [NRSV] and REB). In this sense this word can also be rendered "at one time."

A further textual problem concerns the expression **he who saved**. As the RSV footnote indicates, many manuscripts have "the Lord" or "Jesus" instead of "he." The UBS Greek New Testament prefers the reading "the Lord," although the reading with the strongest textual support is "Jesus," which is the same as "Joshua," as the TEV footnote indicates. It is hard to think of Jude referring to Jesus as leading the Israelites out of Egypt, unless of course we are to think of the preexistent Jesus, but that is quite unlikely. "Joshua" may fit the context, although again we are faced with at least two problems: Joshua did not destroy those who did not believe; and Joshua cannot be the one referred to in the expression "kept by him" in verse 6. Since the Greek text identifies the subject of verse 5 with the person referred to in "kept by him" in verse 6, the participant chosen in verse 5 has to fit the context in verse 6 as well. This is perhaps one reason why the UBS Greek text has decided in favor of "the Lord," and this is reflected in most modern translations. In this case, therefore, "the Lord" refers to God rather than to Jesus Christ. If translators feel that the use of "the Lord" here for the name of God will confuse readers, it will be helpful to say simply "remind you of how God once . . . ."

The term **saved** is not used here in its theological sense of "given a new life" or "rescued from sin and given the gift of eternal life," but in the sense of "brought out safely from a dangerous or perilous situation." The reference is of course to the act of God in rescuing the Israelites from Egypt, where they were slaves. **A people** are the Israelites, information that is given directly in TEV. In certain languages translators can say "helped to become free from Egypt" or "helped to escape out of Egypt."

The rescuing of the Israelites is now contrasted with the punishment or destruction of some of them **who did not believe**. This refers to Numbers 14 (see especially verses 26-35, also 1 Cor 10.5-11 and Heb 3.16–4.2), where God punished those who refused to enter Canaan; they refused to enter Canaan because they heard the discouraging reports of a majority of the people sent by Joshua to spy out the land. Their refusal is a sign of their lack of faith in God, who promised to give them this land. God's decree was that all Israelites, from age 20 and older, with the exception of Joshua and Caleb, would die in the desert and therefore would not set foot on the Promised Land. The Greek word indicates that these people "died" or "were destroyed." In some languages it will be helpful to say "but afterward caused those who did not believe to die (or, be destroyed)."

The whole purpose of this example is to show how God deals with his people. Although he rescues them from danger, he does not hesitate to punish them if they fail to trust in him.

Alternative translation models for this verse are:

(1) Now I want to bring it again to your mind (attention), even though you know all about this, that the Lord (or, God), who once helped the Israelites to escape out of Egypt, afterward caused those who did not believe to die (or, be destroyed).

(2) For even though you know all about this, I want to bring to your attention again how the Lord (or, God), who once . . . .

6	RSV	TEV
	And the angels that did not keep their own position but left their proper dwelling have been kept by him in eternal chains in the nether gloom until the judgment of the great day;	Remember the angels who did not stay within the limits of their proper authority, but abandoned their own dwelling place: they are bound with eternal chains in the darkness below, where God is keeping them for that great Day on which they will be condemned.

Jude now gives a second example, namely, that of the rebellious angels. Some scholars identify these angels with the "sons of God" in Gen 6.1-4. It is, however, more accurate to take this account of the rebellious angels as an expansion or development of the Genesis account. Using this account as the starting point, later Jewish writers created various stories about angels who rebelled against God and consequently were punished by him. It is possible that Jude may have been influenced by these stories and also by some accounts included in a nonbiblical work called the Book of Enoch or 1 Enoch. While this book was not included in the Bible, there is evidence that it was widely used by Jews and Christians alike, and in fact was accepted as authoritative by some church authorities in the second century. The fact that Jude uses information from this writing shows how much it was valued in the early church, particularly by the Christian communities to whom Jude addressed his letter. In this case Jude alludes to certain passages in 1 Enoch where the angels were punished because of pride and disobedience (for example, 1 Enoch 12.4–13.1; 18.13 and following; 21.2 and following). Jude's purpose is to show that even spiritual beings are not exempt from God's punishment. There may be a hidden reference here to the people who claimed to be "spiritual" in contrast to others they regarded as "carnal." **Angels** in a number of languages may be expressed as "heavenly messengers," "messengers from heaven," or "messengers from God."

The word for **position** is literally "rule," "dominion," "domain," "sphere of influence," "authority." **Did not keep** on the other hand means "lose," or "fail to hold on to." The verse is saying that these angels were given a certain status or sphere of authority by God, but they were not content with such a position. Instead **they left their proper dwelling**, that is, they aspired to a higher status and left the place where they lived. In the book of 1 Enoch (12.4; similarly 15.3,7), the dwelling place of the angels is described as "the high, holy, and eternal heaven." A major component of the meaning of "heaven" is the very presence of God, and the angels abandoned that also. The word for **left** is more properly translated "abandoned" (TEV), "deserted."

The passage does not say why the angels rebelled or why they were banished. The verb for **left** is active, which means that the angels were not expelled by God, but that they willfully abandoned their place of abode. Furthermore the sin of the angels is not identified in this verse; however, it is made clear in verse 7 that the angels engaged in sexual immorality, and it is possible to bring this information forward to verse 6.

As a result of their rebellion, the angels received the punishment they deserved. The one who punishes them (**by him**) is the Lord in verse 5 (see the discussion there on "he who saved"). The word for **kept** is the same word as in the first part of the verse (that is, in **did not keep**). One of the rhetorical features of Jude's letter is that of using repetition of words and sounds. Sometimes this is a way of emphasizing or focusing on something, but at other times it is simply a stylistic device. Here there is a play on the word "keep," using it to describe an evil act as well as its punishment. Furthermore, the play on words carries a sense of irony: the angels were too proud to "keep" their God-given position, therefore God has "kept" them in eternal chains. It should also be noted that, in other parts of Jude's letter, the word "keep" is used as a catchword (see for example verses 1, 13, and 21). The angels are contrasted with God's people, who are exhorted to "keep" their position in God's love (verse 21), and whom God will "keep" safe, not for punishment but for salvation at the end of the world (verse 1). It is of course difficult to retain these rhetorical features in translation. However, an awareness of these features opens the possibility for translators faithfully to retain the function of such features in the translation, either by retaining the features themselves where it is possible and natural, or by substituting equivalent devices as necessary.

The word for **chains** is often used in stories regarding the fallen angels, and again Jude may have been influenced by these writings. The chains are described as **eternal**, which does not seem to fit the context, since, as RSV has it, these angels are only chained until the judgment on the last day. A translation like RSV will therefore make little sense in some languages. In such cases the restructuring in TEV will help tremendously, where the angels are represented as being chained eternally and continue to be chained even during the final judgment. Another aspect that needs to be noted is that the expression **have been kept by him in eternal chains** does not mean that God himself chained the angels. Rather it is likely that he had other agents who actually did the chaining. This point needs to be expressed in many languages;

for example, "God had them bound with eternal chains" or "God caused them to be bound with chains eternally (forever)."

The **nether gloom** is literally "darkness" or "gloom" and is used in Greek poetry to refer to the underworld. This is also the case here, where it refers specifically to Sheol, that is, the world of the dead. TEV's "darkness below" is an accurate translation; there may be a problem, however, if for example "below" is understood in a good sense. In such cases the focus can be put on "darkness," since in most languages darkness is considered bad. NRSV has "deepest darkness."

The great day is here used as a technical term for the day of final judgment, that is, the time at the end of the world when God will judge all creation. **Day** of course should not be understood as equivalent to our day of twenty-four hours, but as a short definite period of time. **Judgment** is "punishment" or "condemnation" (TEV). It is not that the angels will be brought before the court to determine their innocence or guilt, but since they are already guilty, they will at that time receive the punishment appropriate to their guilt. **Have been kept . . . until the judgment of the great day** must be restructured in certain languages; for example, "God is keeping them for that great Day when he will judge them."

The purpose of the whole verse is to show what it means if angels, spiritual though they be, are not exempt from God's punishment if they do evil; in the same way even members of God's people will also be punished for their evil deeds. There is of course a great deal of similarity between the angels and the godless people, particularly in their rebellion against God and in their indulgence in sexual immorality, as verse 7 shows.

An alternative translation model for this verse is:

> You should also think about the angels (heavenly messengers) who were not content with the authority (or, position) that God had given them, but abandoned their home in heaven; God had them bound with eternal chains in the darkness below, where he is keeping them for that great Day on which he will condemn them.

7	RSV	TEV
	just as Sodom and Gomorrah and the surrounding cities, which likewise acted immorally and indulged in unnatural lust, serve as an example by undergoing a punishment of eternal fire.	Remember Sodom and Gomorrah, and the nearby towns, whose people acted as those angels did and indulged in sexual immorality and perversion: they suffer the punishment of eternal fire as a plain warning to all.

A third example is now given, namely, the account of the cities of Sodom and Gomorrah, which is regarded by biblical writers as the best example of divine judgment of the wicked. The Gospels contain references to Jesus using this illustration (for example, Matt 10.15; 11.24; Mark 7.11; Luke 10.12; 17.29). The reference here is to Gen 19.11-28, which relates how the men of Sodom had demanded that Lot should surrender to them the angels who had visited him, so that the men of Sodom could have sexual relations with them. This story has similarities with that in verse 6: the presence of angels, sexual immorality, and eternal punishment.

The **surrounding cities** include Admah, Zeboiim, and Zoar, but Zoar was spared God's punishment (see Gen 19.20-22). In some cultures there are no human settlements that are the equivalent of **cities** and "towns" (TEV), but people live in villages or small groups of houses. In such cases it will be necessary to refer to a city or town as "a large group of houses surrounded by a strong wall," or perhaps as "the large (or chief) village." There are small island cultures, however, which have only one word for "place" or "land." In cases like this the equivalent for "city" will be "a place where many people live surrounded by a strong fence." The first clause of this verse can then be rendered as "Remember the big places of Sodom and Gomorrah surrounded by high fences, and the other places nearby where many people lived."

Acted immorally can be understood in a general sense as referring to all forms of sexual sin. The first meaning of **immorally** is "not conforming to established patterns of social conduct and ethics," which is the sin for which Sodom and Gomorrah were destroyed, according to Ezekiel (16.48-51); the secondary sin of excessive sexual misconduct occurs in addition to the primary sin of immorality, and should carry no more weight than that (in the case of Sodom and Gomorrah), while **indulged in unnatural lust** can be understood as referring to a particular kind of sexual immorality. **Likewise** refers back to the angels in verse 6 and indicates that the people of Sodom and Gomorrah are being compared to the angels; that is, they indulged in the same evil acts that were committed by the angels, a fact made clear in TEV. Translators need to investigate the range of vocabulary in their language in so far as "sexual immorality" is concerned. Possible models are "licentious sexual behavior" or "unlawful sexual intercourse."

But what does the expression **unnatural lust** refer to? The Greek simply has "other flesh," or "different flesh." Some scholars have understood this to mean having sexual relations with people of the same sex, as, for example, men with men (see Rom 1.26-27; 1 Cor 6.9). Others take the position that the focus here is not on homosexual acts but on the parallel between the angels and the men of Sodom and Gomorrah; in much the same way that the angels had sexual relations with human beings, so also the men of Sodom wanted to have sexual relations with angels. This latter point of view seems preferable because of the close relation between these two verses. However, it seems that in most languages, as in TEV, **unnatural lust** will be rendered as "sexual perversion," "perverted sexual activity," or "abnormal sexual activity," without being more specific as to the nature of the sexual activity.

The result of such sexual immorality is now revealed as **undergoing a punishment of eternal fire**. The verb for **undergoing** is in the present tense, which means that the inhabitants of Sodom are at the moment going through their punishment. Some scholars suggest that there may be a reference here to the Dead Sea, which is 30 miles from Jerusalem and 1,280 feet below sea level. In Jewish tradition the Dead Sea is a result of the destruction by fire of Sodom and Gomorrah and the surrounding cities; it is even believed that these cities continue to burn underground. This is easy to explain, since the Dead Sea is very hot, with the water getting hotter because of hot springs from the bottom. While it is possible and even likely that Jude had this tradition of the Dead Sea in mind, yet he is primarily referring here to the eternal fires of hell, where the people of these cities continue to suffer; this again relates verse 7 with verse 6, which speaks of the "nether gloom." The word translated **example** is literally "sample"; that is, here is an actual case of sinners being punished; this serves both as proof and as warning to future generations of the reality of divine punishment (note TEV "plain warning").

Eternal fire is the same expression used in some literature of the period leading up to the New Testament (for example 4 Maccabees 12.12) and in the New Testament itself (for example, Matt 18.8; 25.41). There is a problem of interpretation with regard to the positioning of this expression. The problem can be put simply: does **eternal fire** go with **example** or with **punishment**? In other words, is Jude saying that the burning of the cities is an example of how the wicked will be punished with eternal fire, or that the eternal burning of the cities is an example of how the wicked are going to be punished? Either of these interpretations is possible. Some translations follow the first interpretation, as, for example, Mft, "exhibited as a warning of the everlasting fire." But more translations reflect the position taken by TEV, "they suffer the punishment of eternal fire as a plain warning to all." This relates this statement to the tradition that these cities continue to burn. Another possible translation model is "They undergo punishment by being burned with fire eternally (forever), as an example to warn other people what can happen to them."

The godlessness of the people emphasized through the use of Old Testament examples
8-16

RSV

8 Yet in like manner these men in their dreamings defile the flesh, reject authority, and revile the glorious ones. 9 But when the archangel Michael, contending with the devil, disputed about the body of Moses, he did not presume to pronounce a reviling judgment upon him, but said, "The Lord rebuke you." 10 But these men revile whatever they do not understand, and by those things that they know by instinct as irrational animals do, they are destroyed. 11 Woe to them! For they walk in the way of Cain, and abandon themselves for the sake of gain to Balaam's error, and perish in Korah's rebellion. 12 These are blemishes on your love feasts, as they boldly carouse together, looking after themselves;

TEV

8 In the same way also, these people have visions which make them sin against their own bodies; they despise God's authority and insult the glorious beings above. 9 Not even the chief angel Michael did this. In his quarrel with the Devil, when they argued about who would have the body of Moses, Michael did not dare condemn the Devil with insulting words, but said, "The Lord rebuke you!" 10 But these people attack with insults anything they do not understand; and those things that they know by instinct, like wild animals, are the very things that destroy them. 11 How terrible for them! They have followed the way that Cain took. For the sake of money they have given themselves over to

waterless clouds, carried along by winds; fruitless trees in late autumn, twice dead, uprooted; 13 wild waves of the sea, casting up the foam of their own shame; wandering stars for whom the nether gloom of darkness has been reserved for ever.

14 It was of these also that Enoch in the seventh generation from Adam prophesied, saying, "Behold, the Lord came with his holy myriads, 15 to execute judgment on all, and to convict all the ungodly of all their deeds of ungodliness which they have committed in such an ungodly way, and of all the harsh things which ungodly sinners have spoken against him." 16 These are grumblers, malcontents, following their own passions, loud-mouthed boasters, flattering people to gain advantage.

the error that Balaam committed. They have rebelled as Korah rebelled, and like him they are destroyed. 12 With their shameless carousing they are like dirty spots in your fellowship meals. They take care only of themselves. They are like clouds carried along by the wind, but bringing no rain. They are like trees that bear no fruit, even in autumn, trees that have been pulled up by the roots and are completely dead. 13 They are like wild waves of the sea, with their shameful deeds showing up like foam. They are like wandering stars, for whom God has reserved a place forever in the deepest darkness.

14 It was Enoch, the sixth direct descendant from Adam, who long ago prophesied this about them: "The Lord will come with many thousands of his holy angels 15 to bring judgment on all, to condemn them all for the godless deeds they have performed and for all the terrible words that godless sinners have spoken against him!"

16 These people are always grumbling and blaming others; they follow their own evil desires; they brag about themselves and flatter others in order to get their own way.

After giving vivid and somewhat terrifying examples of God's judgment, Jude now resumes speaking directly about the godless people. But he continues to use Old Testament examples in order to emphasize the wickedness of these people. In fact verses 8-16 follow a structure that consists of a series of elements in which a description of the people Jude refers to is followed by an Old Testament allusion. Thus we can outline the whole passage as follows:

> Description of the godless people (verse 8);
> an Old Testament example (verse 9);
> description of the godless people (verse 10);
> an Old Testament example (verse 11);
> description of the godless people (verses 12-13);
> an Old Testament example (verses 14-15);
> description of the godless people (verse 16).

SECTION HEADING. The long heading suggested by the outline may be shortened; for example, "Godless people are compared to some Old Testament characters," "More examples of ungodly people," "Other wicked people," or "God is angry against all other evildoers."

8   RSV   TEV

Yet in like manner these men in their dreamings defile the flesh, reject authority, and revile the glorious ones.[c]

[c] Greek *glories*

In the same way also, these people have visions which make them sin against their own bodies; they despise God's authority and insult the glorious beings above.

The verse starts with three words in Greek, **in like manner**, **yet**, and "also," the function of which is to connect this passage with the verses before it. **In like manner** and "also" indicate the similarities of the people Jude is writing about with the three groups mentioned in verses 5-7, but particularly with the people of Sodom and Gomorrah. However, the term **yet** is difficult and can be understood in two ways: Firstly, it may simply serve to strengthen the whole expression; in this case it can be left untranslated, as in TEV. Or secondly, it may emphasize the contrast between the expected attitude of these people and their actual deeds. A knowledge of what God had done, particularly to the people of Sodom and Gomorrah, should deter them from doing evil, in order to avoid God's punishment. However, despite these examples of divine punishment, these people still continue to commit the same sins. If translators follow this second interpretation, another way of rendering this phrase is "Despite this warning, in the same way also . . ." or "Even though these people received a warning, in the same way also, they . . . ."

These men in their dreamings refers to the godless people mentioned in verse 4. The word for "dream" occurs only one other time in the New Testament, in Acts 2.17, where it is used of prophetic dreams. It is very likely that these people have claimed that through dreams or "visions" (TEV) they receive special revelations from God and thereby gain spiritual insight. Therefore the verse is not suggesting that they perform all these evil acts while experiencing visions, or that they sin in their dreams (which a literal translation may suggest), but that they justify their sinful acts by special revelations they claim to receive from God. If this interpretation is followed, translators may say "These godless people have visions." In languages that do not distinguish between dreams and visions, the translator may have to use the word for "dream." However, another possible translation is "special dream."

Jude mentions three actions that these people try to justify. First of all, they **defile the flesh**. The word for **defile** can also mean "contaminate," "stain," "corrupt," and is used both of ritual and moral defilement. In the present context defilement is related to sexual corruption. **Flesh** on the other hand can be understood as referring to people in general, or as referring to their own bodies in particular (as for example TEV "they sin against their own bodies"). This latter rendering is similar to some references in 1 Enoch, where the fallen angels are described as defiling themselves with women (for example, 1 Enoch 7.1; 9.8; 10.11; 12.4; 15.3,4). We may also translate **defile the flesh** as "making their bodies dirty (defiled) with sexual sins."

Secondly, these people **reject authority**. **Authority** here is understood in various ways:

1. It may be authority in general, both religious and political. This means that these people reject all forms of authority, which would explain their utter disregard of any rule or regulation.
2. It may refer to angelic authority. The Greek word for authority here is *kuriotēta*, and there is a group of angelic beings known as *kuriotētes* (Col 1.16, "dominions"; Eph 1.21, "dominion").
3. It may refer to human authority, both civil and religious.
4. It may be divine authority. Perhaps this is what Jude had in mind. Here again, there is a play on words. The word for "authority," *kuriotēta*, is related to the word for Lord, *kurios*.

It is likely therefore that **reject authority** here is equivalent in meaning to **deny our only Master and Lord Jesus Christ** in verse 4. This alternative is followed by TEV "despise God's authority." Other ways of rendering this are "do not recognize God's authority" or "do not recognize that God is Master (or, Chief)."

Thirdly, these people **revile the glorious ones**. The word **revile** is literally "blaspheme" and can mean "insult," "slander," "speak disparagingly," "speak evil of," "say bad things about," or "spoil a person's name." Languages tend to have a large range of vocabulary in this area. When this word stands by itself without any object, it is directed toward God. Here, however, a definite object of the blasphemy is mentioned, namely, **the glorious ones** (literally "glories"). Some take this to mean noble and illustrious people, while others understand it as supernatural beings in general. Most commentators, however, take "glories" to mean angels, since the Greek term is used of angels in many writings, including the Dead Sea Scrolls, and in Gnostic literature. They are probably called "glories" because they are thought to have a share in the majesty of God. "Glorious beings" can also be rendered as "glorious angelic beings," and in some languages there is special vocabulary reserved for such beings; for example, "the sacred beings." Translators may also need to identify the location of these "beings" in relationship to the world (TEV's "above") and say "The glorious beings in heaven."

Are these angels bad angels or good ones? Some commentators, looking forward to verse 9, think that bad angels are meant. This would mean that in much the same way that Michael did not insult the prince of evil, so these people should not say bad things against the powers of evil. The general opinion, however, is that these are good angels.

How do the godless people insult angels? Here the focus is primarily on words rather than actions: they say evil things about the angels. That the insult is oral is supported by the fact that in verse 9 "reviling judgment" (which translates the same word) definitely refers to words. But what is actually said against the angels is difficult to determine, since the text offers little help in this matter. Three suggestions are worth considering:
1. They insult angels as agents of creation. This would assume a Gnostic background for the whole letter, a system of belief that regards the created material world as evil, and therefore the agents of creation as equally evil. The Gnostic background of Jude is held by many scholars.

2. These people regard themselves as spiritually superior to angels because of their dreams and visions through which they claim to have received spiritual insight and knowledge. This would relate this part more closely to the first part of the verse.
3. They despise the angels, who are the mediators and guardians of the law of God, and who also are guardians of the whole created order. This would relate their attitude toward angels to their attitude toward the law. Since they claim for themselves the right to act in any way they please, with utter disregard for the law, they would despise and insult anyone who would oppose such a law-less way of life.

All of these suggestions are conjectures, of course, and it probably is not necessary to include in the translation the reasons why angels were insulted and the specific ways in which this slander is carried through.

There is, however, one other aspect of the text that is relevant for translation. The order of words in the Greek text seems to indicate that the three negative aspects of these people are somehow related, with the first one being the result of the next two. The Greek text can be restructured as follows: "These men in their dreamings on the one hand defile the flesh, and on the other hand reject authority and revile the glorious ones." The last two are therefore the basis of the first: they sin against their own bodies because they despise God's authority and insult the angels. And all three actions find their justification in the dreams and visions. If this analysis is valid, then it is important to show these relationships in the translation.

Using the restructuring above, an alternative translation model is the following:

> These people have visions (dreams) that make them refuse to accept God's authority, make them say evil things about the glorious beings in heavens, and make them commit dirty sexual practices.

9 RSV   TEV

But when the archangel Michael, con-   Not even the chief angel Michael did
tending with the devil, disputed about   this. In his quarrel with the Devil, when
the body of Moses, he did not presume   they argued about who would have the
to pronounce a reviling judgment upon   body of Moses, Michael did not dare
him, but said, "The Lord rebuke you."   condemn the Devil with insulting words,
                                         but said, "The Lord rebuke you!"

To prove his case against these godless people, Jude cites the example of the archangel Michael, who in confrontation with the Devil did not pronounce a severe judgment on him, but simply said **"The Lord rebuke you."** The logic seems to be as follows: Michael, who is the chief angel, did not claim for himself the right to pronounce judgment on the Devil, who is the chief of all evil forces, but left the whole matter up to God; therefore there is no justification at all for ordinary human beings to treat the angels in such an insulting way.

The title **archangel** means "chief angel" or "ruling angel." In some literature written during the period between the Old Testament and the New Testament, there is a great deal of reference to angels and how these are classified into grades in a descending scale, with archangels at the top. There is also mention of seven archangels, and six of them are named in 1 Enoch 20.2-8: Raphael, Raquel, Michael, Saraqael, Gabriel, and Ramiel. To each of these archangels God assigned a province. **Archangel** can also be translated as "the chief of God's messengers." The phrase **when the archangel Michael . . .** may be rendered in some languages as "when Michael, who is one of the angels that is greater than the others . . . ." **Michael** is mentioned in Dan 12.1 as the guardian of Israel. He was thought of primarily as the angel who protected the people of Israel from the power of Satan or the Devil. In Rev 12.7 Michael is the church's protector against the dragon.

This is the first time in the letter that Jude refers to the Devil. References to the Devil are rare in the Old Testament; they are found in later compositions, as for example in Zech 3.1 and 1 Chr 21.1. During the period leading up to the New Testament, the idea developed that the Devil is the prince of evil, and New Testament usage echoes this understanding. In fact New Testament teaching about the future asserts that, immediately before the final days of this age, the Devil will display his power in order to lead astray even those who already trust in Christ (see for example Matt 24.4-18; 2 Thes 2.3-12; 2 Tim 3.1-9; Rev 20.7-8). By the time of the writing of Jude's letter, **the devil** has already become a technical name for the prince of evil, and that is the reason why TEV capitalizes the word.

The story about Michael and the Devil fighting over the body of Moses is not found in the Old Testament, which simply states that the burial place of Moses is not known by anyone (Deut 34.6). However, in a composition called "The Assumption of Moses" (written about the first century A.D.), it is related that, when Moses died, Michael was given the task of burying the body. The Devil, however, claimed power over the body, since he was lord of the material order. When Michael refused to hand the body over, the Devil threatened to accuse Moses of being a murderer for having killed the Egyptian (as recorded in Exo 2.12). Michael, however, did not respond by rebuking the Devil, but simply proceeded to bury Moses with his own hands.

The fact that Jude makes reference to this story without any background material for his readers indicates that he assumes his readers are familiar with the story; this need not be because they know of "The Assumption of Moses" but because this story was probably widely known among the Jews at that time.

The words **contending** and **disputed** refer generally to a discussion or argument, but they are also used in relation to a legal dispute. In this story it is the Devil who brings a legal case against Moses, accusing him of murder, and therefore of not being worthy of a decent and honorable burial. So the word **contending** does not really have the sense of "quarrel" as in TEV, which refers to a violent argument, but suggests that Michael "challenged the Devil's right" to take Moses' body. Another translation model, then, is as follows: "When he disputed with the Devil, and argued with him as to who . . . ." **Did not presume** should not be translated as "was not brave enough to," as the rendering "did not dare" (TEV and NRSV) may suggest; rather it means that Michael "did not take it upon himself" or "did not feel that it was his prerogative (that he had the authority)."

The word translated **reviling** is the same word used for "revile" in verse 8, which again is a play on words similar to that on the word "keep" in verse 6. Taken with **judgment**, some meanings suggested are "he did not pronounce a sentence on blasphemies spoken by the Devil," "in condemning the Devil, he did not indulge in the language of mere reproach," "in challenging the Devil, he did not revile in turn," "he did not condemn him with insulting words," or "he did not use bad words to reprove the Devil." This contrasts Michael's action with that of the godless people: they insult angels, whereas Michael, the chief angel, refrains from insulting the Devil himself; they show no respect for supernatural beings, whereas Michael respected even the Devil.

The expression **"The Lord rebuke you"** is quoted from Zech 3.2, where the LORD speaks these words to Satan in reply to Satan's accusations against the high priest Joshua (see Zech 3.1-10). **Rebuke** can mean "reprove," "censure," or "reprimand," but perhaps here it has the stronger meaning of "punish" or "condemn." The whole expression **"The Lord rebuke you"** is in the Greek optative mood, expressing a wish or a hope, similar in form to that of blessing or benediction formulas, but used in this context in a negative sense.

An alternative translation model for this verse is:

> Not even Michael, who is one of God's chief angels (messengers), resorted to insult (saying bad things against). For when he disputed with the Devil and challenged his right to take the body of Moses, Michael did not feel that he had the authority to condemn the Devil with bad words; instead he said, "May the Lord speak severely to (reprimand) you.

10

RSV	TEV
But these men revile whatever they do not understand, and by those things that they know by instinct as irrational animals do, they are destroyed.	But these people attack with insults anything they do not understand; and those things that they know by instinct, like wild animals, are the very things that destroy them.

Continuing the theme of "reviling" and going back to the same people, Jude now mentions the consequences of their acts, namely, their own destruction. **These men** is equivalent to the same expression in verse 8 and refers back to the godless people. The word for **revile** is once again "blaspheme," the same word used in verse 8 and in verse 9 ("a reviling judgment").

Here it has the primary meaning of "insult," hence TEV "attack with insults." We may also say "say bad words against" or "use abusive language against."

There is some difficulty in determining what the expression **whatever they do not understand** means. This goes back to verse 8 and refers to their attitude toward angels and God's authority, or in other words, to the spiritual world in general, and so to the Christian message itself in particular. These people claim spiritual superiority, but Jude now asserts that in actual fact they know little if anything of the spiritual world that they despise and abhor. In fact, the opposite is true: they are experts in **things that they know by instinct**. **Instinct** translates a Greek word that means "naturally" as opposed to something learned or developed, and hence the use of natural or instinctive powers as opposed to the use of developed reason or acquired knowledge. Included in this are impulses of appetite, sensual pleasure, sexual desire, and perhaps evil violence and rebellion.

There is definitely a sense of sarcasm here; these godless people are denounced for claiming that they know everything about the spiritual world, when in fact what is true is the opposite—all their knowledge is based on raw and uninformed instinct. Translators will do well to capture this sense of sarcasm in the translation.

In simply following their instincts, these people are compared to **irrational animals**. **Irrational** translates a Greek word that can literally mean "without reason," "unreasoning," "unreasonable," but when used with animals it can mean "wild" (as in TEV). In this sense **irrational animals** will be expressed in many languages as "forest animals" or "jungle animals."

It is the things that they only know by instinct that bring about the destruction of these people. However, it is not the knowing of these things that leads to their destruction, but doing them and acting by them. The expression **by instinct** means negatively "without using reason (logic)." Destruction here refers not primarily to physical sickness or death, or even to moral and spiritual decay, but to God's judgment and punishment, perhaps at the end time.

An alternative translation model for this verse is:

> But those godless people (or, people who do not worship God) use abusive language (or, bad words) to attack anything that they do not understand; and when they act like wild animals and do these things that they know without thinking (without using human reason), they will suffer God's punishment (or, God will punish them).

11   RSV   TEV

Woe to them! For they walk in the way of Cain, and abandon themselves for the sake of gain to Balaam's error, and perish in Korah's rebellion.

How terrible for them! They have followed the way that Cain took. For the sake of money they have given themselves over to the error that Balaam

**committed. They have rebelled as
Korah rebelled, and like him they are
destroyed.**

In this verse Jude continues his attack on the godless people, pronouncing
a curse on them and comparing them with three Old Testament characters
who are well known for their wickedness and rebellion against God.

Woe to them! is a common expression in the Gospels, but outside the
Gospels it is used only here and in 1 Cor 9.16. This expression functions as a
formula that states the certainty of God's punishment and condemnation. So
Woe to them can be translated "How horrible it will be for them," "How
severely they will be punished by God," or "God will surely punish them."

The punishment is directly related to, and is in fact a result of, their
actions, which are similar in nature to the sins of which the three Old
Testament characters mentioned are guilty. This is the significance of the word
For at the beginning of the second sentence, which here gives the sense: "They
are being punished because . . . ." In certain languages it will be helpful to
state this directly. However, the idea of punishment may be included clearly
in the previous sentence, **Woe to them** (compare TEV); for example, "God will
severely punish them!"

The first example given is **Cain**, who is known from the Old Testament for
killing his brother Abel. In first-century Jewish thought, Cain was described
as a person of treachery, lust, avarice, self-indulgence; he was the unloving
person who cared for nothing except his own self-interest; he was a cynical,
skeptical, materialistic person who had little faith in God or in morality, and
who therefore did everything according to his own whims and wishes.
Furthermore Cain was also represented in the tradition as a false teacher who
led the people into licentiousness and immorality. Among the early church
fathers Cain is represented as an example of those who through jealousy,
dissatisfaction, and rebellion against society lead their fellow-believers to death
(1 Clement 4.1-7). It is of course rather unlikely that Jude had all of this in
mind; but at any rate it was easy to take Cain as the first clear example of an
evil person.

The people Jude is attacking are therefore accused of walking **in the way
of Cain**. The word translated "walk" is literally "go" or "proceed," but here it
is used figuratively to mean "conduct oneself," "live." In some languages
translators may keep this metaphor and say "they walk on the same path as
Cain," which means "they live the same kind of life that Cain lived." **The way
of Cain** actually means the kind of life Cain lived, including his thinking,
feeling, and actions. To walk **in the way of Cain** then means to live as Cain
lived, to follow his example, to act as he acted. And if Cain is as bad as Jewish
tradition pictures him, then certainly those who follow his example deserve
God's curse and punishment.

The second example given is **Balaam**. The godless people are said to have
abandoned themselves **to Balaam's error**. The word translated **error** can also
mean "delusion," "deceit," "deception." What was Balaam's error? The
references are in the book of Numbers, chapters 22–24, and in particular 31.16,

where Balaam leads Israel to worship other gods, and all because of a bribe from Balak. Jewish tradition remembers Balaam primarily as a man of greed, who was prepared to commit sin and lead others to sin, for the sake of gaining a reward for himself. In other parts of the tradition, Balaam is represented as a false teacher who perverted the youth of Israel and led them into idolatry and immorality.

The word translated **abandon themselves** can also mean "plunge in," "wallow in," or "devote themselves to." The picture is that of a person who in utter and selfless abandon gives himself or herself to some activity. And the godless ones have done just that; they have devoted themselves to doing exactly what Balaam did, committing sin and leading others to commit sin, all for the sake of monetary or material gain. **For the sake of gain** means "in order to get money" or "in order to enrich themselves."

As a result of their imitating Cain and following the example of Balaam, these people are said to **perish in Korah's rebellion**. The reference here is to Num 16.1-35, where Korah, son of Izhar, together with over two hundred and fifty others, rebelled against the leadership of Moses and Aaron, with the aim of getting hold of a share in the priesthood. The end result is that all those who rebelled, together with all the members of their families, were swallowed through an opening of the earth. Later tradition pictures Korah as a heretic who had utter disregard for the law or for duly constituted ecclesiastical authority. Korah therefore is a good example from Scripture for these people, for they also are disrespectful of authority and have coveted for themselves positions in the Christian community that they have no right to occupy. **Perish** means "to be destroyed," "to die," "to have their breath snuffed out," or "to be wiped off the earth."

Rebellion is a Greek word that can also mean "argument," "dispute," or "hostility"; but here it refers primarily to Korah's rebellion against Moses. The whole expression then means that, because these people are rebelling as Korah did, they will also perish.

It should be noted that all the verbs in this verse are in the aorist tense, which is normally used to express a completed action in the past. In some contexts, however, the aorist may function as a perfect tense; that is, it describes actions that have already taken place or begun to take place, but whose effects continue in the present and even into the future. This seems to be the case here.

In translating the three expressions, **they walk in the way of Cain**, **abandon themselves . . . to Balaam's error**, and **perish in Korah's rebellion**, one must note that past and present events are joined together, with the present event being compared to and explained by what has happened in the past. Translators will do well to make the relationships of the events clear, as TEV has done, for example.

An alternative translation model for this verse is as follows:

> God will punish them for sure! For they live the same kind of life that Cain did. For in order to enrich themselves they have devoted themselves completely to the error that Balaam commit-

ted. They have rebelled as Korah rebelled, and like him God will destroy them (snuff their breath out)."

12-13	RSV	TEV

12 These are blemishes[d] on your love feasts, as they boldly carouse together, looking after themselves; waterless clouds, carried along by winds; fruitless trees in late autumn, twice dead, uprooted; 13 wild waves of the sea, casting up the foam of their own shame; wandering stars for whom the nether gloom of darkness has been reserved for ever.

[d] Or *reefs*

12 With their shameless carousing they are like dirty spots in your fellowship meals. They take care only of themselves. They are like clouds carried along by the wind, but bringing no rain. They are like trees that bear no fruit, even in autumn, trees that have been pulled up by the roots and are completely dead. 13 They are like wild waves of the sea, with their shameful deeds showing up like foam. They are like wandering stars, for whom God has reserved a place forever in the deepest darkness.

Jude now continues his description of the godless people. In the first part of verse 12, he describes their actions during worship meetings of the Christians, particularly in the love feasts, or fellowship meals. The remainder of this verse, together with verse 13, is full of figurative language giving four pictures from the world of nature.

First of all Jude describes the behavior of these people during the gatherings of the community. In this regard he mentions three things. The first of these is that they are **blemishes on your love feasts**. The **love feasts** were evening meals in the early church, during which members came together as an expression of their close relationship with God and with one another. The "love feast" usually ended with the sacrament of holy communion. This practice of coming together for a common meal has as its primary background the common meals that Jesus ate with his disciples both before his crucifixion and after his resurrection. Mention of these common meals is found in descriptions of the early church in the book of Acts (see 2.46; 20.7,11) and in Paul's first letter to the Corinthians (see 11.20-34). However, the term "love feast" actually occurs only here and perhaps in 2 Peter 2.13. TEV's "fellowship meals" is a more natural English translation of the term.

The word translated **blemishes** is a very rare word, occurring only here in the New Testament. Some of the meanings of the Greek word are:
1. "Blot," "blemish," "spot" (compare verse 23, which is the verbal form, meaning "to defile"). Sometimes this word can be used to describe spots and markings on rocks. This would fit the context; however, some claim that this meaning came to be popular only very much later, perhaps in the fourth century.

2. The word can be taken as an adjective that means "dirty," or "polluted." A similar word occurs in verse 13, where it is translated "spotted" (TEV "stained"). This also fits the context, since the godless are polluted by their sexual perversity.
3. It can also mean half-submerged rocks, or coral "reefs," which can easily cause shipwrecks. In this sense Jude is saying two things: first, that these people will destroy the love feasts, in much the same way that reefs cause ships to sink; secondly, that close association with them, especially during the fellowship meals, is dangerous and can cause other people to lose their faith. Therefore contact with these people should be avoided as much as possible, in much the same way as a pilot tries to steer clear of the dangerous reefs.

Both the first and the third of these meanings are possible and appropriate to the context.

Given these interpretations, two possible translation models are as follows:

(1) They are like dirty spots that defile you as you eat your fellowship meals together.
(2) They are like coral reefs (or, half-submerged rocks) that cause disharmony as you eat your meals together.

Jude further describes what takes place during the love feasts: **they boldly carouse together**, and they are only **looking after themselves**. The Greek word translated **carouse** can have a neutral meaning "to eat together," but in the present context it has a derogatory meaning: they eat together without any regard for the greater group or for the spiritual significance of the meal. This means that, instead of regarding the fellowship meal as a time for communion with the Lord and with their fellow Christians, they used it simply as an occasion for physical satisfaction. And all of this they did **boldly**, that is, "without reverence," or "shamelessly" (as in TEV). The sense of "shameless carousing" (TEV) may be rendered as "partying uproariously with no shame." Their whole attitude and behavior during these common meals is summarized by the statement **looking after themselves**, which is literally "shepherding themselves." In other words they are shepherds who take care only of themselves and not of their sheep. This may be an allusion to Ezek 34.2, where the rulers of Israel are compared to shepherds who took care of themselves at the expense of the sheep. In much the same way, these people were supposed to be leaders and therefore servants of the community, but instead they were exploiting the community for their own benefit and selfish interests. In this sense this statement can be connected with the common meal, but at the same time it can also be understood as a more general description of the people Jude is referring to in their dealings with the Christian community.

The godless people are now further described in four metaphors or pictures drawn from nature. These figures are chosen from each of the four parts of the universe: clouds in the air, trees on the earth, waves in the sea, and stars in the sky. Nature is usually portrayed as operating according to regular laws. Jude, however, chooses examples that seem to transgress rather than follow natural laws, and these examples are pictures of the lawless behavior of these people. It has been noted by some scholars that these metaphors may have been influenced by parts of 1 Enoch (2.1–5.4 and 80.2-8; rain is mentioned in 80.2, fruits in 80.3, and stars in 80.6).

It should be noted that RSV retains the metaphorical form, whereas TEV has transformed the metaphors into similes (as, for example, **waterless clouds** [RSV], "like clouds . . ." [TEV]). Both are possible in translation, and the choice of one or the other depends on many factors, the most important of which is the ability of the intended readers to grasp, understand, and appreciate the message.

The first picture is taken from the region of the air, namely, the **waterless clouds, carried along by winds. Waterless clouds** are a figure of worthlessness. This may be an allusion to Pro 25.14: "Like clouds and wind without rain is a man who boasts of a gift he does not give." Some commentaries note that, on summer days in the Middle East, clouds can sometimes be seen approaching land and giving hope of rain, but then they pass on, blown by the wind and, instead of giving rain, aggravate the already excessive heat. **Carried along by the wind**, on the other hand, symbolizes lack of willpower. This picture of the waterless clouds carried along by the wind stands for the people who make great claims about their spirituality and the doctrines that they teach, but in the end do not benefit anyone and have nothing to offer for the spiritual growth of members of the Christian community.

The second picture from nature is taken from the earth, namely, **fruitless trees in late autumn**. There are two interpretations of this metaphor:
1. These are trees that are expected to have fruit, because late autumn is the end of the harvest season, when fruits become ripe. In this sense the godless people do not really do anything beneficial to anyone, although they have all the opportunity to do so.
2. These trees are really fruitless, since at the end of autumn trees shed their leaves and are really without any fruit. When applied to the godless people, this means that they don't do anything that would contribute to the building up of the Christian community.

RSV can be interpreted either way. Most commentaries, however, favor the first of these alternatives. In this sense it provides a clear parallel to the waterless clouds: just as the clouds promise rain but only contribute to the heat, so the trees promise fruit but produce nothing.

The word for **autumn** in many languages is "season when leaves drop from trees." But in cultures that recognize only two seasons, namely, "cold" and "hot" or "hot" and "rainy," it may be helpful to say "they are like trees at the end of the hot season that bear no fruit." A more basic problem is that in many parts of the world the season when trees bear their fruit is not the time when they drop their leaves. Therefore a better translation may be "they are like trees that bear no fruit in the fruit-bearing season."

As a result of the fruitlessness of the trees, they are described as **twice dead** and **uprooted. Twice dead** refers more to the people than to the trees and can be understood in two ways. It may refer to the apostasy of these people. Having returned to the state they were in before they became

Christians, they are in a sense twice dead, the first death being the time before they accepted the Christian message. Or it may be a reference to the second death, that is, to the fate of evil people at the last judgment (see, for example, Rev 2.11; 20.6,17; 21.8).

The term **uprooted** is a figure that is still related to the fruitless tree. In much the same way that a dead, fruitless tree is **uprooted**, so also these people will be **uprooted**, that is, they will be judged, pronounced guilty, and then given the punishment due them. Some suggest that "uprooting" may mean that these people are no longer members of the Christian community, an interpretation that seems unlikely. But even though they remain members, their relationship with Jesus Christ has been broken, and this ultimately leads to their separation from Christ.

In TEV "twice dead" and "uprooted" are put in reverse order, which makes the relationship between the two much clearer. It is when trees are uprooted that they die; therefore "uprooted" is the cause, and "twice dead" is the result. So this may be expressed as "people have pulled them up by the roots, and they are completely dead."

Alternative translation models for verse 12 are as follows:

(1) These people are like dirty spots. They defile you as they carouse shamelessly while you eat your fellowship meals together. They are like clouds that the wind blows along, but bring no rain (have no rain). They are like trees that bear no fruit in the season for bearing fruit. They are completely dead, for people have pulled them up by the roots.

(2) These people are like coral (or, rock) reefs that will ruin your fellowship meals as they carouse shamelessly . . . .

The third picture, beginning in verse 13, is taken from the sea, namely **wild waves . . . casting up the foam of their own shame**. This is probably an allusion to Isa 57.20: "But evil men are like the restless sea, whose waves never stop rolling in, bringing filth and muck" (TEV). The figure of waves is also used in James 1.6, although we cannot be sure whether Jude knew James. **Wild** can also be translated "stormy," and the word for **casting up** can also mean "cause to splash up." When the waves dash against the shore, they toss up dirt and filth; these are collected in foam and are cast up and left on the seashore. In much the same way the godless people scatter their abomination everywhere, resulting in the confusion of Christians and causing them to doubt the truth of the Christian message.

The expression **casting up the foam of their own shame** refers more to the godless people than to the waves; the waves can of course produce foam, but they do not experience shame, nor can they produce shameful deeds. The actions and erroneous teachings of these people, on the other hand, can be considered shameful in that these bring shame and disgrace on themselves.

In certain island cultures where **waves of the sea** are ever present, translators can simply say "wild waves (storm waves)." Alternative translation models for the beginning of verse 13 are:

40

(1) These godless people are like wild waves, casting up the foam (dirt) of their shameful deeds on the beach.
(2) These godless people are like storm waves of the sea tossing up dirt and filth on the shore like their shameful deeds.

The fourth picture is taken from the sky, namely, **wandering stars**. This term is understood by some commentaries to refer to shooting stars or meteors that fall rapidly from the sky and quickly disappear in the darkness. There are a number of scholars, however, who argue that the **wandering stars** refer to planets, which according to modern astronomy are not actually "stars." In fact the name "planet" in English comes directly from the Greek word *planētoi*, which is the word translated **wandering** here. In the ancient world the planets were always a mystery because of their irregular movements, which seemed to violate the orderly rules of movement in space. These irregular movements were explained as originating from the disobedience of the angels who controlled these planets, and who were punished by imprisonment. This is referred to in some parts of 1 Enoch (see especially 18.13-16; 21.1-10). At any rate, whether these wandering stars are planets or shooting stars, the important thing to note is they are assumed to have strayed from their proper course. They are therefore an appropriate figure for the people who have also gone off course.

The punishment of the **wandering stars** is confinement in the **nether gloom of darkness**, which refers to the place of future punishment, which is often described as a place of intense darkness. The more popular way of speaking of the last judgment is punishment by eternal fire. Jewish thought, however, also knows the idea of imprisonment in eternal darkness (see for example 1 Enoch 63.6; Matt 8.12; 22.13; 15.39). The image of darkness is much more appropriate for stars. When applied to the godless people, this focuses on the fact that they have wandered from the way of truth and can therefore be described in some way as giving forth light that misleads themselves and others as well. As a result they will be confined to darkness forever, where they will receive their just punishment.

The expression **has been reserved** is one of the so-called divine passives, with God as the unnamed agent—a fact that is made clear in TEV.

Alternative translation models for the last part of verse 13 are:

(1) They are like stars that have strayed from their proper course (path). So God has reserved a place for them forever in darkness where there is no light at all (where everything is completely black).
(2) They are like stars . . . forever in the completely dark place of punishment (where they will be punished, or where God will punish them).

14   RSV   TEV

It was of these also that Enoch in the seventh generation from Adam prophesied, saying, "Behold, the Lord came with his holy myriads,

It was Enoch, the sixth direct descendant from Adam, who long ago prophesied this about them: "The Lord will come with many thousands of his holy angels

Jude continues his criticism of the godless people; **of these** refers back to these people. To describe them Jude quotes a prophecy of Enoch, who is described here as **in the seventh generation from Adam**. In Gen 5.1-24 we find that, counting Adam as the first, Enoch is the seventh in the list of ancestors. This means that Enoch is in fact the sixth descendant of Adam, and TEV has expressed it in this way: "the sixth direct descendant from Adam." However, the number 7 is regarded as the perfect number, and its function here is probably to enhance the authority of the prophecy of Enoch; so the actual number is important in this verse, and if possible it should be retained in translation, provided that the meaning of the verse is clear. In some languages this idea will be expressed through the use of the equivalent of "ancestors," placing the phrase **in the seventh generation from Adam** at the end of the verse; for example, "It was Enoch . . . . From Enoch back to Adam there were six ancestors." It is of course recognized that in many cultures people do not remember or take their kinship systems as far back as the seventh generation; in such cases the restructuring of TEV is perhaps the best thing that can be followed. It is important to make clear in translation that a line of generation is meant, and not that the one man Adam has seven sons.

The word **prophesied** here means "predicted," "foretold," or "said beforehand that something would happen." The quotation itself comes from 1 Enoch (see the explanation on page 23), and it starts with a Greek word that can literally be translated "Behold" or "Look," and whose primary function is to catch the attention of the hearer or reader. Many translations have left this word untranslated (for example TEV, NEB); others give a literal rendering (for instance AT "See," Translators New Testament [TNT]) "Look"; while still others try to recapture the function of the word by using some other expression such as "I tell you" (The Jerusalem Bible [JB]).

The expression **the Lord** is not found in 1 Enoch but has been added by Jude in order to make the quotation a Christian one, with **the Lord** probably referring to Jesus Christ. See verse 4 on the translation of **Lord**.

The verb **came** is translated literally in RSV from the Greek, which uses an aorist form here (past tense, completed action). Most commentaries, however, interpret the aorist here as having a future sense, since in 1 Enoch the quotation is about God coming as judge in the future. It is quite common for a biblical prophet to speak in the past tense when he is referring to a future event, thus emphasizing his faith that God will surely fulfill what he has predicted. This form of speech (past tense for future events) is likely to create problems for modern-day readers, especially when such a form does not exist in their own language. Accordingly some translations have used the future tense here; for example, TEV "The Lord will come"; others have used the present; for example, AT "the Lord comes."

The expression **his holy myriads** most probably refers to angels; many translations include this information. There are quite a number of references that speak of Christ coming to earth accompanied by angels (Matt 16.27; 25.31; Mark 8.38; Luke 9.26; 2 Thes 1.7). The word **myriads** can mean the number ten thousand but can also mean countless thousands, hence TEV "many thousands," NIV "thousands upon thousands." One may also say "so many they cannot be counted." These countless angels are described as **holy** primarily in the sense that they are dedicated to God and continually serve him. Since the word for **holy** in many languages means "pure" or "clean," it will be best for translators in such languages to translate "holy angels" as "his angels," meaning "God's angels (messengers)" or "God's heavenly servants."

15	RSV	TEV
	to execute judgment on all, and to convict all the ungodly of all their deeds of ungodliness which they have committed in such an ungodly way, and of all the harsh things which ungodly sinners have spoken against him."	to bring judgment on all, to condemn them all for the godless deeds they have performed and for all the terrible words that godless sinners have spoken against him!"

The purpose of the Lord's coming is now stated, namely **to execute judgment on all** people and to punish them for their evil deeds.

The meaning of **judgment** here depends on how we understand the word **all**. If **all** refers to all people, both good and bad, then **to execute judgment** means to judge all people in the sense of determining whether they are innocent or guilty. The next two clauses then refer to judgment or punishment given to the guilty. Another way of putting it is that the first part of the verse talks of universal judgment, whereas the next two clauses refer to the punishment inflicted on those judged to be wicked. This is the interpretation found in some translations; for example, TNT "to bring universal judgment, and to convict all the ungodly ones . . ."; JB "to pronounce judgment on all mankind and to sentence the wicked . . . ." In some languages **to execute judgment** in this sense is rendered idiomatically; for example, "to tie the words of." In other languages people may say "to decide the right or wrong of."

If, however, **all** is understood as referring to the godless, then "to execute judgment" is equivalent to bringing about conviction and punishment. This will also mean that the godless are the objects of judgment throughout the verse.

A third interpretation is to understand **to execute judgment** as including the punishment, and that the object of judgment for the whole verse is all of humanity. This is the interpretation followed by RSV and TEV; in both translations it is clear that the object of judgment is the same throughout the verse. While this interpretation does not seem as logical as the first alternative, it is the one that is closest to the Greek text, which can be translated literally: "to do (or, bring about) judgment (or, justice) on all and to convict every life (or, soul) concerning all their godless works that they have committed in a godless way, and concerning all the hard (or, defiant) things (or, words) that godless sinners spoke against him."

For **ungodly** see comments on verse 4. This word and related forms seem to be a favorite word in Jude. In the present verse it is repeated three times, and the repetition is a very effective rhetorical device, emphasizing the wickedness of the ones he is referring to. Such a device can be retained in translation, provided that it is natural in the language, and that such repetition will have the same function as it has in the biblical text, namely, to highlight and focus on the godlessness of these people. However, if repetition results in an unnatural expression, or weakens rather than strengthens the point that the verse wants to emphasize, namely, the godlessness of the false teachers, then repetition as a rhetorical device should not be used. In this case rhetorical devices with equivalent functions should be employed. For example, in some languages a series of different words of similar meaning will have such a function of emphasis and focus.

The expression **which they have committed in such an ungodly way** translates a single Greek verb, which is the verb form of the word "ungodliness" or "godlessness." There seems to be no way, in English at least, of translating this in a natural way. TEV has restructured the whole clause in order to make it more natural; it has translated the verb simply as "performed," leaving the quality of godlessness to be understood from the context, since such information is also present in the previous expression "godless deeds." Some other translations have similar solutions; for example, JB "the wicked things they have done," NEB "the godless deeds they have committed." One other way is simply to omit translating the verb altogether, since the expression "godless deeds" already includes the element of doing (as, for example, TNT "their ungodly deeds"). While this solution results in a very natural translation in many languages, it has the problem of not retaining the rhetorical device of repetition that is employed in the Greek text, and also of not compensating for such a device through the use of an equivalent rhetorical device in the translation. One can partially retain these devices by translating "to condemn all those people who do not worship God, for all the evil deeds they have performed against him."

The last part of this verse deals with **things**, which means "words." The word translated **harsh** can also mean "hard," "rough," "stiff," "defiant" (JB), "unpleasant," "terrible" (TEV), or "insolent." These words are spoken by "ungodly sinners," who should be identified with the "ungodly" in the second part of the verse, except that now they are also described as "sinners." This identification should be made clear in translation, otherwise the meaning may come out that the "ungodly" are being punished for the harsh words that other people, namely "godless sinners," are saying. An example of identifying the two is that of TNT: "the harsh things which they, godless sinners, have said against him." In all languages there is a natural way of marking old information, and this should be done with "ungodly sinners" here. One way of doing this is to say "for all the terrible words (hard to hear) that these godless sinners . . . ."

Him refers back to **the Lord** at the beginning of the quotation in verse 14.

In many languages it is more natural to put "words" before "deeds," and some translators may want to reverse the order here. However, there is a further consideration: the next verse (verse 16) deals primarily with words, and the connection of the two verses may be much clearer if the present order is retained. This of course does not prevent a translator from reversing the order, provided the connection between the two verses can still be established clearly.

Alternative translation models for this verse are:

> (1) to bring judgment on all people; to condemn those godless sinners for all the terrible words they have spoken against him and for the godless deeds they have performed (against him).

Reversing the order of the final clauses:

> (2) to bring judgment on all people; to condemn them all for the evil deeds they have performed against God and for all the terrible words that they have spoken against him.

In both these models the phrases "against God" or "against him" bring out the idea of **ungodly**.

16 RSV	TEV
These are grumblers, malcontents, following their own passions, loud-mouthed boasters, flattering people to gain advantage.	These people are always grumbling and blaming others; they follow their own evil desires; they brag about themselves and flatter others in order to get their own way.

In this verse Jude elaborates on verse 15, giving five examples of the evil words and deeds. With the exception of the third ("following their own passions"), these examples refer primarily to words; perhaps this is because, in the first part of the letter, he has already mentioned the evil deeds of the godless people, and now he wants to concentrate on their words or teachings.

These of course refers to the same people referred to in verse 15. The first thing mentioned about them is that they are **grumblers** or "murmurers." One way of rendering "grumble" is "speaking against." And in certain languages there are idioms that capture the meaning of this word; for example, "have a brittle mouth."

Who are these people grumbling against? There are three possibilities: they are grumbling against God or against other people, or against both. Some translations such as RSV translate the text literally and come out with an ambiguous rendering (in addition to RSV, also NEB, TNT "they do nothing but grumble and complain."). Other translations make other people the object (TEV for instance).

A case can be made for God being the object of these grumblings. The use of this word is probably suggested by the experience of the Israelites in the desert, when they continually complained against God. This matter has already been mentioned in verse 5. The complaints of the Israelites are described in both biblical and nonbiblical literature as "murmurings" or "grumblings" (for example, Num 14.2,27,29,36; Deut 1.27; Psa 106.25). Korah's revolt (mentioned in verse 11) is also described in the Old Testament as "murmuring." If it can be accepted that Jude has the desert experiences of the Israelites in mind, then "grumblings" can be related directly to "harsh things" in verse 15, and these grumblings therefore are directed more to God than to other people. Such an interpretation will also take seriously the literary style of Jude, who likes to build on things he has already mentioned.

The second description of these people is that they are **malcontents**. The Greek word here describes people who are "fault-finding," "complaining," or "discontented," never satisfied with their state and always blaming others about their situation. The word is used only here in the whole New Testament; in nonbiblical literature it is sometimes used as a term meaning the same as **grumblers**.

As to who this discontentment is directed against, again the possibility is either God or other people. If **malcontents** and **grumblers** are taken as being parallel terms, then their object is the same. It is possible, of course, to distinguish between the two and understand the object of "malcontents" as other people rather than God (as in TEV "blaming others"). In this case we may also say "saying that others are wrong" or "finding fault with others."

The third description of the godless people is that they **follow their own passions**. The Greek word translated **passions** can be understood either in a general sense, referring to every human desire as opposed to God's, or in a more limited sense, referring to desires in a bad sense, "evil desires" (TEV), "selfish desires" (TNT). The Greek word for **follow** is literally "going the way of" and contains the elements of "living according to" or "conducting oneself." Alternative translation models for this clause are "They give themselves over to do the evil things their hearts want them to do" or "They continuously do the evil things . . . ."

The fourth description is that these people are **loud-mouthed boasters** (literally "their mouth speaks in an excessive [or, bombastic] way"). The word for "excessive" is used only here and in 2 Peter 2.18 and literally means "huge," but it is used figuratively here to characterize boastful, bombastic, or arrogant speech. If the meaning is taken as "boastful," then the object of the boasting is "themselves" (as in TEV "they brag about themselves"). If, however, we take the meaning as "arrogant," then this arrogance is directed toward God. Most translations render this expression in an ambiguous way, without making clear the intended object, although those taking the meaning of "boastful" can be understood as favoring the first of these two options (for instance, NEB "Big words come rolling from their lips," JB "with mouths full of boastful talk," or idiomatically "big mouths").

The fifth description of these people is **flattering people to gain advantage**. The Greek word for **flattering** people is literally "to admire (or, marvel at) a face," and the expression does not appear elsewhere in the New Testament. As far as its Old Testament background is concerned, the expression has the following meanings:

1. It may mean to show respect to people. Used in this general sense the term is not necessarily bad; in fact it may have a positive tone.
2. It may mean to show partiality, in a bad sense. The equivalent Old Testament idiom very often refers to showing favoritism in the administration of justice, usually as a result of taking bribes.
3. It may mean to flatter people. This is another possible meaning, although there are very few examples in the Old Testament where this meaning is clearly intended.

What is clear from the context is that this expression has to be related to the words of the godless people, that is, to the content of their teaching and the way they teach. Therefore a general meaning of "showing favoritism" will not do, since that would refer primarily to deeds rather than words. What it seems to mean here is that these people show partiality in their teaching; that is, they teach in such a way so as to cater to the wishes and whims of some people. Their teaching therefore is compromised to the extent that they will change it if that will please some important people in the community. And they do this for a very selfish reason: **to gain advantage**. This expression can refer either to material benefits or to political gains: they cater to these people so that they, the false teachers, can have their own way (compare TEV). In certain languages translators may use idioms in this context; for example, "sweet talk others" or "have sweet mouths with others in order to . . . ."

Alternative translation models for this verse are as follows:

(1) These people are always speaking against God and finding fault with him; they continuously do the evil things that their hearts want to do; they have big mouths and flatter (sweet talk) other people in order to get their own way.
(2) These people are always speaking against other people and finding fault with them; . . . .
(3) These people are always speaking against God and finding fault with other people; . . . .

Ethical guidance for the recipients of the letter
17-23

RSV

TEV

Warnings and Instructions

17 But you must remember, beloved, the predictions of the apostles of our Lord Jesus Christ; 18 they said to you, "In the last time there will be scoffers, following their own

17 But remember, my friends, what you were told in the past by the apostles of our Lord Jesus Christ. 18 They said to you, "When the last days come, people will appear who will

ungodly passions." 19 It is these who set up divisions, worldly people, devoid of the Spirit. 20 But you, beloved, build yourselves up on your most holy faith; pray in the Holy Spirit; 21 keep yourselves in the love of God; wait for the mercy of our Lord Jesus Christ unto eternal life. 22 And convince some, who doubt; 23 save some, by snatching them out of the fire; on some have mercy with fear, hating even the garment spotted by the flesh.

make fun of you, people who follow their own godless desires." 19 These are the people who cause divisions, who are controlled by their natural desires, who do not have the Spirit. 20 But you, my friends, keep on building yourselves up on your most sacred faith. Pray in the power of the Holy Spirit, 21 and keep yourselves in the love of God, as you wait for our Lord Jesus Christ in his mercy to give you eternal life.

22 Show mercy toward those who have doubts; 23 save others by snatching them out of the fire; and to others show mercy mixed with fear, but hate their very clothes, stained by their sinful lusts.

After describing the godless people at length, Jude now addresses his readers directly and gives them guidance on how they should conduct themselves in view of the threat that comes from these people. He first of all reminds them that the emergence of these people was predicted long ago by the first Christian apostles. Then he advises them on how they should live and how they should relate to other Christians.

SECTION HEADING. The heading suggested by the outline of Jude is covered more simply by the TEV section heading "Warnings and Instructions." This may also be rendered as "How Christians should live," "Jude warns and instructs the Christians," or "Jude instructs Christians how they should live."

17   RSV   TEV

But you must remember, beloved, the predictions of the apostles of our Lord Jesus Christ;

But remember, my friends, what you were told in the past by the apostles of our Lord Jesus Christ.

But you is emphatic and indicates a sharp contrast between Jude's readers and the godless people referred to in the previous section. The last mention of those people was at the beginning of verse 16.

Must remember is an imperative; that is, it is grammatically a command. However, the readers are not exactly commanded to remember something in the sense of putting some new fact into their memory; rather they are exhorted to call to mind or recall something they already know. Therefore **you must remember** can be rendered as "it is necessary for you to recall," or "it is important for you to bring to mind," or ". . . not to forget."

What they are supposed to recall or remember are **the predictions of the apostles of our Lord Jesus Christ. Predictions** is literally "words spoken before" or "words said beforehand." The focus is not so much on whether these words are **predictions** or prophetic utterances, but on the fact that these were spoken before the time of the writing of Jude's letter.

This is the first time in the letter that Jude uses the word **apostles**, which describes persons who are sent with a message and a mission, and who can

48

speak and act with the authority of the sender. The word has both a restricted and a general usage. It refers in particular to the first disciples of Jesus (sometimes known as the Twelve). This list includes Matthias, who took the place of Judas Iscariot (Acts 1.26). Generally, however, **apostles** is used to refer to Christian missionaries, evangelists, and other Christian workers (Acts 15.5; Rom 16.7; 2 Cor 8.23). In the early church the apostles were recognized as people of authority; they derived this authority from the fact that they were with Jesus while he was on earth and were eyewitnesses to the events in Jesus' life. It is therefore proper for Jude to appeal to apostolic authority. The plural form here, **the apostles**, perhaps refers not to the general meaning of the term but to its restricted usage, meaning the original twelve disciples of Jesus. This is probably why Jude clearly excludes himself from the group. In some languages **apostles** will be referred to as "sent ones" or "messengers of Jesus Christ"; but in others a term similar to "ambassador" will be used, referring to an individual who is sent by someone to convey a message—in this case the Good News. So one may translate "ambassadors from Jesus Christ," or even "special ambassadors from . . . ."

For **Jesus Christ** see comments on verse 1; and for **Lord** see comments on verse 4. The close relation between the Christians and Jesus is indicated by the use of the pronoun **our**. It should be translated here in an inclusive sense, to include Jude and his readers.

An alternative translation model for this verse is:

> But it is important for you, my dear fellow Christians, not to forget (to bring to mind) the words that the apostles spoke in the past about our Lord Jesus Christ.

18	RSV	TEV

they said to you, "In the last time there will be scoffers, following their own ungodly passions."	They said to you, "When the last days come, people will appear who will make fun of you, people who follow their own godless desires."

They said to you can be understood in two ways. First, it can mean that the communities to whom Jude is writing have been evangelized directly by the apostles, and that the Christians in those communities have actually heard the apostles speak to them in person. But it is more likely that what is meant here is not that the apostles necessarily spoke directly to the recipients of Jude's letter, but that, when they spoke, what they said was relevant not only for their own immediate listeners but for all believers, including those of later generations. This interpretation allows the quoted material to be part of a body of Christian teaching that was in circulation during Jude's time.

A literal translation of course favors the first interpretation, and this is true of most translations, including RSV and TEV. However, some translations do allow for the possibility that the apostles did not speak directly to Jude's readers; for example, Phps has "the words that the messengers of Jesus Christ gave us beforehand when they said . . . ."

The statement that follows is also found in 2 Peter 3.3 but nowhere else in the New Testament or in any existing writings attributed to the apostles. And since 2 Peter is dependent on Jude, it becomes obvious that the source for Jude's quotation does not exist today. It is of course possible that this is not a quotation but a summary of the apostles' thinking regarding this matter. This understanding is allowed by the Greek text itself and may be reflected in a translation by avoiding the use of quotation markers. Most translations, however, translate the statement as a quotation.

In the last time is literally "In the end of time" and is a popular New Testament expression for the period between the time of Jesus' earthly life and his coming again. It was the belief among the early Christians that the coming of Jesus began a new era in history, characterized by a new way of God dealing with his people. This new era will come to its climax at the second coming of Jesus, at which time all of God's plans for the universe and for all humankind will be completely fulfilled. There are variations in the form of this expression, as for example "in the last days" or "in the last times," but these have the same meaning. The use of the term to describe the time of Jude indicates that Jude himself believed that he was living in the last days, and that the end of the world was about to come. We may also translate this phrase as "in the days just before the end time."

The word **scoffers** occurs in the Old Testament and describes people who make fun of or despise anything that has to do with God, religion, or morality. As such these people are clearly contrasted with righteous people, that is, people who obey God and live according to his way. These scoffers make fun not only of God and the gospel, but also of people who profess to live by the gospel. This more narrow position is reflected in TEV, which states the object of the ridicule ("make fun of you"; we may also say "laugh at you"). But the broader position (that is, making fun of both God and people) seems preferable in this case.

The scoffers are characterized further as **following their own ungodly passions**. For **following** and **passions** see verse 16, where the same words are used. The word for **ungodly** is the word used in verse 4 (for which see discussion there) and repeated three times in verse 15. As already noted, it is one of Jude's favorite words.

An alternative translation model for this verse is:

> They warned you, "When the days just before the end time come, people will appear who will make fun of (or, laugh at) God and you. These are people whose lives are controlled by their own lusts (or, evil desires)."

19   RSV   TEV

It is these who set up divisions, worldly   **These are the people who cause divi-**
people, devoid of the Spirit.   **sions, who are controlled by their natu-**
                                                   ral desires, who do not have the Spirit.

The scoffers are further described in three ways: they **set up divisions**, they are **worldly people**, and they are **devoid of the Spirit**.

The expression **set up divisions** translates a rare Greek word that is used only here in the New Testament. There are two possible senses in which Jude uses it.

1. The word can mean "to define," or "to make a distinction." In this sense Jude may have meant that these scoffers make distinctions within the Christian community. Some scholars suggest that the people referred to are Gnostics and regard themselves as spiritual and therefore superior to other Christians, who are regarded as worldly and carnal.

2. The word can also mean "to divide," "to separate," and therefore to cause divisions within the Christian community. The scoffers create and cause divisions and factions within the church because of their teaching and their attitude toward others. By classifying people into spiritual and carnal, they have created a group within the church who consider themselves spiritually superior to others.

It is also possible that these people have actually separated themselves from other Christians. It is, however, preferable to understand that they have not actually started a separate group, but that they have created or caused the creation of factions and cliques within the Christian community. In certain languages we may translate **set up divisions** as "cause a strong difference of opinion among people," "a strong difference between groups of people," "cause separations" (Thai), or "cause the believers to separate into groups."

The term translated **worldly people** is a Greek word that can be translated literally as "natural" or "pertaining to the soul (or life)." In the New Testament it is used of people who put emphasis on the physical rather than on the spiritual, and who depend on their natural instincts rather than on the help of God's Spirit. This distinction is found in Paul's letters; for example, in 1 Cor 2.14 this word is used to refer to people who "do not have the Spirit (are unspiritual)." Perhaps in this context it means "people . . . who are controlled by their natural desires" (see TEV) or "whose natural evil desires control them." Apparently these people considered themselves spiritual and other Christians as nonspiritual or natural, but here Jude turns what they say around and applies to them the same negative term that they have applied to others.

Finally the godless people are described as **devoid of the Spirit**, literally "not having the Spirit." This is directly related to the term we have just discussed. **Worldly people** are also **devoid of the Spirit** because they depend solely on their own strength and not on the power of the Spirit. **The Spirit** here refers to the Spirit of God. Here again Jude turns the arguments around. While these people declare themselves to be spiritual, Jude asserts the opposite: they do not have the Spirit of God, nor are they guided by the Spirit.

In languages that do not use capital letters, it will be helpful to state that this is the Spirit of God.

An alternative translation model for this verse is:

> These are the people who cause the believers to divide into separate groups. Their evil natural desires control them, and they do not have the Spirit of God.

20   RSV   TEV

But you, beloved, build yourselves up on your most holy faith; pray in the Holy Spirit;	**But you, my friends, keep on building yourselves up on your most sacred faith. Pray in the power of the Holy Spirit,**

In the next four verses Jude gives direct advice to his readers on how they should respond to the threat of the godless people among them. He instructs (or, teaches) them first how to conduct themselves within the Christian fellowship, and then how to deal with those who have been influenced by these people.

For **But you, beloved**, see comments on verse 17.

With regard to living out their lives within the fellowship, Jude gives his readers four pieces of advice. First, he exhorts them to **build yourselves up on your most holy faith**. The use of the building (or the temple) as a metaphor for the Christian community is found frequently in the New Testament, especially in Paul's letters, but also in 1 Peter (see 1 Peter 2.5). It is perhaps out of this metaphor that the idea of "building up" the Christian community developed. The meaning of the figure is not that each Christian should build up his or her own Christian life, but that Christians should help and encourage one another so that they may grow in their faith and collectively contribute to the growth and well-being of the church.

Your most holy faith can be connected with what is before it in two ways: either with "in" or with "on." This is because the Greek itself does not explicitly use a preposition, and since the noun is in the dative, the prepositions "in" and "on" are both possible. If "in" is chosen, it means that Jude is exhorting his readers to help one another to grow in the knowledge and practice of their faith. If, however, "on" is chosen (as in RSV and TEV), then it means that the **holy faith** is the foundation upon which the Christians are going to build. This latter interpretation is quite appropriate here, since the Christians to whom Jude is writing are facing the threat of heresy and false teaching.

What does **faith** here mean? If the first interpretation above is chosen, then faith can mean "trust in" or "commitment to" Jesus Christ; or perhaps **faith** can also be understood as a Christian virtue, although this would not go very well with **most holy**. This is perhaps enough reason for choosing the second interpretation above (using the preposition "on" rather than "in"), in which case **faith** is understood either as a technical term for the Christian religion, or as a body of Christian teaching. The second alternative seems quite appropriate here, since Jude is combating heretical teaching, and it is therefore logical for him to contrast Christian teaching or doctrine with the heretical views that are being put forward. (For further comments on **faith** see the discussion on Jude 3.)

The word **holy** can also mean many things, but here it can refer to the content of the faith (that is, it is about sacred or divine matters), or the source of the faith (it is from God and therefore unique). **Most** is not used here with a comparative function (meaning that their faith is the "holiest"), but with an intensifying function, being understood as "really," or "truly," or "very very."

The second instruction that Jude gives is that his readers should **pray in the Holy Spirit**. This again is a familiar command in the New Testament (see Rom 8.26; Eph 6.18). The preposition **in** here most probably means "in the control of," "under the inspiration of," "guided by," or "by means of the power of." In other words Jude is exhorting his readers that when they pray they should always seek and follow the guidance of the Spirit, so that by the Spirit's power they are able to pray properly and according to God's will. So we may also say "You should pray through the power of the Holy Spirit," ". . . guided by the power of the Holy Spirit," or "When you pray, the power of the Holy Spirit will guide you."

The **Holy Spirit** is used here as a technical term referring to what Christians now understand as the third person in the Trinity. In translating this term, translators should of course use whatever term is already in use in the Christian community for whom they are translating.

An alternative translation model for this verse is:

> But you, my beloved fellow Christians, must keep on helping each other to build upon (grow in) the message that God has given you. You should pray guided by the power of the Holy Spirit.

Or:

> . . . has given you. As you pray you should let the power of the Holy Spirit guide you.

21	RSV	TEV
	keep yourselves in the love of God; wait for the mercy of our Lord Jesus Christ unto eternal life.	and keep yourselves in the love of God, as you wait for our Lord Jesus Christ in his mercy to give you eternal life.

Jude's next instruction to his readers is to **keep yourselves in the love of God**. The Greek text can mean "Keep yourselves in your love for God," and some commentators follow this interpretation. This is possible, since in the two previous exhortations Jude is urging his readers to some course of action, and here he may also be exhorting them to continue loving God.

Most commentators, however, take the genitive construction of this phrase as meaning "God's love for you," which would be parallel to **the mercy of our Lord Jesus Christ** in the next part of the verse. In this case Jude is telling his readers that they should live and act with the consciousness that God loves them; if they believe that God loves them, then such a faith demands an appropriate response: their life must show that they are indeed controlled by God's love. As previously noted, **keep** is a favorite term of Jude (see verses 1, 6, and 13). So we may translate "You should continue to live knowing (or, with the assurance) that God loves you."

Finally Jude exhorts his readers to **wait for the mercy of our Lord Jesus Christ unto eternal life**. It is obvious that this RSV rendering is not a natural English sentence; the reason for this is that it translates the Greek text literally.

The word for **wait for** is used in the New Testament for the Christian's expectation of things in the future; that is, the Christian waits with confidence for the coming of the end time, when Jesus Christ will be fully revealed at his coming again. Thus the object of the Christian's waiting is really Jesus Christ himself, who will show mercy; the object is not his mercy, as a literal translation of the verse seems to indicate. Another way of translating this is "wait expectantly for the Lord Jesus Christ to mercifully . . . ."

Mercy may also be rendered as "pity," "compassion," "kindness," "goodness," or "love." Like **wait for**, **mercy** is also a term associated with the Christian's hope regarding the future; it is used to refer to divine compassion that is to be shown at the end of time. In the literature before the New Testament period, this mercy was attributed to God. The New Testament generally attributes it to Jesus Christ, and Jude's wording clearly reflects the Christian interpretation of this hope. The clause **wait for the mercy of our Lord Jesus Christ** may be translated as "You must wait expectantly (with confidence) for our Lord Jesus Christ to show his love."

The expression **eternal life** is one of the most common expressions in the New Testament. It has two components of meaning: quality (real life, life that God has promised, life lived according to God's will) and length (unending, continuous, endless). So we may say "real life that lasts forever." Eternal life is to be given to the Christians in the end time as a result of Christ's mercy on them. This is the meaning of the preposition **unto**.

Perhaps after this analysis the meaning of the clause is much clearer. We can summarize it as follows: The Christians are exhorted to wait with patience for the last days, at which time Jesus Christ will give to them eternal life. He will do this because he has compassion on them.

An alternative translation model for this verse is:

> You should continue to live knowing (or, with the assurance) that God loves you. Wait expectantly for our Lord Jesus Christ to let you have eternal life. He will do this because he loves you.

22-23   RSV   TEV

22 And convince some, who doubt;   22 Show mercy toward those who
23 save some, by snatching them out of   have doubts; 23 save others by snatch-
the fire; on some have mercy with fear,   ing them out of the fire; and to others
hating even the garment spotted by the   show mercy mixed with fear, but hate
flesh.^e   their very clothes, stained by their sinful
                                           lusts.

^e The Greek text in this sentence is
uncertain at several points

There is a textual problem in verse 22: some manuscripts have "convince,"
while others have "have mercy." The two verbs are quite similar in the Greek,
both in form and in sound, and this obviously gave rise to the textual problem.

In addition to this variation, an early papyrus indicates a shorter version
of verses 22-23a that can be translated thus: "Snatch some from the fire, and
have mercy with fear on those who doubt . . . ." This seems to be the text
translated by Mft: "Snatch some from the fire, and have mercy on the
waverers, trembling as you touch them." Some commentators are of the opinion
that this text is the original text written by Jude.

Most modern translations, with the exception of RSV, translate the text
used by TEV. This is also the text that is in the UBS Greek New Testament,
although the rating for this text is "C," which means there is a considerable
degree of doubt as to what the original text is. At any rate, the verb "have
mercy" primarily means "have pity," "have compassion," "be kind," or "having
a loving heart toward."

This mercy is directed toward fellow Christians **who doubt**. The word used
here already appears in verse 9, but there it has the meaning "dispute." Some
scholars take the position that it also has the same meaning here, referring to
members of the Christian community who argue against other Christians, and
who justify their ungodly behavior by means of the heretical teachings of the
godless. This goes well with the verb "convince" or "refute" and produces the
following translation: "refute those who dispute the Christian faith."

However, the word here is in the form of a passive participle, and in the
passive the verb frequently means "to be doubtful," "to waver," "to hesitate,"
and this is the meaning reflected in RSV and TEV, and in many other
translations. These are the Christians who begin to have doubts about the
truth of the Christian faith and of particular Christian doctrines because of the
influence of those who are giving false teaching. Perhaps we can say "those
who are uncertain about what they believe."

A third possible meaning of this word is "to be under judgment" and refers
to people who have been reproved or perhaps separated from the Christian
community because of their stubborn and unrepentant attitude. While this is
possible, and it fits the context quite well, no translation examined for this
Handbook follows this interpretation.

Save in the next clause primarily means "rescue" or "keep from." **Fire**, on
the other hand, can refer to two things:

1. It can be a reference to the fires of the final judgment (as in verse 7), during which time the wicked will receive the punishment they deserve. This is in keeping with the tone of urgency about the future found in the letter. Most commentaries prefer this first possibility.
2. On the other hand, **fire** can refer to the trials and difficulties that the Christians were experiencing at that time. This also is appropriate, since Jude describes a community of believers that is beset by many problems arising from the presence of godless people among them.

Both options are equally valid. A literal translation does not offer any clue as to which meaning is preferred.

Who are the people who should be saved? Some commentators suggest that it is the same people spoken of in verse 26, that is, those who doubt. Others identify this group with the people mentioned in the next clause. Still others, however, are of the opinion that there are three groups mentioned in verses 22-23, one group in verse 22 and two other groups in verse 23. This is the position taken by both RSV and TEV.

The expression **snatching them out of the fire** is an allusion to Zech 3.1-5, especially verses 3-4. The word for **snatch** can also mean "take by force," "carry off." If **fire** is taken to refer to the final judgment (as in the first possibility above), then the whole act of snatching people out of the fire is keeping them from going to hell or from eternal destruction at the end of the age. However, if **fire** refers to difficulties experienced in the present, then snatching people out of the fire means taking them out of their difficult situations, or making sure that these difficult situations cease and no longer affect the believers in a negative way.

It is clear from both RSV and TEV that **snatching them out of the fire** is the means by which saving these people is achieved. This relationship needs to be expressed clearly in the translation. In some languages it is much more natural to express **save** as the purpose or result of the act of snatching, as for example "Snatch them out of the fire in order to save them" or ". . . and, as a result, save them." In this context the word for **snatch** does not seem to indicate "force." If that is true, perhaps we may translate "Help them to get out of." Keeping in mind the two possible interpretations for the meaning of **fire**, it is possible to translate this clause as: (1) "Rescue other people by snatching them from the fire of judgment," or (2) "Rescue other people by saving (snatching) them from the trials and difficulties that are like a fire."

Jude now mentions a third group and exhorts his readers to **have mercy with fear** toward this group. The word for **mercy** is the same word used with reference to the first group. But what does **have mercy with fear** mean? A literal translation will be misleading, since it will have the meaning "mercy characterized by fear" or "fearful mercy." But here Jude is talking about two attitudes: being merciful and being fearful. And **fear** here can mean two things. Firstly, it may be fear of being contaminated by the sins of these people. In this sense Jude is saying that, while they should have mercy and compassion on these people, they should also be aware of the danger of their sins and should guard themselves against being influenced by them. So this fear has in it the elements of carefulness and caution. See, for example, JB, "there are others to whom you must be kind with great caution." On the other hand, **fear** can mean "fear of God." In this sense Jude is exhorting his readers to continue to have awe and reverence for God. And since they know that God will punish those who sin against him, their fear of God will prevent them from being influenced by these evil people within their fellowship.

While both of these interpretations can be justified by the text, the first one seems to be preferred because it fits the context much better, especially the words that follow.

The expression **hating even the garment spotted by the flesh** seems to explain further what **fear** means. In this case Jude exhorts his readers to be very cautious in dealing with these people, in order to avoid contamination of any kind. The word translated **garment** is the piece of clothing that is worn next to the skin. This is sometimes known as the inner garment, in contrast to the coat or robe that is known as the outer garment. This inner garment is described as **spotted by the flesh**. **Flesh** is the same word used in verse 8; here it refers either to sinful human nature or to actual sinful acts, primarily sexual immorality. The whole expression **the garment spotted by the flesh** can be understood literally; that is, their clothes are dirty and soiled as a result of their sinful acts. Or it may be expressing the primitive belief that spiritual and demonic powers can reside in and be communicated through a person's clothes (see Mark 5.27-30; Acts 19.11-12). It is more likely, however, that here we have a figure of speech known as hyperbole, or exaggeration. The idea seems to be that these people are so sinful and so evil that even the very clothes they wear are affected and defiled.

What does Jude mean by exhorting his readers in this manner? Some commentators suggest that here he is advising his readers not to have any contact with these sinners—a position that finds support elsewhere in the New Testament. To hate even their garments then means that any contacts with these people, however casual or slight, should be avoided at any cost. However, it seems more likely that Jude's intention is not for his readers to avoid contact with such people, but to exercise caution and care in dealing with them. The object of their hate is not the sinners but their garments; the sinners on the other hand should be the object of their mercy and compassion, with the aim in view of leading them out of their errors and sinful ways. If this is the case, we may translate "as if their clothes have been stained by their sinful evil lusts" or "as if their sinful evil lusts have made their garments filthy."

An alternative translation model for these verses is:

> 22 Show compassion (or, Have a loving heart) toward those people who are uncertain about what they believe; 23 rescue others by snatching them from the fire of judgment. And there are other people to whom you must be kind, but at the same time be very cautious. You must hate their very clothes, as if their sinful lusts have made these garments filthy.

Doxology
24-25

RSV   TEV

Prayer of Praise

24 Now to him who is able to keep you from falling and to present you without blemish before the presence of his glory with rejoicing, 25 to the only God, our Savior through Jesus Christ our Lord, be glory, majesty, dominion, and authority, before all time and now and for ever. Amen.

24 To him who is able to keep you from falling and to bring you faultless and joyful before his glorious presence—25 to the only God our Savior, through Jesus Christ our Lord, be glory, majesty, might, and authority, from all ages past, and now, and forever and ever! Amen.

Unlike other New Testament letter writers, Jude does not include in his conclusion greetings to individual members of the community he is writing to. But like some other letters he ends with a doxology, following the traditional New Testament doxology form. This form has four parts:
1. the person being praised, usually in the dative case;
2. the word of praise;
3. the indication of time; and
4. the word "Amen."
While Jude follows this form, he introduces several modifications and expansions, as we shall see.

SECTION HEADING: "Doxology" may also be rendered as in TEV, "Prayer of praise," or else "Concluding prayer" or "Concluding doxology." A full clause may be "Finally Jude praises God."

24   RSV   TEV

Now to him who is able to keep you from falling and to present you without blemish before the presence of his glory with rejoicing,

To him who is able to keep you from falling and to bring you faultless and joyful before his glorious presence—

The person to whom praise is addressed in the doxology is God. **To him** is linked with "to the only God, our Savior" in verse 25. In many languages translators will need to introduce "God" at this point rather than at the beginning of verse 24 and say, for example, "The only God, our [inclusive] Savior, is able to keep . . . ." (See the alternative translation model at the end of the comments on verse 25.) Jude does not simply refer to God, but he mentions two functions of God that are directly related to Jude's readers. First, he describes God as **able to keep** them **from falling**. The expression **to him who is able** is used in two other doxologies (Rom 16.25; Eph 3.20) and emphasizes God's power and sufficiency. The word translated **falling** is literally "stumbling" and is a very popular metaphor in the Old Testament, particularly in the book of Psalms, where the psalmist refers to God's power to prevent him from falling into the traps laid down by the enemy (see Psa 140.4-5; 141.9;

142.3). In Jude **falling** may have the general meaning of being defeated by any problem or difficulty, or of giving in to sin. But perhaps here it focuses on the particular meaning of a person losing faith and ceasing to be a follower of Christ, together with the consequences of receiving judgment. This of course happens if Jude's readers rely on their own strength in dealing with the godless. But in the end it is God who will give them victory over these people and their false teachings.

The second attribute of God is his ability to make people sinless and bring them into his very presence. The formula used by Jude is similar to formulas present in other New Testament doxologies (Col 1.22; Eph 1.4), indicating that this is a standard formula. **To present you** is to put you in front of, to put you before. The word for **without blemish** was used originally to describe animals that were brought for the temple sacrifice; they were to be perfect in every way, without defect of any kind (see 1 Peter 1.19 for example). In other parts of the Bible this word is used of the moral purity and integrity that should characterize people who come to worship God (for example Psa 15.2; Pro 11.5; Eph 1.4; Heb 9.14). This is the sense in which it is used here. **Glory** refers to God's being and presence, characterized by radiance, majesty, and greatness. Here it perhaps has overtones of the manner in which God appears at the end of time. The whole expression **before the presence of his glory** therefore simply means "before his glorious presence" (TEV).

With rejoicing further characterizes those who are presented before God. This also has overtones of the joy and exultation of God's people when he reveals himself to them at the end of the age. The Greek construction clearly suggests that **with rejoicing** is parallel to **without blemish**, suggesting perhaps that joy is a result of being pronounced not guilty at the final judgment. If this is correct then the translation must show clearly this relationship. Some translations have tried to do this, like TEV "faultless and joyful," JB "bring you safe to his glorious presence, innocent and happy," and TNT "present you, blameless and rejoicing, in his glorious presence."

25	RSV	TEV
	to the only God, our Savior through Jesus Christ our Lord, be glory, majesty, dominion, and authority, before all time and now and for ever. Amen.	to the only God our Savior, through Jesus Christ our Lord, be glory, majesty, might, and authority, from all ages past, and now, and forever and ever! Amen.

The pronoun "him" in verse 24 is now made clear by the expression **the only God**. One of the famous creeds of the Jews is that God is the only God and cannot tolerate rivals. God is described as **Savior**, which is also a traditional Jewish term for God (note the Old Testament phrase "the God of our salvation" in Psa 64.6; 94.1). God is called "Savior" because he rescued the people of Israel from slavery in Egypt, and because he saves them from trouble, difficulty, and the threat of enemies. The title "Savior" is used eight times in the New Testament to refer to God, but more frequently (sixteen times) it is used of Jesus Christ. It is possible that the use of the term for Jesus has as its background the Old Testament usage. It is not unusual for functions and attributes of God in the Old Testament to be used of Jesus.

It is also possible that the term **Savior** has as its background its use in the popular religions of that period, where the term was used of Greek gods and various rulers. If there is truth in this, then this is one case where the pagan environment has influenced the proclamation of the Christian faith, or where the Christian faith has used pagan culture in order to more meaningfully proclaim and communicate the gospel of Jesus Christ.

As for the meaning of the term itself, it refers to the work of "salvation," for which see the discussion on Jude 3. Considering the focus of the letter on the future, perhaps salvation here also refers to the gift of new and real life at the end of time.

The expression **through Jesus Christ** is often found in New Testament doxologies and is distinctively a Christian addition to the traditional doxology form (see Rom 16.27; 1 Peter 4.11). But how does this relate to the whole doxology? Is it related to the function of God as Savior in the sense that God saves us through Jesus Christ, as the RSV punctuation has it, or does it relate to the words of praise that follow, giving the sense that it is through Jesus Christ that we ascribe glory and majesty to God? Most translations indicate by the punctuation they use that they prefer the second of these alternatives.

There are four qualities ascribed to God. **Glory** can mean either "praise" (that is, God is worthy to be praised) or greatness. **Majesty** describes the awesome splendor of God (see 1 Chr 29.11). The next two terms are similar in meaning, with **dominion** referring to God's absolute power, and **authority** to God's sovereignty as ruler. All four terms are commonly used in traditional doxologies.

But the question still remains, how do we ascribe all of these to God through Jesus Christ? This can be understood to mean either that it is Jesus Christ who enables people to do this, or else that it is because of Jesus Christ (that is, their relationship to him) that they are now able to praise God and acknowledge his majesty, power, and authority.

These qualities are ascribed to God for all eternity. That is what Jude means by **before all time** (that is, before any time that is past), **and now** (that is, the present), **and for ever** (that is, any time in the indefinite future). **Before all time** is similar to "before the ages" (1 Cor 2.7), "before the foundation of the world" (John 17.24; Eph 1.4; 1 Peter 1.20), and other similar expressions. It refers to the time before the creation of the world and includes any time that is past.

The closing word **Amen** is a Hebrew affirmation that is regularly used at the conclusion of prayers and doxologies. The meaning of the expression is "so be it," or "may this come true," or "may this happen as we have said." This term is now used among Christians, usually at the end of a prayer. If it is strange to use it at the end of a doxology formula, then of course it will have to be restructured, in order to avoid confusion between a prayer and a doxology.

In many languages translators will need to restructure these two verses and say, for example:

> 24 The only God, our [inclusive] Savior, is able to keep you from giving in to sin, and to bring you to stand in the dazzling light before him, having no faults and with a joyful heart. 25 May Jesus Christ our Lord cause people to give honor to God and praise him. May they recognize that he has power and authority from the beginning of time, presently, and always forever. Amen.

Or:

> . . . 25 Because people belong to Jesus Christ, they are now able to give honor to God. . . .

The Second Letter from Peter

Title

Translators should follow the same format as that used for the title of *The First Letter from Peter.*

Outline of Contents

As is the case in Jude, there are various ways of outlining the contents of *The Second Letter from Peter.* The outline suggested below is followed in this Handbook.

1.1-2 Salutation
1.3-11 A call to live according to God's call
1.12-15 Aim and purpose of the letter
1.16-21 The reliability of the prophetic message regarding Jesus Christ

2.1-3 False teachers who misinterpret and misuse the prophetic message
2.4-10a Old Testament examples to show that God punishes the wicked
   and rewards those who are faithful to him
2.10b-22 A further description of the false teachers
   2.10b-16 The sins of the false teachers
   2.17-22 The punishment of the false teachers

3.1-18 A discussion on the Parousia
   3.1-2 Introductory statement about a former letter
   3.3-10 The Parousia and reasons for its delay
   3.11-15a Ethical implications of the Parousia and the disaster connected
      with it
   3.15b-16 A mention of Paul and his letters as supporting the above ideas
3.17-18 Closing doxology

As far as section headings are concerned, translators may want use TEV as a model. In this case they may wish to use alternative ways of rendering the section headings, and some suggestions will be made at the appropriate places in the Handbook.

Chapter 1

Salutation
1.1-2

<table>
<tr><td align="center">RSV</td><td align="center">TEV</td></tr>
<tr>
<td>

1 Simeon Peter, a servant and apostle of Jesus Christ,

To those who have obtained a faith of equal standing with ours in the righteousness of our God and Savior Jesus Christ:

2 May grace and peace be multiplied to you in the knowledge of God and of Jesus our Lord.

</td>
<td>

1 From Simon Peter, a servant and apostle of Jesus Christ—

To those who through the righteousness of our God and Savior Jesus Christ have been given a faith as precious as ours:

2 May grace and peace be yours in full measure through your knowledge of God and of Jesus our Lord.

</td>
</tr>
</table>

The beginning of the letter follows the traditional letter form, which starts with the name and a brief description of the writer, followed by the names of those the letter is addressed to, and then a blessing. In the case of *The Second Letter from Peter,* the writer is named as **Simeon Peter, a servant and apostle of Jesus Christ**. (Please note that earlier editions of RSV used the spelling "Simon," but since the 1971 edition the spelling has been **Simeon.**) Those who receive the letter are not referred to by name but are described as sharing the writer's faith. The blessing is contained in verse 2 and is very similar to the blessing used in *The First Letter from Peter,* 1.2b.

Even though the writer of this letter identifies himself in the Greek as *Symeōn Petros,* there are problems in determining his real identity (see "Translating Jude and 2 Peter," page 1, and the comments on verse 1). Nevertheless it is clearly the intention of the writer to identify himself with the writer of *The First Letter from Peter,* who in turn is traditionally identified as the apostle Peter. For the purposes of this Handbook, the author of *The Second Letter from Peter* will simply be designated as "Peter," following the tradition of the church.

SECTION HEADING: "Salutation" may also be rendered "Greetings" or "Peter greets his readers."

1.1

<table>
<tr><td align="center">RSV</td><td align="center">TEV</td></tr>
<tr>
<td>

Simeon[x] Peter, a servant and apostle of Jesus Christ,

To those who have obtained a faith of equal standing with ours in the right-

</td>
<td>

From Simon Peter, a servant and apostle of Jesus Christ—

To those who through the right-eousness of our God and Savior Jesus

</td>
</tr>
</table>

eousness of our God and Savior Jesus Christ:[a]

Christ have been given a faith as precious as ours:

[x] Other authorities read *Simon*
[a] Or *of our God and the Savior Jesus Christ*

As indicated in RSV, the first name of Peter (Simon) is given in its Hebrew spelling **Simeon**, which is a Greek transliteration of the Hebrew form. This spelling is used only here and in Acts 15.14, although several other people in the New Testament have the name "Simeon" (see Luke 2.25,34; 3.30; Acts 13.1; Rev 7.7).

There are some scholars who find the use of *Symeon* significant here, especially since the Greek form "Simon" is the more popular form in the New Testament. Among the reasons given for the use of the Hebrew form are:

1. to emphasize the Jewish origin of Peter;
2. to stress the fact that Peter was an eyewitness of the events in Jesus' life, and therefore to affirm his authority as valid in opposition to the false teachers mentioned in the letter; and
3. to establish the authenticity of the letter.

Many interpreters, however, do not see any particular significance in the use of the Hebrew form, and simply understand it as a variation of the Greek form that was more commonly used during the first century.

At any rate, since "Simon" is the more common and familiar form, it means that in all likelihood *Symeon* was the form used to designate the author of this letter. A formal type of translation will reflect this feature of the text, which is what RSV has done. In such a case it is important to make sure that the name is spelled according to the way words are formed in the translator's language. For instance, in a language that lacks the cluster "sym," *Symeon* will have to be spelled according to what is allowed in the language, such as "Simeon" or "Simyon." However, in translations that focus on meaning, especially on a common language level, the variations in the spelling of a name do not have to be retained. What is more important is that the reader is aware that a particular name refers to a particular person. That is why, in common language translations, only one name (and one spelling) is used for a person, even if that person is known by different names, or even if there are different spellings of the same name.

Peter calls himself **a servant and apostle of Jesus Christ.** The Greek word for **servant** is literally "slave," which puts emphasis on being owned by Jesus Christ and being committed to follow and obey him completely. It is possible, however, and even likely, that the Greek word for "slave" here translates the Hebrew word (literally "servant"), in which case the emphasis is on serving Christ rather than being a slave of Christ. In the Old Testament the term "servant" is used as an honorific title of many Israelite leaders, including Abraham (Psa 105.42), Moses (Neh 9.14), David (Psa 89.3), and Daniel (Dan 6.20). In the New Testament the term is used both of believers in general and of particular individuals. The focus is on their being called by God and designated to perform certain tasks within the Christian fellowship, and as a result to become examples to all the believers of what it really means to be a follower of Christ.

Certain languages maintain a clear distinction between a person who works for a fixed salary and one who is a personal servant or attendant supported by his master but who does not have a fixed salary. It is this latter term that should be used in this context, if it is necessary to make such a distinction. There are also languages where people say "I am Jesus Christ's man," meaning "I work for Jesus Christ."

For **apostle** see discussion on Jude 17.

The apostles were recognized as having authority in the early church. They traveled from one place to another, encouraging the believers and taking care of problems encountered by the congregations, especially in matters of doctrine and church government. Peter uses the title here to remind his readers not only that he is one of the twelve original disciples, but that what he writes should be taken seriously, since he writes as one whose authority comes from Jesus Christ himself.

In many languages it is impossible to maintain the structure **Simeon Peter, a servant and apostle of Jesus Christ**, in which a noun phrase is in apposition with the name of a person. In such cases we may translate this sentence as "I, Simeon Peter, who am a servant and . . . ." Some translators will find it helpful to begin this epistle in a way that is more natural to letter writing in their own languages, instead of following the English or Greek; for example, "I, Simon Peter, who am a servant and apostle of Jesus Christ, write this letter to . . ." or "This letter comes from me, Simeon Peter, who am a servant and . . . ." It also may be necessary in certain languages to combine the initial clause with what follows and say, for example, "I, Simeon Peter, who am . . . write this letter to those who . . . ." The phrase **to those** may also be rendered as "to those people," or even "to those people among you."

The readers are not identified in terms of race, nationality, or geographical location. Any statement regarding them must be derived from a study of the letter itself. If it can be assumed that those who received the letter are the same as those who received *The First Letter from Peter,* then we can know more definitely who they are and what their situation is, since *The First Letter from Peter* makes various references to the situation of its readers. In fact some scholars accept this position, primarily because of 3.1, where this letter refers to a first letter. However, such an assumption is held in doubt by many scholars. It is therefore necessary to examine the letter itself in order to identify the readers, and to understand the situation in which they find themselves, together with the problems that confront them. The letter tells us that those it is addressed to have also received Paul's letters (3.15). Because of this some have come to the conclusion that they are primarily Gentiles. However, this is hard to justify, since Paul wrote to churches that were composed of both Jews and Gentiles.

The word for **obtained** (TEV "has been given") primarily means "to receive." In translating this term we should avoid the idea that faith is acquired through a person's own effort or that it is given as a reward for what a person has done. Faith itself, or the power to trust in Jesus Christ, is a gift from God. In the phrase **To those who have obtained** (TEV "To those who . . . have been given"), it is clear that God is the one who causes people to accept or receive this **faith**. Therefore it is possible to translate this phrase as "To you whom God has caused to receive the . . . ."

What does **faith** mean in this case? It can refer to trust in and commitment to Jesus Christ, or to a body of authoritative teaching, or else, to the Christian faith as a religious movement. There is, however, no one view among commentaries or translations as to what **faith** here means. While English translations in general retain the word **faith**, they show their preference by the use of an indefinite article (for instance **a faith**, as in Mft, NIV, RSV, TEV) or by the absence of an article (as in Knox, NEB).

In the light of our interpretation above, we may translate **To those who have obtained a faith** as "To you who have received the teachings about Jesus Christ," or "To you whom God has caused to trust in Jesus Christ," or even "To you whom God has caused to receive the teachings of the Christian religion." Note also the discussion of the term in the comments on Jude 3.

The phrase **of equal standing** may be understood with the meaning "of the same kind" or "of equal value," thus accenting the quality of such a faith. These possibilities are expressed in translations such as NIV, the Spanish common language version (SPCL), and TEV by the phrase "as precious as ours." The choice of meaning is in some sense influenced by how **faith** is understood (see above). If **faith** in this context is understood to mean "a body of teaching," then we may translate the phrase **obtained a faith of equal standing** as "received teachings about Jesus Christ just like the ones we did" or "received the same teachings about Jesus Christ as we did." If, however, **faith** is understood as trust in Jesus Christ, then the phrase may be translated "trusted in Jesus Christ in the same way we did" or "who trust in Jesus Christ as fervently as we do."

The pronoun **ours** may refer: (1) to Peter and the other apostles, as contrasted with the intended readers, who were not apostles or eyewitnesses; (2) to Peter and the other Jewish Christians, as contrasted with the intended readers, who were most probably non-Jewish believers; or (3) to Peter and the Christian community to which he belongs, as contrasted with the intended readers, who obviously don't belong to Peter's immediate group. All three are possible, but most commentaries choose either the first or the second possibility. It seems, however, that the first possibility is to be preferred for the following reasons: firstly, the Jewish-Gentile conflict is not in focus in the letter; and secondly, in the light of 1.16-18 it is more likely that Peter is referring to the apostles as eyewitnesses rather than to Jewish Christians as a whole. Therefore **ours** can be translated as "that of us apostles." In any case, whatever possibility is chosen, the pronoun **ours** should be understood and translated as exclusive, that is "we" (Peter and others) excluding "you" (the intended readers).

This **faith** is given **in the righteousness of our God and Savior Jesus Christ**. The expression **our God and Savior Jesus Christ** may also be rendered as "our God and the Savior Jesus Christ," as the RSV footnote shows. The problem here can be made clear by a question: does the expression refer to two persons (God and Jesus Christ), or to only one person (Jesus Christ)? Those who interpret the expression as referring to both God and Jesus Christ put forth the following arguments:

1. The very next verse (verse 2) clearly distinguishes between God and Jesus Christ.
2. Similar expressions within the letter refer to Jesus Christ not as "God" but as "Lord."
3. The term "God" is rarely used of Jesus in the New Testament.

Arguments for understanding the expression as referring only to Jesus Christ include the following:

1. The Greek text itself favors this position. A word-for-word translation looks like this: ". . . of the God our and of Savior Jesus Christ." That the text favors the understanding that the whole expression refers to Christ is shown by the presence of only one definite article, which is placed before God. If the expression were intended to refer to both God and Jesus Christ, a definite article would have been placed before "Savior."
2. Elsewhere in the letter the same grammatical construction is used, and it is clear that in those other contexts the whole phrase refers to Jesus Christ (for example, 1.11; 3.18, except of course that in these expressions "Lord" is used instead of "God").
3. The term "God" is used of Christ elsewhere in the New Testament (see John 1.1; 2 Thes 1.12; and possibly Titus 2.13; 1 John 5.20) and in extra-biblical writings by the beginning of the second century (as in Ignatius' letter to the Ephesians 1.1; 7.2; 18.2; 19.3; and so on).

Considering all the arguments, it is probably best to understand the expression as referring to one person, namely, Jesus Christ, rather than to both God and Christ.

The other title used of Jesus Christ is **Savior**, for which see the discussion on Jude 25.

The expression **in the righteousness** can also be understood as "by the righteousness" or "through the righteousness" (TEV). This is because the Greek preposition *en* can mean "in," "by," or "through." In the last case the **faith** is given to the readers through or by means of **the righteousness** of Christ. But what does **righteousness** mean here? This word is one of those biblical terms that are rich in meaning and can be translated in various ways, depending on their context. For example, the expression "the righteousness of God" appears in different contexts with different meanings and emphases. In Rom 1.17 the righteousness of God refers to God's activity of putting people into a right relationship with himself (as TEV correctly translates). In Matt 6.33, however, the righteousness of God refers to what he requires people to do in order that they will be pleasing to him. In the present verse righteousness has been interpreted in the following ways:

1. It refers to Christ's righteous, redemptive work. It is through Christ's righteousness (that is, his dying on the cross) that Christians are given the power to put their trust in him.

67

2. It refers to Christ's righteous character as Savior and Redeemer. It is because of Christ's righteousness (that is, his sinlessness, holiness, uprightness, goodness) that he is able to do his work as Savior and redeemer.
3. It refers to Christ's righteous sense of justice, generosity, fairness and impartiality. This means that Christ is no respecter of persons; he plays no favorites. When applied in the realm of faith, it means that Christ makes it possible for anyone, Jew or Gentile, apostle or nonapostle, to have the same faith.

In the light of the context, and in the light of the usage of "righteousness" in the rest of the letter, the second and third meanings seem to be the more logical choices. A literal translation (as in TEV, RSV, and most other translations) will of course allow all three possibilities, but it is not meaningful to most readers, since it does not give them any clue as to what the word really means. A much better approach, although a more risky one, is to make a choice in the translation and put alternative renderings in the notes, provided these alternatives can be justified. Therefore it is possible to translate the phrase **in the righteousness of our God and Savior Jesus Christ** as "who through the fairness and impartial generosity of our God and Savior Jesus Christ" or "through the goodness and uprightness of Jesus Christ."

Alternative translation models for this verse are:

(1) I, Simon Peter, who am a servant and apostle of Jesus Christ, write to you. You have received through the fairness and impartial generosity of our [inclusive] God and Savior Jesus Christ the same teachings about him as we did.

(2) I, Simon Peter, who am a servant and apostle of Jesus Christ, write to you. Our God and Savior Jesus Christ has been fair and generous. He has impartially given you the same teachings about him as we received.

(3) I, Simon Peter . . . write this letter to you who through the goodness of our [inclusive] God and Savior Jesus Christ have come to trust in him as we did.

1.2	RSV	TEV

May grace and peace be multiplied to you in the knowledge of God and of Jesus our Lord.	May grace and peace be yours in full measure through your knowledge of God and of Jesus our Lord.

Verse 2 begins with the traditional Christian greeting **grace and peace**. **Grace** (*charis*) resembles a greeting (*chaire*) commonly used among Greek speakers, and it refers to God's undeserved love and favor. **Peace**, on the other hand, reflects an expression used among Jewish people, and it denotes total health, total well-being, or in other words, everything that God bestows on people for them to enjoy life in all its abundance. Both of these words are now combined in a Christian greeting which, judging by its presence in other letters as well, seems to have been the traditional and popular greeting among Christians. It is very tempting to take these words in their full theological meaning and impact. We should remember, however, that these are part of a greeting formula and therefore must be translated according to their function within that formula.

The type of impersonal request for blessing in the clause **May grace and peace be multiplied to you** must be expressed in a number of languages by naming the person who gives, and also by proposing an expression of prayer or request; for example, "I pray that God may give you grace and peace in abundance" or "I pray that God may give you a great deal of grace and peace." Since in a number of languages **grace** is most closely related to a term for "love," we may translate **May grace . . . to you** as "May God show his love to you." **Peace** may be expressed in certain languages as "well-being." In other languages **peace** will be translated idiomatically; for example, "live in coolness and have happiness." Therefore in such a language **May grace and peace be multiplied to you** (TEV "May grace and peace be yours") can be expressed as "May God show his love and cause you to live in coolness and have happiness."

"Be yours in full measure" (TEV) is literally **be multiplied to you** and is a distinctive feature of Jewish prayers (compare Dan 4.1; 6.25). It conveys the hope that the readers will receive **grace and peace** continually, and that their lives will therefore be blessed and made more pleasant as a result (compare NAB "be yours in abundance"; JB "may you have more and more"). In certain languages **May grace and peace be multiplied to you** will be rendered as "May God show his love to you greatly and cause you to have much peace."

Knowledge is one of the major themes of this letter. The word translated **knowledge** here is used four times, while another form of the word is found in three other places. Interpreters suggest that this emphasis on knowledge may be due to the fact that some teachers from the Gnostic groups were proclaiming that, in order to attain a life that is pleasing to God, people should have a special kind of knowledge about the universe and about the very nature of God (the name "Gnostic" comes from *gnōsis,* the Greek word for knowledge). In contrast to this, Peter puts emphasis on knowing God and Jesus Christ. **Knowledge** here is more than just having information; it includes being in a very close relationship with someone, perhaps experiencing that person's power in our lives.

The phrase **in the knowledge** may be rendered as "because you know" (simple reason), "because you have come to know" (causative), "by means of your knowing" (instrumental), "as a result of your knowing" (result), or even "as a result of your experiencing the presence (or, power) of . . . ."

As noted in the comments on verse 1, the Greek of verse 2 clearly distinguishes between **of God** and **of Jesus . . .** as two distinct personalities. **Lord** means "the one who controls," "the one who commands," or "the one who rules us," so in certain languages a possessive pronoun should not be used, since that would give the impression that we own the one who controls us. It then is better to say "the one who commands (or, rules) us." Thus the phrase **Jesus our Lord** may be expressed as "Jesus who controls us," "Jesus who rules us," or "Jesus who commands us."

An alternative translation model for this verse is:

> May God show his love to you greatly and cause you to have peace, because you have come to experience the presence (or, power) of God and Jesus our Lord (or, the one who controls us).

A call to live according to God's call
1.3-11

RSV   TEV

God's Call and Choice

3 His divine power has granted to us all things that pertain to life and godliness, through the knowledge of him who called us to his own glory and excellence, 4 by which he has granted to us his precious and very great promises, that through these you may escape from the corruption that is in the world because of passion, and become partakers of the divine nature. 5 For this very reason make every effort to supplement your faith with virtue, and virtue with knowledge, 6 and knowledge with self-control, and self-control with steadfastness, and steadfastness with godliness, 7 and godliness with brotherly affection, and brotherly affection with love. 8 For if these things are yours and abound, they keep you from being ineffective or unfruitful in the knowledge of our Lord Jesus Christ. 9 For whoever lacks these things is blind and shortsighted and has forgotten that he was cleansed from his old sins. 10 Therefore, brethren, be the more zealous to confirm your call and election, for if you do this you will never fall; 11 so there will be richly provided for you an entrance into the eternal kingdom of our Lord and Savior Jesus Christ.

3 God's divine power has given us everything we need to live a truly religious life through our knowledge of the one who called us to share in his own glory and goodness. 4 In this way he has given us the very great and precious gifts he promised, so that by means of these gifts you may escape from the destructive lust that is in the world, and may come to share the divine nature. 5 For this very reason do your best to add goodness to your faith; to your goodness add knowledge; 6 to your knowledge add self-control; to your self-control add endurance; to your endurance add godliness; 7 to your godliness add brotherly affection; and to your brotherly affection add love. 8 These are the qualities you need, and if you have them in abundance, they will make you active and effective in your knowledge of our Lord Jesus Christ. 9 But whoever does not have them is so shortsighted that he cannot see and has forgotten that he has been purified from his past sins. 10 So then, my brothers, try even harder to make God's call and his choice of you a permanent experience; if you do so, you will never abandon your faith. 11 In this way you will be given the full right to enter the eternal Kingdom of our Lord and Savior Jesus Christ.

Verse 3 is the beginning of the body of the letter. Most modern translations indicate this by starting a new paragraph at this point. Furthermore, in translations that have section headings, a section heading is put right before verse 3. There is, however, no agreement as to where this section ends. Some translations treat verses 3-15 as one section and verses 16-21 as another (TEV). Others end the first section at verse 11 and treat verses 12-21 as the second section in the chapter (NIV). Still others treat verses 3-21 as a single section.

An analysis of the passage in question will guide us in making a decision as to how to divide it. In verses 3-4 the readers are reminded of the gifts from God that empower them to live as God's chosen people. In verses 5-9 they are urged to cultivate certain Christian virtues such as goodness and knowledge. In verses 10 and 11 they are admonished to take God's call seriously. In verses 12-15 they are informed that they will always be reminded of these matters. Verses 16-18 contain an eyewitness account of the transfiguration of Jesus. Finally, verses 19-21 deal with the nature of the prophetic message.

In the light of the above analysis, it looks as if verses 3 to 15 are logically related, whereas there is an obvious change of subject matter from verse 16 onwards. Therefore it seems more logical to divide the passage into two sections, verses 3-15 and verses 16-21, which is what TEV has done.

Some scholars note that verses 3-11 follow a standard homiletic pattern in Jewish and early Christian literature. The pattern consists of three parts:
1. a historical or theological opening, recalling God's acts for and on behalf of his people (3-4);
2. ethical teaching, guiding the readers to right conduct (5-10); and
3. a concluding part, which promises either salvation or judgment (verse 11).

This homiletic pattern appears in some farewell speeches in other Christian writings of the time that are called the Pseudepigrapha, and the pattern is intended to summarize a teacher's message so that it will be remembered even after his death. This seems to be the purpose here as well (see verses 13-14).

SECTION HEADING: the heading from the outline may be rendered as a full clause such as "Christians are urged to live according to God's call" or "Christians should live as people called and chosen by God." Similar to the heading in the Handbook outline is the TEV section heading, "God's call and choice," which may also be rendered "What it means to be called and chosen by God." The TEV heading is intended to cover verses 3-15, but it is also suitable for this shorter section, verses 2-11.

1.3   RSV   TEV

His divine power has granted to us all things that pertain to life and godliness, through the knowledge of him who called us to[b] his own glory and excellence,

God's divine power has given us everything we need to live a truly religious life through our knowledge of the one who called us to share in his own[a] glory and goodness.

[b] Or *by*

[a] to share in his own; *some manuscripts have* through his.

A special problem is raised by verses 3 and 4 with regard to determining whether God or Jesus is the person referred to by the third person pronouns. Decisions reached on this matter will affect the interpretation of these two verses. It is because of this that a more detailed analysis of this problem is presented below.

*1. Who does **His** refer to in the expression **His divine power**?* The choice is of course between God and Christ. Many translations simply have **His** here, thus retaining the ambiguity of the text. However, TEV has resolved the ambiguity by translating "God."

It should be noted first of all that verse 3 begins with a Greek particle sometimes translated "as" or "seeing that"; this has led many interpreters to connect verse 3 with verse 2, and then to regard verses 3 and 4 as an expansion of verse 2. This opinion is by no means universal, since there are some other interpreters who favor connecting verse 3 with what follows. One primary reason for this preference is that verse 3 doesn't have a finite verb but has a Greek form called "the genitive absolute," which is usually used at the beginning of a paragraph. In view of this, many translations leave the particle untranslated and treat verse 3 as a new sentence.

Whether verse 3 is treated as a new sentence or as a part of verse 2, the fact remains that, in the latter part of verse 2, both God and Jesus are mentioned, with Jesus being mentioned last. It would be logical then to take Jesus as the subject of the very next clause. In fact, were it not for the paragraph break, the Greek text would easily favor Jesus Christ as the person referred to by the pronoun "his." It should be noted, however, that connecting verse 3 with verse 4 would favor "God" (as in TEV).

A further consideration is the expression **divine power**, which was a popular term in Greek literature. In the New Testament, however, it is used only here, which is one indication of how this letter has been influenced by Greek literature. It should be mentioned, however, that the Greek adjective for **divine** is used also in Paul's speech at the Areopagus (Acts 17.29, "the Deity" or "divine likeness"), and that the equivalent expression "the power of God" is frequently used in the New Testament. "Divine power" is of course a natural way of describing God's power; and this seems to favor "God" as the one referred to by "his." It should be noted, however, that in verse 1 the letter has just used the expression "the righteousness of our God and Savior Jesus Christ." There is of course a possibility of rendering this as "our God and the Savior Jesus Christ," as indicated in the discussion of verse 1. But considering all the arguments, it is probably best to understand the expression as referring to one person, namely, Jesus Christ, rather than to both God and Christ. If this is the case, then it will not be strange to talk of Jesus as having "divine power," and this expression does not necessarily exclude Jesus as the person indicated by **His**.

*2. Who is referred to by **him** in **the knowledge of him who called us**, and who is referred to by **his** in **to his own glory and excellence**?*

It would be logical to identify the person referred to here with the person referred to in the first part of this verse. This in fact is what most translations do; that is, if God is the subject of the first part of the sentence, then God is kept as the subject of all of verses 3 and 4.

It should be noted that, in the New Testament, the function of calling people to become God's people is usually assigned to God and not to Jesus

Christ (see Rom 8.30; 2 Tim 1.9; 1 Cor 7.15; 1 Peter 5.10; and other passages). This favors God as the one referred to here. However, we cannot be dogmatic at this point, since there are just too many passages where "called" is in the passive form, with the implicit agent either God or Jesus Christ.

3. Who does "he" refer to in the clause at the beginning of verse 4, "by which he has granted us"? Again "he" can refer to either God or Christ. If we take the position that **him** in **of him who called us** is God, then it is logical to conclude that God is also the one referred to in "by which he has granted us." The same holds true of course if we come to the conclusion that these clauses refer to Jesus Christ.

In summary, then, the following alternatives are possible:

A.   "his divine power" — God
      "through the knowledge of him who called us" — God
      "by which he has granted us" — God
B.   "his divine power" — Christ
      "through the knowledge of him who called us" — Christ
      "by which he has granted us" — Christ
C.   "his divine power" — Christ
      "through the knowledge of him who called us" — God
      "by which he has granted us" — God
D.   "his divine power" — God
      "through the knowledge of him who has called us" — Christ
      "by which he has granted us" — Christ

Most translations follow one of the above alternatives. Our preference for this Handbook is alternative C.

A translator's decision as to whether the subject of this verse is Christ or God will determine how **divine power** is translated. If the subject is Christ, then we may say "Christ, through his power as God," but if God is the subject, then a possible translation is "God, through his own power." In the light of the discussion above, we recommend the former as the more reasonable interpretation, namely "Christ, through his power."

Has granted translates a Greek verb that means "to give, bestow, present something to someone," but is used especially when the giver is either a king, a high official, or God himself (see Mark 15.45).

A literal translation would give the understanding that it is **divine power** that is the source of these gifts. It is clear, however, from the analysis of the verse that it is Christ (or God) who bestows these gifts, and he bestows them through (or because of) his divine power. In other words, Christ (or God) has made use of his divine power in order to grant his people what they need.

Who are the people who receive the gift? Who does **us** refer to? There are three possibilities:

1. It can refer to Peter and the other apostles. This position has some validity, since there seems to be a contrast between "us" in verses 3 and 4a and "you" in verse 4b. Understood this way, "us" then will be translated in the exclusive form in languages that make a distinction between the exclusive and inclusive ("we not including you" as contrasted with "we including you"). It is, however, unlikely that it is only the apostles that are meant

here, considering the purpose of the gifts of God, which is to enable someone to live a godly life.

2. It can refer to Peter and his readers, in which case "us" is inclusive.

3. It can refer to Christians in general. This would explain why Peter switched from "us" to "you" in the second part of verse 4. He has been talking about all Christians in verses 3 and 4a, but in verse 4b he addresses his readers directly.

Therefore it is best to translate **us** as inclusive in those languages that make a distinction.

The expression **all things** accents the completeness of God's gift. He has given us all things **that pertain to life and godliness**, that is, everything that we need in order to live a life of piety and godliness.

The expression **life and godliness** is best understood, not as two separate elements, but as two related words, with one word describing the other. Such a construction is known as "hendiadys," meaning one thing is expressed by saying two things. An example of this construction is "grace and apostleship" in Rom 1.5, which means "the grace (or the privilege) of being an apostle." So here **life and godliness** means "godly life" or "the way God wants us to live." The word for **godliness** is used elsewhere in this letter (1.6,7; 3.11; and see also 2.9). It is a Greek term and is used many times in the Pastoral letters (1 Timothy, 2 Timothy, Titus). Outside of Jewish-Christian usage it meant piety toward the gods. In this letter it covers both worship of God and proper conduct arising out of such worship; see TEV "a truly religious life," and NEB "true religion." We may also say "to live as a Christian really should live," or idiomatically, "to walk one's life as a Christian should really walk (or, live)."

The phrase **through the knowledge of** is similar to "in the knowledge of" in verse 2 above, except that the Greek preposition for **through** used in this verse puts emphasis on the instrumental relationship, hence "by means of our knowing" (or ". . . knowledge of"), although it is also possible to render it as "because we have come to know." The expression **of him** (TEV "the one") may be too vague in many languages. It may be necessary to identify who **of him** refers to; for example, "God, the one . . ." or "Christ, the one . . ." (see the discussion under "C," page 73).

Who has called us: as we have noted above, **us** refers to Christians in general. **To his own** (TEV "share in his own . . .") can also be translated as "to have a part in his own . . . ." **Glory** is one of those New Testament words that are hard to translate because they can be interpreted and understood in so many ways. For instance, **glory** can refer to God's greatness or majesty, to a bright light from God, to God's power, to honor and praise, or to a blessed state in the presence of God. Central to the meaning of **glory** is the praise and honor people express toward God, but here it seems best to understand **glory** as referring to the very nature or the very person of God, whom people praise, and to the privilege God gives his people of sharing the praise God receives, simply because they are God's people and have been welcomed into his presence. **Excellence** refers to God's moral excellence or goodness (see verse 5 for a more detailed discussion on "goodness").

In many languages it will be necessary to break the complex sentence in this verse into two sentences; for example:

> Jesus, through his own power, has given us everything we need to live as Christians really should. This is possible because we have come to know God. He is the one who has called us to have a part in his greatness and moral goodness.

1.4   RSV   TEV

by which he has granted to us his precious and very great promises, that through these you may escape from the corruption that is in the world because of passion, and become partakers of the divine nature.	In this way he has given us the very great and precious gifts he promised, so that by means of these gifts you may escape from the destructive lust that is in the world, and may come to share the divine nature.

The expression **by which** (TEV "In this way") may refer to what comes immediately before, in which case it is through God's glory and goodness that we receive God's promises. More likely, however, **by which** refers to all of verse 3, especially the first part. What Peter is saying then is that, when Christ (or God) gives us all that we need to live a godly life, he also gives to us those blessings that he has promised. Another way of saying **by which**, then, is "Because of this . . ." or "Because of these things . . . ."

For **he has granted** see 1.3. In both instances the perfect tense is used, indicating that the promises have already been given and continue to be effective even into the unknown future. **He** most probably refers to God, and this can be made clear in the translation, especially if in verse 3 translators have identified "him" in the final clause as Jesus.

The word for **promises** is used only here in the New Testament and is usually understood in one of two ways: it can refer to the things promised, that is, the content of these promises (for example, "blessings," or TEV "gifts"), or it can refer to promises for the future that are mentioned in the latter part of the letter, such as the promise of a new heaven and a new earth (3.4,9,13, and other verses). As we shall see, a decision on which meaning to take depends somewhat on how the second part of verse 4 is interpreted.

The gifts are described as **precious and very great**. **Precious** translates a Greek word that refers to high honorable status when used of people, and to having considerable worth or value when used of things. In the present case **precious** can therefore be rendered as "valuable," or even "invaluable" or "priceless" (that is, it is impossible to estimate its worth). The Greek word translated **very great** puts emphasis on importance, so it may be translated "very important" or even "extremely important." These two attributes taken together stress the extreme significance and value of the gifts.

Through these can mean "by means of God's blessings" (as in TEV "by means of these gifts") or "by means of God's promises," that is, by receiving the blessings that come as a result of the fulfillment of God's promises. It is more likely, though, that "gifts" are meant here. Therefore another possible rendering is "by using these gifts." This translation helps to avoid the impression that the "gifts" caused the **escape**. Rather, they are the means used to escape.

The result of all this is that the believers **escape from the corruption that is in the world** and **become partakers of the divine nature**. The word for **escape** is used only in this letter in the New Testament (see also 2.18,20). The Greek form (aorist participle) clearly indicates that escaping from corruption comes before participating in the divine nature. **Escape** here does not mean "run away from" or "flee" but puts the main focus on being free or being delivered from something, which in this case is **the corruption that is in the world**. So the phrase **through these you may escape from** may be rendered "through these gifts you may be free from," or even "that these gifts may help you to avoid," or "that these things (blessings) that God has given to you may help you to avoid."

Corruption literally refers to the decomposition of a dead body after it is buried; this has led many scholars to understand it primarily in a physical sense, with the stress being on the fact that life here on earth is temporary and not permanent. However, there are others who understand the term to include an ethical aspect as well, referring to moral deterioration and the resulting loss of character and immortality.

This corruption is described as being **in the world**, which can be understood simply as the created order, which is temporary and exposed to decay, or it can be understood as an evil force opposed to God and therefore subject to God's judgment. Furthermore this corruption is related to or caused by **passion**. The Greek word used here means generally "desire" but in a negative sense means "sinful desire," "evil desire," "lust" (TEV), that is, desire to do evil or sinful things, desire for things that are against the will of God. While Greek concepts are used here, particularly the opposition between the material and the spiritual, yet Greek thought is also modified in the sense that corruption is not simply a natural result of the physical world but is caused by sinful and evil desire.

How are these three words (**corruption, world, passion**) related to one another? One possibility is simply to follow the ordering of the Greek, in which case corruption is located in the world and is caused by passion (as in RSV, and note Phps "to escape the inevitable disintegration that lust produces in the world"). Another way is to understand corruption as a quality of passion, hence, evil desires that destroy, as in TEV "destructive lust that is in the world." Still another way is to understand passion as a quality of the world (as in JB "to escape corruption in a world that is sunk in vice"). All of these are possible interpretations of the Greek text, although the first two are preferred by the majority of commentaries and modern translations. Therefore, keeping in mind these two interpretations, the clause **you may escape from the corruption that is in the world because of passion** may be rendered in many languages as "you may escape from the evil desires (lusts) in the world that destroy people" or "the evil desires (lusts) in the world that destroy people will not corrupt you."

Having escaped from corruption, the believers can now **become partakers of the divine nature**, which can be understood in two ways: being given some characteristics that are reserved for the divine, in this case immortality and incorruptibility, and sharing in the life and nature of God himself (as in Phps "to share God's essential nature," and NEB "to share in the very being of God"). We may also render this phrase as "to share in God's own nature," "become like God," "share in God's heart."

Many commentators note here the use of Greek concepts. The word for **divine** (see also 1.3) is used in only one other place in the New Testament, and that is in Acts 17.29, as part of Paul's speech to the Athenians at the Areopagus, and in which he aptly uses a term that is popularly known, especially among the educated Greeks (RSV "a [divine] representation"). The Greeks believed that human beings had in themselves a part of the divine nature which, however, was obscured by the material and physical elements. It was by escaping from the material world that they would come to share fully in the very nature of the gods. Salvation therefore was escape from the bondage of the physical and material. Peter uses what is popular in Greek thought, but he modifies it in such a way that it becomes compatible with Christian thought. He makes it clear that people become partakers of the divine nature, not because they already have it, or because of their own efforts, but primarily because of God's grace and goodness; it is God and God alone who makes this possible.

We should note that there is a change here from the first person plural (**us**) to the second person plural (**you**). From this point on until verse 15, Peter addresses his readers directly. This change of pronouns is also found in verses 16-21, where the first person plural pronoun is used in verses 16-19a, and the second person from verse 19b to the end of the chapter.

A further question to be resolved in this verse is when all of this takes place. When will believers escape from corruption and decay and share in the divine nature? Firstly, this may be understood as a present reality, in which case escape from corruption and sharing in the divine nature are related to the Christian experience of conversion and baptism. Secondly, this may be understood as referring to the last days, in which case escape from corruption and sharing in the divine nature are related to the Christian experience at the end of time. The highly ethical nature of the immediately following verses (verses 5-15) favors the first alternative, while the many other references to the end of all things in the letter itself favor the second. At any rate, the first alternative goes well with the understanding that the **promises** are the blessings and gifts that are contained in it; while the second possibility goes well with the understanding that the **promises** are for the future, and their fulfillment will be at the end of the age. We propose that the former is the most likely interpretation.

An alternative translation model for this verse is:

Through all this God has given us the very great and precious gifts that he promised. By using these gifts we can escape from the evil desires in the world that destroy people, and may come to have a part in God's own nature.

1.5   RSV   TEV

For this very reason make every effort to supplement your faith with virtue, and virtue with knowledge,	**For this very reason do your best to add goodness to your faith; to your goodness add knowledge;**

Having reminded his readers of their great and glorious destiny, he now invites them to demonstrate this in their lives, that is, to lead lives that are morally and ethically acceptable.

For this very reason can refer to verse 4 ("Because you are meant to share the divine nature"), or more likely to verses 3-4 ("Because Christ [or God] has done all this"); or we can say "Because of what God has done for us." Others understand it with the sense "to attain this" (so JB; and note also the Living Bible "But to obtain these gifts.")

The expression for **make every effort** is found only here in the whole New Testament and is an invitation to do your best, regardless of the cost. (See JB "You will have to do your utmost yourselves," and Phps "you must do your utmost from your side.") In its secular usage the expression is an appropriate introduction to a list of virtues. This imperative may be rendered in many languages as "you must do your best" or "you must try as hard as you can."

The word for **supplement** presents some difficulties in translation. The word can also mean "to furnish" or "to provide at one's own expense." The noun form of the verb was used of prominent and wealthy citizens who underwrote the expenses for the choirs needed in the performance of Greek plays. Later on the verb came to mean "to give lavishly" or "to give generously" (see verse 11, "will be richly provided"). In this context it stresses the great efforts that Christians must make to insure that their basic faith in Christ is supplemented by other important virtues as well. In many languages, when translating the list of qualities that follow, it will be necessary to follow the TEV word order (action-virtue-faith) rather than that of RSV (action-faith-virtue) and translate **supplement your faith**, for example, as "add the following qualities to your trust in Christ." The whole clause **make every effort to supplement your faith** can be expressed as "you must try as hard as you can to add the following qualities to your trust in Christ" or "along with trusting Christ you should make every effort to add these following qualities."

What follows is a string of eight qualities that were familiar in Greek culture in general, and to Stoic thought in particular. There seems to be no apparent underlying reason for the order in which these qualities are listed; the only thing significant is that the list begins with **faith** and ends with **love** (verse 7), thus giving the impression that these qualities are needed in order to live a truly Christian life. The number 8 has significance, for it symbolized perfection in the ancient world. These eight qualities are in pairs, with the second member of each pair becoming the first member in the next pair.

Faith here is basically trust in and commitment to Jesus Christ, although it is possible to understand it as loyalty to Christ or faithfulness to Christian teaching. The fact that it is mentioned first is significant, indicating that faith is the basis of all Christian life.

Virtue (TEV "goodness") can be understood in a general sense, referring to moral excellence, or in a more restricted sense, referring to moral courage or strength. In this context it probably has the first sense, namely, "moral excellence." This can be rendered in some languages as "beautiful goodness" or even "the ability to do good and beautiful deeds." TEV's "goodness," however, is a very general virtue, and to translate it generally in some languages may be too vague. So it will be necessary to say, for example, "ability to be good toward other people."

Knowledge can be understood generally as either philosophical knowledge or understanding and discernment of God's will and purpose in the world, and in a narrower sense as either knowing the difference between good and evil or the wisdom and discernment that Christians need in order to live virtuous lives. In non-Christian lists, **knowledge** is usually first or last, but in Christian lists it has been replaced in this position by faith and love. In many languages it will be necessary to say what kind of knowledge is referred to; for example, "knowledge about God," or "knowing more of what it means to be a Christian," or "knowing what it means to be part of God's people."

Keeping in mind what we have said above, an alternative translation model for this verse is:

> Because God has done all this for us, you must try as hard as you can to add the following things to your trust in Christ: first of all you must add goodness; then to your goodness add knowledge about God.

However, in many languages it will be difficult to talk about adding abstract Christian qualities to a person's Christian life. Therefore it may be necessary to rephrase the verse as follows:

> Because God has done all this for us, along with your trust in him you must try as hard as you can to gain the ability to be good to other people along with your trust in God; and this goodness should be accompanied by true knowledge of God.

1.6 RSV	TEV
and knowledge with self-control, and self-control with steadfastness, and steadfastness with godliness,	to your knowledge add self-control; to your self-control add endurance; to your endurance add godliness;

Self-control is once again a Greek virtue, one which is possessed by people who are masters of their own selves and who by self-discipline can tame their passions and desires and thus refrain from excessive physical indulgence. While it is rare in the New Testament, it is nevertheless mentioned several times (see, for instance, Gal 5.23; Acts 24.25; 1 Cor 7.9; 9.25; Titus 1.8), indicating that it was a recognized Christian virtue. Its mention here is significant in that it contrasts the disciplined Christian life with the licentiousness and animal-like lifestyle of the false teachers (see, for example, 2.2,12; 3.3). In some languages this virtue of **self-control** can be expressed as "knowing how to control (restrain) yourself," or "being able to refuse what your body wants to do," or "having control of your desires."

Steadfastness is mentioned many times in the New Testament (Rom 5.3,4 "endurance"; 1 Tim 6.11; 2 Tim 3.10; Titus 2.2; Rev 2.19; and many other places). In Greek culture it refers primarily to personal courage and endurance in the face of suffering and evil. As a Christian virtue **steadfastness** stems not so much from a person's own bravery as it does from the believer's trust in God and hope for the fulfillment of all of God's promises. Here it perhaps refers in particular to the patient waiting for the return of the Lord, which is discussed in chapter 3. It will be necessary in many languages to translate **steadfastness** as "the ability to endure." However, in certain languages translators will have to render this expression in an idiomatic way; for example, "have a heart (liver) that endures" or "have a big heart."

Godliness is the same word used in verse 3. In Christian lists it appears only here and in 1 Tim 6.11. Its rare use is not only because it is a Greek characteristic, but because it is too general, since it includes both devotion to God and a sense of duty toward human beings. Its mention here is appropriate, since later on the false teachers are labeled as "ungodly" (2.6; 3.7). In this context its main meaning is probably devotion to or complete commitment to God. Translators can thus render it as "complete commitment to God," "have a life wholly devoted to God," or "turn your life over completely to God, doing what God wants us to do."

1.7   RSV   TEV

and godliness with brotherly affection,   to your godliness add brotherly affec-
and brotherly affection with love.   tion; and to your brotherly affection
                                             add love.

Brotherly affection is used many times in the New Testament. In secular usage this word was used to describe affection between brothers and sisters and other family members. Later on it was used to describe a person's concern for his or her own nation (for example, Jeremiah in relation to the Israelites, 2 Maccabees 15.14). In the New Testament, and among Christians, the word came to mean affection between fellow-believers, including sympathetic concern for others and the care of those in need. Other ways to translate this term are "love and affection for your fellow Christians" or "concern for one another as brothers and sisters ought to have for each other." Some languages will have a special word for love and affection of brothers and sisters for each other. That is the term to use here.

The last thing on the list is **love**, which appears also in other New Testament lists (2 Cor 6.6; Gal 5.22; Eph 4.2; 1 Tim 4.12; 6.11; 2 Tim 2.22; 3.10; Titus 2.2; Rev 2.19; and so on). As contrasted with brotherly affection, love is first of all not limited to family members or to fellow-believers but is universal in scope and has as its object all people. Secondly, **love** is unmotivated, that is, it doesn't expect anything in return, whereas **brotherly affection** has the element of a mutual love, which will be returned by the other person. **Love** in this context, then, is not referring to "love for God" but "love for others" and should be translated in this way. In certain languages love will be expressed using bodily parts such as the heart or liver; for example, "heart is warm towards," "hold other people in one's heart," or "stomach moves for others."

1.8	RSV	TEV
	For if these things are yours and abound, they keep you from being ineffective or unfruitful in the knowledge of our Lord Jesus Christ.	These are the qualities you need, and if you have them in abundance, they will make you active and effective in your knowledge of our Lord Jesus Christ.

This verse together with verse 9 explains the importance of possessing the virtues just mentioned. Verse 8 describes the benefits for people who possess these virtues, while verse 9 describes the negative condition of people who lack these virtues.

If these things are yours and abound: this stresses two things. In the first place these virtues must truly be possessed and fully at a person's disposal; and secondly, these virtues must continue to be developed in a person's life. Other ways of translating this clause are: "You need to have these qualities, and if you have them in a great measure . . . ," or idiomatically, "You need to . . . and if they grow strong in your heart . . . ."

The result of possessing and fostering these virtues is stated negatively: it keeps the believers **from being ineffective or unfruitful in the knowledge of our Lord Jesus Christ. They keep you** is a causal construction; in some languages it may be expressed as "they will cause you to." The words for **ineffective** and **unfruitful** are very similar in meaning and stress the importance of good actions in the Christian life. It must be noted that both of these words are negatives that sometimes can be translated positively. Thus **ineffective** can also be "useless" (NEB), "complacent" (Phps), or positively, "active" (TEV), "to have ability." **Unfruitful** can also be "barren" (NEB), "unproductive" (Phps), or positively, "effective" (TEV), "successful," "useful." Hence this whole negative construction can also be expressed positively, as in TEV "they will make you active and effective in your knowledge of our Lord Jesus Christ."

How are these virtues related to the knowledge of our Lord Jesus Christ? First of all, knowledge of Christ may be viewed as the goal of the virtuous life; a life of virtue leads to a fuller and more effective knowledge of Jesus Christ. (See JB "they will not leave you ineffectual or unproductive: they will bring you to a real knowledge of our Lord Jesus Christ.") But secondly, however, the Greek preposition for **in** can be taken with the meaning "with reference to" or "in respect to." If the preposition is taken in this manner, the knowledge of Christ becomes the root of the virtuous life; the lives of believers are determined by their knowledge of Christ.

An alternative translation model for this verse is the following:

> These are the qualities you need, and if you really know our Lord Jesus Christ, you will have them strong in your heart. This will produce good results in your life.

1.9   RSV   TEV

For whoever lacks these things is blind and shortsighted and has forgotten that he was cleansed from his old sins.	**But whoever does not have them is so shortsighted that he cannot see and has forgotten that he has been purified from his past sins.**

This verse describes the life of people who do not possess the qualities mentioned in verses 5-7. First of all, such people are **blind and shortsighted.** This combination may present some translation problems, since **blind** is stronger than **shortsighted**, and since obviously, if a person is blind, that person cannot be shortsighted at the same time. A better way of understanding this is to take **shortsighted** as having the effect of causing blindness: a shortsighted person is in effect blind, hence TEV "is so shortsighted that he cannot see." Furthermore this should not be taken literally but in a metaphorical sense, that is, being morally and spiritually blind; this metaphor is a popular one in the New Testament (see, for example, Matt 15.14; John 9.40-41; Rev 3.17). In many languages this metaphorical usage must be made clear by using a simile such as "is like a person who is so shortsighted that he cannot see."

Secondly, these people have **forgotten** that they were **cleansed** from their **old sins. Forgotten** is literally "having received forgetfulness," a typical Greek expression. The metaphor of cleansing from sin has its origin in the Old Testament, where it is connected with the Jewish sacrificial system. This metaphor was also widely used in the early church and is found in many parts of the New Testament (for instance Titus 2.14; Heb 1.3; 9.14; 1 John 1.7,9). Most commentaries are agreed that the reference here is to the purification that a person receives at baptism, during which a person is forgiven of his or her past sins before baptism. Baptism therefore signifies the end of the old and the beginning of the new: it marks a break between the old life of sin and disobedience and the new life of virtue and obedience to God. Many languages cannot literally translate the passive construction **he was cleansed from his old sins** but will need to name God as the one who does the cleansing, or else use a construction with a verb such as "receive." In such cases this clause will be rendered "that God has cleansed him from his past (old) sins" or "that he has received from God cleansing from his past sins." In still other languages it will be necessary to make a direct reference to baptism and say "that God has cleansed his past sins through baptism."

An alternative translation model for this verse is:

> But whoever does not have these qualities is like a person who is so shortsighted that he cannot see (or, is blind), and has forgotten that God has cleansed him from his old sins.

1.10 RSV	TEV
Therefore, brethren, be the more zealous to confirm your call and election, for if you do this you will never fall;	So then, my brothers, try even harder to make God's call and his choice of you a permanent experience; if you do so, you will never abandon your faith.[b]

> [b] abandon your faith; *or* fall into sin.

Therefore connects this verse with verses 8 and 9, meaning, in effect, "in the light of the blessing in verse 8 and the warning in verse 9 . . . ." At the same time it recalls verse 3, where God's call is first mentioned. **Brethren** is a common form of address in early Christian letters and is used in a general sense to refer to all believers, including women. This general sense should be reflected in the translation; that is, whenever possible, a term that is inclusive of both men and women should be used. We may also translate this expression as "(my) fellow Christians," or "(my) elders and youngers."

The word for **zealous** is used in the New Testament for moral effort (Heb 4.11; Eph 4.3; see also 2 Peter 1.15 and 3.14). The whole expression **be the more zealous** means strive harder, eagerly exert greater effort (as in TEV "try even harder," and JB "work all the harder." Other ways of saying this are "You must make a greater effort than before" or "You must try even harder than before."

The verb **confirm** can be understood in a legal sense as meaning "to ratify," "to guarantee," "to make certain of," "to make sure," "to make secure."

Call and election is yet another example of Peter's use of a pair of words of very similar meaning. If a distinction is to be made between them, we can say that **election** is a prior decision to select someone from a group (as, for example, God selecting Israel out of the nations to be his people), while **call** is the actual process of inviting the elected ones to share in the privileges and responsibilities of their election. The one who does the calling and choosing is God; this information can be included in the translation (as TEV has done).

These two terms stress the fact that it is through God's initiative that people experience a new relationship with God.

But how do people confirm their call and election? We should of course avoid translating this in such a way as to make the calling and election dependent on human action rather than on divine initiative. God is the one who calls, but those who are called must show by their action that their call is real and that their election is absolutely certain. In this way they themselves, as well as people from outside the church, won't have any doubt regarding the genuineness of God's call. This emphasis on the importance of the human role in the Christian life serves to remind the readers that there are teachers who would like to lead them into a morally lax existence. Some translators will find even TEV's model a difficult one. In such cases it is possible to restructure the ordering of these clauses completely and say, for example, "My brothers, God has called you to follow him and has chosen you to be his people. So, if you want to insure that this experience lasts permanently, you must try even harder than you have up to now" or ". . . Therefore try even harder to act in a way that will prove to yourselves and others that God has really called you to follow him and has chosen you to be his people."

If you do this can refer to what comes immediately before, that is, making sure of your call and election, or else to the virtues in verses 5-7, since literally this reads "if you do these things." The word for **fall** is literally "stumble," which in this context can refer to committing error or sinning, or falling away from the faith and becoming unfaithful to Christ. Some commentators take this in a future sense, taking "stumble" as referring to the inability of reaching final salvation. The Greek negative here is emphatic, with the sense of "never, never," or "never at any time." If the translator understands the phrase **if you do this** to refer to the virtues listed in verses 5-7, and **fall** to refer to "becoming unfaithful to Christ," an alternative translation model is the following; "If you follow these qualities you will never stop trusting in Christ." However, if **fall** is understood as committing error or sinning, then one can translate "if you follow these qualities you will never fall into sin." However, if translators understand **If you do this** to refer to what comes immediately before this text, an alternative translation model is the following: "if you insure that God has called you and chosen you, you will never stop trusting in Christ (or, never fall into sin)."

1.11	RSV	TEV

RSV	TEV
so there will be richly provided for you an entrance into the eternal kingdom of our Lord and Savior Jesus Christ.	In this way you will be given the full right to enter the eternal Kingdom of our Lord and Savior Jesus Christ.

This verse continues the thought of verse 10 and mentions in a positive way the reward that comes to believers as they make sure of their call and election. It begins with the word **so** (TEV "In this way"), again referring back to the virtues mentioned earlier. In many languages this can be rendered as "By doing all these things . . . ."

The idea of an **entrance** being **richly provided** stresses that people have the right to enter not because they deserve it but because the privilege is given to them as a free gift. This is captured in many modern translations such as TEV "you will be given the full right to enter," and NEB "you will be afforded full and free admission." Some other translations interpret **richly provided** as indicating a warm welcome; hence Phps "a rich welcome awaits you as you enter," and NIV "you will receive a rich welcome." However, many languages cannot reproduce this passive form, so translators will need to state directly the agent (God) of the "providing" and say "God will give you the full right," "God will open the door wide for you," or "God will welcome you." Phps has "God will open wide to you the gates of the eternal kingdom." Some languages will need to use a direct quotation here, such as "God will generously say to you, 'Come . . . .'"

The **eternal kingdom of our Lord and Savior Jesus Christ** focuses both on a place and a reign, that is, a place where Jesus Christ will reign eternally. The idea of Christ's kingdom as eternal is also found in Luke 1.33 (and see Rev 11.15). Jesus in his ministry proclaimed the kingdom of God, but in *The Second Letter from Peter*, what is proclaimed is the kingdom and the glory of Christ himself. This kingdom will be fully revealed at the end of the age, and in particular at the second coming of Christ, at which time Christians will be united with their God through Christ. This kingdom is **eternal** in the sense that Jesus Christ will be king forever in this kingdom, and those who are in union with him will be citizens of this kingdom forever. In many languages it will be necessary to use a verbal expression for **kingdom**. In such a case we may say "to enter the place where our Lord and Savior Jesus Christ rules eternally (forever)."

Jesus Christ is here referred to as **Lord and Savior.** This exact combination is found in the New Testament only in this letter (see also 2.20; 3.2,18). **Lord** translates a word that can mean "owner" or "master" but has the more precise meaning of one who rules and who is acknowledged as king and as worthy to be served and obeyed (see the comments on 1.2). For **Savior** see comments on 1.1. The pronoun **our** should be understood as inclusive, referring to all believers. In some languages it will be necessary to make it clear that **Lord** and **Savior** refer to the same person. We can render this as "of our Lord who is our Savior Jesus Christ."

Aim and purpose of the letter
1.12-15

RSV

TEV

12 Therefore I intend always to remind you of these things, though you know them and are established in the truth that you have. 13 I think it right, as long as I am in this body, to arouse you by way of reminder,

12 And so I will always remind you of these matters, even though you already know them and are firmly grounded in the truth you have received. 13 I think it only right for me to stir up your memory of these matters as long

85

14 since I know that the putting off of my body will be soon, as our Lord Jesus Christ showed me. 15 And I will see to it that after my departure you may be able at any time to recall these things.	as I am still alive. 14 I know that I shall soon put off this mortal body, as our Lord Jesus Christ plainly told me. 15 I will do my best, then, to provide a way for you to remember these matters at all times after my death.

These four verses state very clearly the aim and purpose of the letter: Peter wishes to leave an authoritative statement to which his readers can refer again and again, especially after his death. This kind of a statement has developed into a literary genre, or form of writing, known as the *testament,* examples of which are found in other parts of the New Testament (for instance Acts 20.17-38; 2 Tim 3.1–4.8). The two customary marks of the testament form that are present in these verses are, firstly, that the author knows that his death is near, and secondly, that he wishes his teachings to be remembered after his death. Several other things need to be noted:

1. These four verses serve as a transition between the summary of his teachings in 1.1-11 and his defense of this teaching in the rest of the letter.
2. The use of the testament form clearly indicates that the letter presents no new teaching but reproduces the traditional teachings of the apostles and applies these same teachings to the readers' situation at that time.
3. The readers are invited to continue recalling these things even after the author's death. Note for example, **I intend always to remind you** in verse 12, **to arouse you by way of reminder** in verse 13, and **you may be able at any time to recall these things** in verse 15.

SECTION HEADING: the outline refers to verses 12-15 as "Aim and purpose of the letter." A shorter form is "The purpose of this letter." A full clause may be, for example, "Peter writes (or, has written) so that they will remember these things" or ". . . remember to behave in the right way."

1.12   RSV   TEV

Therefore I intend always to remind you of these things, though you know them and are established in the truth that you have.	And so I will always remind you of these matters, even though you already know them and are firmly grounded in the truth you have received.

I intend is in the future tense in the Greek; this is reflected in TEV "I will always remind you," (and see also NEB "I will not hesitate to remind you"). A translation should be avoided that excludes this letter, that is, one which gives the idea that Peter will in the future remind his readers by writing yet another letter. A more appropriate way of understanding the future tense here is in the sense of including the present: "I will always remind you, as I am doing now." In this sense NRSV is quite appropriate: "I intend to keep on reminding you." We can also express this sentence as "I will continually bring these matters to your attention" or "I will continually cause you to remember these things." In some languages there will be idioms that will capture this meaning quite satisfactorily; for example, the English idiom "jog your memory."

These things refers back to verses 3-11, which contain a summary of Peter's message and of the apostolic message in general.

You know them refers back to *The First Letter from Peter,* which forms a background to *The Second Letter from Peter* and which the readers are assumed to have read. Many of the things discussed in 2 Peter are also found in 1 Peter, such as the importance of being steadfast (1 Peter 1.3-9) and the possibility of sharing in divine glory (1 Peter 1.8; 5.1).

Are established translates a verb that indicates solid grounding in and firm commitment to something, as in TEV "firmly grounded," and NEB "well grounded." **Are established** in many languages can be rendered as "are deep in your heart" or "are firmly fixed in your heart."

The truth that you have refers to the Christian message that the believers have been taught since their conversion and baptism. **Truth** is often used in the New Testament to designate the Christian message in general (see, for instance Gal 2.5; Eph 1.13; Col 1.5; 2 Thes 2.12-13; 2 Tim 2.15; James 1.18). Here we can see the development of a body of authoritative Christian teaching to which believers have to give their allegiance. This truth that the believers **have** is something they received as a result of proclamation and teaching (NRSV "the truth that has come to you"); it was handed down to them through the Christian community's ministry of preaching and nurture. Some translators may be able to follow NRSV "that has come to you." However, in certain languages it will be difficult to talk about an abstract idea such as truth performing an action, that is, "coming." In this case we can say "you heard the true teachings" or "the true teachings were preached (or, taught) to you."

An alternative translation model for this verse is:

> Therefore I will continually cause you to remember those things, even though you know them already. The true teachings that were taught to you are also firmly fixed in your heart (or, mind).

1.13	RSV	TEV
	I think it right, as long as I am in this body,[c] to arouse you by way of reminder,	I think it only right for me to stir up your memory of these matters as long as I am still alive.

[c] Greek *tent*

I think it right includes the two elements of rightness and duty; so JB has "I am sure it is my duty," and Phps has "I consider it my duty."

As long as I am in this body is literally "as long as I am in this tent," as the RSV footnote shows. Two explanations have been given regarding this metaphorical language:

1. The Greek word for "tent" was a popular term for the body, conveying the idea that the body is a temporary dwelling place of the immortal soul, which leaves it after death. Taken in this manner it is another example of the influence of Greek thought within the letter.
2. Another possible background for the metaphor is the nomadic life of God's people in the Old Testament. During the journeys of the Israelites in the wilderness, they carried tents that they put up whenever they camped.

Whatever the background may be, the whole expression refers to the state of being alive, temporary though it may be, and this can be stated directly in the translation (as in TEV "as long as I am alive"). So, while Peter is still alive, he wants to **arouse** (NRSV "refresh") the memory of the readers. This is literally "to rouse you up in remembrance." Some translations give the idea that what is meant here is rousing people up to action by reminding them of some important things (for example, JB "keep stirring you up with reminders," and Phps "to stimulate you by these reminders.") It is more likely, however, that this simply means to refresh the memory, which is what NRSV and TEV follow. Other ways of expressing this are "cause you to remember these things" or "cause you to think about these things again."

1.14 RSV	TEV
since I know that the putting off of my body[c] will be soon, as our Lord Jesus Christ showed me.	I know that I shall soon put off this mortal body, as our Lord Jesus Christ plainly told me.

[c] Greek *tent*

If a translator ends verse 13 with an incomplete sentence as in RSV, it will be necessary to begin this verse with a connecting word such as "since" or "because."

The putting off of my body is literally "the putting off of my tent" (as in TEV "I shall soon put off this mortal body")—which is another way of saying simply "my death." The figure is not perfect here, since a tent is actually folded and not taken off like a garment. But such mixing of metaphors is quite frequent in the Scriptures (see for example 2 Cor 5.1-4). If the metaphor of **body** has been used in the previous verse, it will be helpful for a translator to keep the same metaphor in the present verse. But if the translator has avoided the metaphor in verse 13 and used a word for "alive," it will make a better balance to talk about "dying" in this verse; for example, "I know that very soon I will die." Note that TEV has added the word "mortal" to "body." In some languages this idea can be expressed as "this body, which will die," or "this impermanent body." **Will be soon** points to the nearness of Peter's death. Some commentaries want to understand this to mean violent and unexpected death, but such an interpretation seems to be influenced by reading this passage in the light of John 21.18, where Jesus refers to the way Peter will die some day. The Greek word itself simply suggests swiftness, not violence.

The verb translated **showed me** can also mean "inform" or "indicate" and is used of special revelations (as in 1 Cor 3.13; 1 Peter 1.11). In the testament form of writing, the hero usually receives some kind of advance warning of his approaching death, and in this context that warning comes from the Lord. That Jesus gives a special communication to Peter is made clear in some translations; for instance, TEV has "as our Lord Jesus Christ plainly told me," and NEB "indeed our Lord Jesus Christ has told me so." This is perhaps a reference back to John 21.18.

1.15   RSV   TEV

And I will see to it that after my depar- I will do my best, then, to provide a
ture you may be able at any time to   way for you to remember these matters
recall these things.   at all times after my death.

Will see to it translates the same verb used in verse 5 (RSV "make every effort") and in verse 10 (RSV "be the more zealous"). The future tense of the verb has created some problems for translation and interpretation. Some possible ways of understanding the future tense are as follows:

1. It is possible that Peter is here referring to a future effort that will remind his readers of these things even after his death. This effort most probably includes a letter, but one which is not the same as the present letter. Some have even speculated that such a letter was written, but that it has been lost. Others conjecture that what is meant here is Mark's Gospel, since the ancient church regarded it as related to Peter and enshrining his testimony regarding Jesus Christ. Most if not all of this is of course speculative, that is, based only on what some think is possible.
2. The verse does not refer to the writing of any letter, either in the present or in the future, but to Peter's effort of insuring that his testament (that is, the things mentioned in the present letter) is preserved and remembered even after his death.

The verb **see to it** can be rendered in many different ways; for example, "try as hard as I can" or "do whatever I can to."

Departure is a very dignified euphemism, or way of avoiding the unpleasant word "death." (The same euphemism is used in Luke 9.31.) A literal translation may give the wrong idea, such as the departure of the soul from the body, which is a Greek but not a Christian idea. Instead of translating literally, an equivalent euphemism can be used in the translation; for instance "after I am gone" (NEB) or "after I have passed away." It is advisable to use the same expression as in verse 14 if a euphemism is used there. If no euphemism is available, then the meaning can be stated directly, as in TEV "after my death."

You may be able at any time to recall these things is literally "you may be able always to have remembrance of these things." **These things** refers to the contents of Peter's testament, which as suggested above is perhaps identical to the present letter. It is important for the readers of Peter's letter to have continuous access to these important matters, even and especially after Peter's death, since that is the main purpose of a testament. The expression for **recall** appears only here in the whole letter. For **you may be able** TEV has "provide a way for you"; this is an excellent model for translators. Another way to say this is "cause you to."

An alternative translation model for this verse is:

> I will try very hard, then (or, as hard as I can), to give you a way (or, cause you) to remember these matters continually after I have passed away (or, died).

The reliability of the prophetic message regarding Jesus Christ
1.16-21

RSV   TEV

Eyewitnesses of Christ's Glory

16 For we did not follow cleverly devised myths when we made known to you the power and coming of our Lord Jesus Christ, but we were eyewitnesses of his majesty. 17 For when he received honor and glory from God the Father and the voice was borne to him by the Majestic Glory, "This is my beloved Son, with whom I am well pleased," 18 we heard this voice borne from heaven, for we were with him on the holy mountain. 19 And we have the prophetic word made more sure. You will do well to pay attention to this as to a lamp shining in a dark place, until the day dawns and the morning star rises in your hearts. 20 First of all you must understand this, that no prophecy of scripture is a matter of one's own interpretation, 21 because no prophecy ever came by the impulse of man, but men moved by the Holy Spirit spoke from God.

16 We have not depended on made-up stories in making known to you the mighty coming of our Lord Jesus Christ. With our own eyes we saw his greatness. 17 We were there when he was given honor and glory by God the Father, when the voice came to him from the Supreme Glory, saying, "This is my own dear Son, with whom I am pleased!" 18 We ourselves heard this voice coming from heaven, when we were with him on the holy mountain.

19 So we are even more confident of the message proclaimed by the prophets. You will do well to pay attention to it, because it is like a lamp shining in a dark place until the Day dawns and the light of the morning star shines in your hearts. 20 Above all else, however, remember that no one can explain by himself a prophecy in the Scriptures. 21 For no prophetic message ever came just from the will of man, but men were under the control of the Holy Spirit as they spoke the message that came from God.

In this section Peter uses the Transfiguration story (Matt 17.1-8; Mark 9.2-23; Luke 9.28-36) to show that the prophetic message about Jesus is true, and that prophecies in the Scriptures are reliable.

SECTION HEADING: the heading of the outline, "The reliability of the prophetic message regarding Jesus Christ," may also be rendered "The prophetic message (regarding Christ) is reliable" or ". . . can be trusted," or "The apostles learned that the prophetic message about Jesus Christ was true," or else "You can trust the prophetic message about Jesus Christ." The TEV heading emphasizes the reliability of the apostles, which is also appropriate,

"Eyewitnesses of Christ's glory." This may also be rendered "Peter and the other apostles saw Christ's glory."

1.16   RSV   TEV

For we did not follow cleverly devised myths when we made known to you the power and coming of our Lord Jesus Christ, but we were eyewitnesses of his majesty.	We have not depended on made-up stories in making known to you the mighty coming of our Lord Jesus Christ. With our own eyes we saw his greatness.

In this context **we** refers to Peter and the other apostles, hence it is exclusive, since it does not include the readers of the letter. The switch from the singular "I" to the plural "we" is a device by which Peter identifies himself with the group of apostles who were with Jesus on earth and who therefore have authority over the church.

Did not follow may be rendered in some languages as "did not use," "did not depend on" (see TEV), here denying the implied idea that these myths were regarded by the apostles as true and valid. In certain languages this first clause will be expressed idiomatically; for example, "We did not weave made-up stories . . . ."

Myths here is used in a derogatory, negative sense, referring to stories that are not true or that are just imaginary tales, but which are proclaimed and believed by some people to be true. This has not always been the understanding of the term "myth." The old Greek myths, for instance, were used to express religious, moral, and philosophical truths, and therefore were regarded very highly. So what were these **cleverly devised myths** that Peter is referring to here? Commentaries suggest two possibilities:

1. They were speculations of the Gnostic teachers regarding God, the origin of the world, and especially regarding Jesus Christ. In contrast to these Gnostic teachers, Peter is saying that what he and the other apostles proclaim about Christ is solidly founded on history and prophecy and not on speculations.

2. The apostles' message about Jesus was being branded as "myth" in the derogatory sense by Peter's enemies, and Peter is answering that charge. It is very likely that what is especially being attacked as false is the Christian proclamation regarding the Parousia, or the second coming of Christ, which is mentioned in the second half of the verse and is the subject matter of much of chapter 3. The difficulties related to the Parousia, particularly the long delay in its coming, had led some believers to ridicule this belief, and false teachers had taken advantage of the situation in order to accuse the apostles of confusing myth with the truth. Peter vehemently denies all this. Instead he asserts that his message about Christ, and particularly about his second coming, is based both on prophecy and on reliable historical evidence.

91

Cleverly devised translates a Greek word that can also mean "cleverly made up," "cleverly concocted," "invented," or "fabricated." Cleverness here is understood in a derogatory sense. **Myths** can be translated in this context as "stories" (TEV), "tales," "legends," "fairy tales." In certain languages it is possible to talk about "binding stories," meaning "making up stories cleverly," or, as in English, we can say "spinning clever tales."

We made known to you translates a verb that is frequently used in the New Testament for imparting a mystery or a special message received from God (see as examples Luke 2.15; John 15.15; Rom 16.26; Eph 6.19 "proclaim"; Col 1.27). This may also be rendered as "We told you." What is made known here is **the power and coming of our Lord Jesus Christ**. **Power and coming** is another pair of words that may be interpreted in two ways:

1. They can be taken separately, with **power** being an attribute of Christ that was shown during his life and ministry, and especially at his resurrection. **Coming**, on the other hand, is a Greek term for the appearance of a god (*parousia*); when used of Christ it refers primarily to his future coming in glory (see Matt 24.3,27; 1 Cor 15.23; 1 Thes 3.13; 4.15; James 5.7-8; 1 John 2.28). Some translations indicate clearly that these terms are taken separately: JB "the power and the coming," and NEB "the power of our Lord Jesus Christ and his coming."

2. On the other hand, the two terms can be taken together and treated as a hendiadys, with power describing coming, hence "coming with power," "coming in power," "powerful coming," or "mighty coming" (TEV). In other parts of the New Testament, power is closely linked with the second coming of Jesus (Matt 24.30; Mark 9.1; 13.26; Luke 21.27).

There is also another opinion to the effect that **coming** refers not to a future coming, but to Jesus' first coming, that is, to his ministry, death, and resurrection. The reasons for this are, firstly, that the event referred to in this section is the Transfiguration, which in the Gospel narratives points forward to the resurrection rather than to the second coming, and secondly, that the writer at this point would not refer to an event that has not yet taken place, since he wants to argue from things that he was directly involved in.

Against the above it is argued that the term *parousia* is not used elsewhere in the New Testament for Jesus' first coming, but only for his future coming. There is also some slight evidence in the early church that the Transfiguration was interpreted as anticipating the future coming of Christ.

On the whole, then, it is best to take **coming** here as referring to the return of Christ, and **power** as describing this return. Therefore in many languages the clause **we made known to you the power and coming of our Lord Jesus Christ** can be rendered as "we told you how our Lord Jesus Christ will be coming in power" or "we told you how . . . will come and reveal his power."

Peter describes himself and the apostles as **eyewitnesses**. The Greek word for this occurs only here in the New Testament; it was a technical term in the mystery religions, used of people who had gone through all the stages of initiation and were then allowed to watch the secret ritual. It is possible that this usage is echoed here, and that Peter was aware that, as eyewitnesses of the Transfiguration, he and the two other disciples had been privileged to see with their own eyes a special revelation from God. It is, however, also possible that the term is used here in its ordinary sense of being a spectator (see 1 Peter 2.12 and 3.2, where the verb form is used with this ordinary meaning, "see"). TEV's "with our own eyes we saw" is a good alternative model.

What the disciples saw with their own eyes was Jesus' **majesty**; the Greek word is usually used of divine greatness (Luke 9.43; Acts 19.27). Here it accents the supernatural quality of Jesus and the divine majesty that he received from God at the Transfiguration. **Majesty** may be translated in many languages as "dazzling light" or "splendor," and the final sentence may be expressed as "We saw his dazzling light (or, splendor) with our own eyes."

1.17 RSV	TEV
For when he received honor and glory from God the Father and the voice was borne to him by the Majestic Glory, "This is my beloved Son,[d] with whom I am well pleased,"	We were there when he was given honor and glory by God the Father, when the voice came to him from the Supreme Glory, saying, "This is my own dear Son, with whom I am pleased!"

[d] Or *my Son, my* (or *the*) *Beloved*

One important thing to note is that, in the Greek, verses 17 and 18 form one sentence, with verse 17 as a dependent clause and verse 18 as the main clause of the sentence. If this is retained in translation (as in RSV and other formal translations), the sentence becomes too long, and at least in English it does not conform to good style. Most modern English translations divide these verses into two separate sentences, thus making the sentences shorter and making the translation conform to natural style as well. In certain languages, though, where dependent clauses always come before the main clause, it may be helpful to maintain verses 17 and 18 as one long sentence.

Since verse 17 is a dependent clause in the Greek, it has to be related to verse 18 in some way. And since the focus of verse 18 is the presence of the disciples at the scene, this should also be the focus of verse 17. This feature is captured in TEV by starting verse 17 with "We were there when . . . ." Another way is to combine these two verses in order to come up with a clearer and more natural translation. For example, the place setting of the whole episode is given in verse 18, "the holy mountain." In many languages this place setting needs to be put at the beginning of the episode. A possible restructuring is as follows:

> We were with him on the holy mountain when he was given honor and glory by God the Father. At that time the voice came to him from the Supreme Glory, saying, "This is my own dear Son, with whom I am pleased!" We ourselves heard this voice coming from heaven.

The Transfiguration scene is now described. First, Jesus **received honor and glory** from God. These two words are paired in many parts of the Bible (for instance Psa 8.5; Rom 2.7; 1 Tim 1.17; 1 Peter 1.7; Rev 4.9). Various possibilities of interpreting these are as follows:

1. Taken separately, **honor** refers to the exalted status that Jesus received as a result of being named as the beloved Son of God, and **glory** refers to the radiance of his appearance when he was transfigured before the disciples (Mark 9.3).
2. Taking the two terms together, **glory** can be interpreted as describing **honor**, hence "great honor," or "honored greatly."
3. **Glory** can be understood as a way of honoring Jesus, which means that God conferred honor on Jesus by glorifying his appearance, that is, by making his appearance glow with heavenly light.
4. A fourth possibility is to take **glory** as meaning "praise" and therefore having the same meaning as **honor**.

Of these possibilities, the first two seem to be the most likely alternatives. The expression **he received glory and honor**, or even the form "was given" (TEV), may be rendered in the active form in many languages; for example, "God the Father honored him and caused him to be radiant (show glory)." However, if the second alternative is chosen above, we may render this as "God the Father honored him greatly."

It is therefore clear that the source of honor and glory is God himself. This is an important declaration in view of the Greek background of the readers, since in those days there was popular belief in the idea of a "divine man." Jesus was not such a "divine man" but true God who became a real human being and was invested by God with honor and glory because of the task he was sent to perform. **God the Father** will be expressed in a number of languages as "God who is the Father."

In certain languages it will be helpful to insert the words "At that time" before the phrase **the voice was borne to him** and say "At that time the voice came . . . ," "It was at that time that the voice came . . . ," or "When we were there the voice came . . . ." In many languages it will be difficult to translate **the voice was borne to him**, or even "the voice came to him" (TEV). In such cases it will be helpful to introduce the information that Jesus heard the voice (see below), and say "when he heard the voice from God the Supreme Glory saying . . . ."

The term **majestic glory** (TEV "Supreme Glory," JB "Sublime Glory," NEB "sublime Presence") is a euphemism for God and is used in order to avoid mentioning the divine name. In some writings during the first and second centuries B.C. (the intertestamental period), God is called the "Great Glory," as in Testament of Levi 3.4; 1 Enoch 14.20. A meaningful translation of this term can be used provided it is understood by the readers as a reference to God. Another possible way is to include the name of God in the translation; for example, "God the Supreme Glory," "God the Sublime Presence," or "God the Sublime Glory."

God's declaration is called literally **the voice**. The quotation is taken from Matt 17.5 minus the last part ("Listen to him"). In Matthew's setting the saying was addressed to the disciples and not to Jesus; here it is stated that the voice came to Jesus himself. Most commentators are of the opinion that there is a conscious echo here of Psa 2.7, where the words of the Lord God are addressed to the king. This psalm has been interpreted as a messianic psalm, and the king in the psalm has been identified with the Messiah.

"This is my Son, my Beloved" is the wording in many important Greek manuscripts, as the RSV footnote makes clear, while some others have **my beloved Son**. In translating this, however, there may not be that much difference between the two versions of the text, since they practically come out the same in the translation. In many languages, for instance, it is not natural to say "my son, my beloved," but it is perfectly natural to say "my beloved son" or "my son whom I love." The adjustments made will be translational decisions rather than decisions based on the text and its interpretation.

Some scholars interpret this part of the quotation in the light of Old Testament passages. For example, if interpreted in the light of Gen 22.2 ("your only son"), it will indicate the uniqueness of Jesus' divine sonship. If, however, it is interpreted in the light of Isa 42.1 ("my chosen"), then it emphasizes Jesus' election to the messianic office. No matter how valid these opinions are, it is still an essential part of the translation task to remain faithful to the text through the use of valid principles of translation and interpretation, and to avoid any translation that is not based on the text.

The second part of the quotation, **with whom I am well pleased**, is taken from Isa 42.1. The verb is in the aorist tense, indicating past completed action, which means that God's pleasure in choosing Jesus has already occurred in God's eternal time, before it was declared publicly at the Mount of Transfiguration. A further point to note is that in the Greek the pronoun **I** is in the emphatic position; it is God and God alone who chooses Jesus and pronounces good pleasure on his chosen one. The unspoken argument is that, if this is the case, then everything said about Jesus, including his imminent return, is not a human legend but is firmly grounded on God's will and purpose. In many languages it will be helpful to divide this final complex sentence into two sentences and say "This is my son whom I love. I am very pleased with him."

An alternative translation model for this verse, using information from verse 18, is the following:

> We were with him on the holy (or, sacred) mountain when God the Father honored him and caused him to be radiant (or, show dazzling light). When we were there he heard the voice from God, the Supreme Glory, saying, "This is my own son whom I love. I am very pleased with him."

1.18   RSV

TEV

we heard this voice borne from heaven, for we were with him on the holy mountain.

We ourselves heard this voice coming from heaven, when we were with him on the holy mountain.

"We ourselves" (TEV) accurately translates the Greek, where **we** is emphatic. The point here is not "we heard it and others didn't" but "we heard it and therefore our witness is reliable." However, where exclusive pronoun forms exist, they must be used, as this is referring to Peter and his two fellow-disciples James and John. Furthermore, in some languages that have a special expression referring to three people (for example, "we three"), this expression should be used.

The declaration from heaven is "this voice borne from heaven" (TEV "coming from heaven"). **Heaven** can be interpreted as another euphemism avoiding the name of God (as in the expression "kingdom of heaven," which means "kingdom of God"). Here again the name of God can be included in the translation; for example, "this voice from God," "this voice from God in heaven," or even "God's voice from heaven," or "God's voice speaking from heaven." It has been noted also by some commentaries that a voice from heaven is a standard feature of apocalyptic visions, that is, visions that are revelations of God's future plans and actions (see Dan 4.31; Rev 10.4,8; 11.12; 14.13; and other passages). This means that the Transfiguration has been understood in some circles of the early church as a revelation of this type.

In the Gospel accounts the Transfiguration occurred on a high mountain (see Matt 17.1). Here this high mountain is described as **the holy mountain**, that is, a particular place considered sacred and set apart for the worship of God. It is not very likely that during the time of the writing of *The Second Letter from Peter* a special site for the Transfiguration had been identified and set aside by the Christian community. It is therefore very possible that this is a deliberate reference to Mount Zion, through a hint taken from Psa 2.6, where Zion is identified as a holy hill. It is not that the Transfiguration site is identified with Mount Zion, but that the significance of the Transfiguration is explained in the light of the prophecy of Psalm 2. In languages that have a word similar in meaning to the English word "sacred," the translator should use that word in this context. Otherwise, if the only word available is one that means basically "pure" or "clean," then the translator should say instead, for example, "God's mountain." See further discussion on **holy** at Jude 14.

1.19 RSV	TEV
And we have the prophetic word made more sure. You will do well to pay attention to this as to a lamp shining in a dark place, until the day dawns and the morning star rises in your hearts.	So we are even more confident of the message proclaimed by the prophets. You will do well to pay attention to it, because it is like a lamp shining in a dark place until the Day dawns and the light of the morning star shines in your hearts.

From a discussion of the Transfiguration, Peter now moves into a consideration of the prophetic message as a whole. The Transfiguration becomes the basis for affirming the reliability of the Parousia, or second coming of Jesus, and it also confirms and proves the reliability and dependability of the prophetic message. So now it is necessary to say something about the nature of the prophetic message.

The expression **prophetic word** (TEV "the message proclaimed by the prophets," JB "prophecies," Phps "word of prophecy") can refer to many things, among which are: Old Testament messianic prophecy, Old and New Testament prophecies, one particular Old Testament prophecy, 2 Peter 1.20-21 as a prophecy, the Transfiguration itself as a prophecy of the Parousia, and the whole Old Testament understood as messianic prophecy. This last suggestion seems to be the most likely, since the expression itself is almost always used to refer to the Old Testament Scriptures and is in fact interchangeable with the word "Scripture." The Jews themselves regarded all inspired Scripture as prophecy, and the Christians viewed all Scriptures as a prophecy of Jesus, his life, ministry, death, and resurrection, and his return. In view of this, **the prophetic word** can be translated as "the Scriptures written or spoken by the prophets," "the Holy Writings proclaimed by God's messengers," or "what (or, the things that) people speaking for God say in the Scriptures."

More sure: the full clause is literally "we have more sure the prophetic word (NIV "more certain," JB "we have confirmation," TEV "we are even more confident"). This may mean that, in the light of the Transfiguration proving the reliability of prophecy, the prophetic message can now be regarded with greater confidence. Another way of interpreting this is to take the comparative **more sure** as having a superlative meaning, hence "very, very firm." It is not that there was little or no confidence in the prophetic message before it is proved reliable by relating it to the Transfiguration, but that such confidence has been strengthened beyond limits. And since there is no doubt at all regarding the certainty of the prophetic word, there is also much greater confidence that the prophetic word regarding the Parousia will be fulfilled. The phrase **more sure** refers to the writer's confidence and belief in the credibility of this message. In certain languages this confidence will be expressed idiomatically; for example, "to have a firm heart."

The expression **you will do well** is a polite command often equivalent to "please" (as in James 2.3; 3 John 6; and as statements, Phil 4.14 "it was kind of you"; Acts 10.33 "you have been kind enough"), and so Mft has "Pray attend to that word." It is, however, possible to take this expression as having a stronger force in this context, where the readers are invited or urged to give greater attention to the prophetic word, and consequently are warned against misusing or neglecting it. **You will do well** may be rendered as "You will do a good thing if . . ." or "It is a good thing for you to . . . ."

To pay attention can also mean to heed, to follow, to take seriously. This phrase in many languages is rendered idiomatically; for example, "take your heart and place it in." **To this** of course points to the prophetic word, which is compared to **a lamp shining in a dark place.** In Psa 119.105 the Word of God is compared to a lamp, which is a similar comparison. The **dark place** here can be the world, which is marked by evil and sin (as in Gal 1.4), or the human mind, which is not illumined by the prophetic message. In the midst of this darkness, the prophetic message gives light and awakens hope (see Eph 6.12;

1 John 2.8). Other ways of translating this metaphor are "just as if it were a lamp shining in a dark place" or "as you would to a lamp shining in a dark place."

The day here is a technical term for the Parousia (see Rom 13.12), or for the Day of salvation (Luke 1.78), the time when Christ returns to inaugurate the new age and establish a new heaven and a new earth. On that Day the darkness of the present age will be banished in much the same way as the night is banished by the dawning day. In certain languages it will be helpful to expand the phrase **until the day dawns** as follows: "until the light of that Day appears," or more figuratively, "until the sun rises on that Day."

The **morning star** is *phōsphoros* in Greek, a word that refers to the planet Venus and the Greek goddess Artemis. Some scholars have argued that, since *phōsphoros* means "daybreak," it cannot refer to Venus but to the sun. But in ordinary usage *phōsphoros* does refer to Venus, which rises with the dawn and, in a manner of speaking, introduces light into the world. Once again we see Greek culture being used as a vehicle for the Christian message. Here the **morning star** stands for the Messiah, or Christ (see Num 24.17; Rev. 22.16), who will bring light into the **hearts** of believers, in much the same way as the morning star brings light into a dark world. As the morning star banishes darkness from the world, so Christ in his return banishes darkness from the hearts of believers, removing all doubt and uncertainty, and transforming their inner selves into the very image of Christ himself.

Alternative translation models for this verse are as follows:

(1) So we are even more confident in the message of the Holy Scriptures proclaimed by God's prophets. This message is like a lamp shining in a dark place. It shines until the Day dawns and the light of Christ shines into your hearts, just as the morning star brings light to the world. You will do a good thing if you pay attention to this message.

(2) So we are even more confident in what the people speaking for God said in the Holy Scriptures. You will do a good thing if you pay attention to this message, because it is like a lamp shining in a dark place until the Day dawns and the light of Christ shines in your hearts, just as the morning star brings light to the world.

1.20	RSV	TEV

First of all you must understand this, that no prophecy of scripture is a matter of one's own interpretation,	Above all else, however, remember that no one can explain by himself a prophecy in the Scriptures.

Peter's reference to the prophetic message now leads him to expound on the nature of prophecy and how it is interpreted. It is possible, as has been suggested in the discussion of the previous passage, that the false teachers have raised this issue and have objected to the way the prophetic word is being used to prove the truth of certain Christian teachings. It is in answer to these objections that Peter now explains the nature of prophecy. In this verse an individualistic approach to the interpretation of prophecy is rejected.

The expression **First of all you must understand this** marks out the statement that follows as very important and deserving of special attention. Similar phrases are used in other parts of the New Testament, such as Luke 12.39 ("But know this"), Gal 3.7 ("So you see"), and 2 Tim 3.1 ("But understand this"). In many languages the mention of "first" demands a "second," but since there is no "second," then the sense of importance needs to be substituted for "first"; for example, "The most important thing is that you understand . . . ." It is not clear whether the information about to be shared is new or already known to the readers.

What is the meaning of the statement **no prophecy of scripture is a matter of one's own interpretation**? **Scripture** most certainly refers to the Old Testament, and **prophecy** to particular parts of the Old Testament, primarily those parts that foretell future events. However, it is possible to take **prophecy** here and in verse 21 with the meaning "message from God," in which case **prophecy of scripture** can be translated "the message of God contained in the Scriptures," or possibly "a message announced by one of God's messengers, which is contained in the Scriptures."

Interpretation is a Greek word that occurs only here in the New Testament. Both the noun and the related verb are used for the explanation of riddles, puzzles, dreams, parables, and difficult passages of scripture. The Greek word translated **is a matter of** in this context can also be translated "belongs to" or "comes under the scope of." But who is referred to in the expression **one's own interpretation**? As we will see, the answer to this question is decisive in determining the meaning of the whole statement, as the following possibilities show:

1. If **one's own** is understood as referring to any person, then the statement can mean that no one can explain or interpret a prophecy of scripture with the use of his or her own powers alone. This meaning is echoed in some translations such as TEV "no one can explain by himself a prophecy in the Scriptures," Phps "no prophecy of scripture can be interpreted by a single human mind," and AT "no prophecy of scripture can be understood through one's own powers." This connects the interpretation to the guidance of the Holy Spirit, as stated in verse 21.
2. The statement can mean that what is being denied is private individual interpretation of prophecy; in this case what is being indirectly affirmed is the importance of the church or the Christian community. This is echoed in some translations as well; for example, JB "the interpretation of scriptural prophecy is never a matter for the individual."
3. If, however, **one's own** is taken to refer to the prophet himself, then the statement would mean that the interpretation of scripture is not dependent on the prophet's own ideas or efforts. Again, this is echoed in some translations; for example, NIV "no prophecy of Scripture came about by the prophet's own interpretation."

Of these three alternatives, the first two seem preferable, with the second having a slight preference over the first. Taken as a whole, then, the statement is not suggesting that personal reading, reflection and interpretation of scripture is wrong. Rather the statement most probably asserts that the prophetic message should not be interpreted according to a person's whims and fancies. This is of course directed at the false teachers referred to in the next two chapters, who are diluting Christian teaching and twisting it to suit their own fanciful ideas.

Alternative translation models for this verse are:

> The most important thing is that you understand that no one is able through his own ability (or, power) to explain a prophecy of God (or, a message announced by one of God's spokesmen) which is contained in the Scriptures.

Or:

> . . . that you understand that one's own interpretation of prophecy in the Scriptures is not the most important.

1.21   RSV   TEV

| because no prophecy ever came by the impulse of man, but men moved by the Holy Spirit spoke from God.[e] | For no prophetic message ever came just from the will of man, but men were under the control of the Holy Spirit as they spoke the message that came from God. |

[e] Other authorities read *moved by the Holy Spirit holy men of God spoke*

This verse explains why verse 20 is true. The first assertion is that the interpretation of the prophetic message is not dependent on human power, because the prophetic message did not come about **by the impulse of man**. Another way of saying it is that no prophecy is of human origin, since it always originates from God. This first clause may also be rendered "Because no one from his own power (intelligence) ever announced God's message," or we can say "No prophecy ever originated in a human being."

The second assertion, however, defines the place of people in the interpretation of prophecy: people are **moved by the Holy Spirit**. **Men** here does not refer just to males, but means people in general (human beings). It was God's Spirit that carried them along and enabled them to say what God wanted them to say. Apart from the Spirit, the prophetic message does not exist and cannot be understood. It is of course clearly understood that the Spirit belongs to the church, which is created by the same Spirit and therefore plays an important role in the interpretation and preservation of the prophetic message. So people who are **moved** by the Holy Spirit are enabled to proclaim and interpret the prophetic message. The term for **moved** can also be translated "carried away," "have their hearts stirred up," or "The Holy Spirit stirred up their hearts" (note TEV "under the control," NEB "impelled," Phps "inspired," NIV "carried along"); and this somehow suggests a state of ecstasy in which the Holy Spirit takes full control of a person. At any rate, this expression belongs to the vocabulary of prophetic inspiration that was in use within the Greek-speaking section of Judaism. In certain languages translators will need to render this clause in the active rather than the passive; for example, "But the Holy Spirit stirred up people's hearts (inspired them) as they spoke the message that came from God."

The third assertion is that these people **spoke from God**. The vocabulary may have been their own, but the message that they proclaimed "came from God" (TEV). This anticipates chapter 2, where false prophets are mentioned; in contrast to true prophets, these people proclaimed a message that did not come from God but was a product of their own mind.

Chapter 2

After discussing how the Scriptures should be truly interpreted, Peter now deals with people who have been misinterpreting and misusing the prophetic message in order to lead believers into immoral behavior. Many of the examples in this chapter are taken from the book of Jude; it is very likely that Peter had a copy of Jude and referred to it constantly while writing this part of his letter. He did not, however, simply quote Jude but modified it in order to suit his own thinking and purpose. The similarities and differences will be discussed as they appear. In working with this chapter it will be good for translators to have the book of Jude opened before them.

False teachers who misinterpret and misuse the prophetic message
2.1-3

RSV

TEV

False Teachers

1 But false prophets also arose among the people, just as there will be false teachers among you, who will secretly bring in destructive heresies, even denying the Master who bought them, bringing upon themselves swift destruction. 2 And many will follow their licentiousness, and because of them the way of truth will be reviled. 3 And in their greed they will exploit you with false words; from of old their condemnation has not been idle, and their destruction has not been asleep.

1 False prophets appeared in the past among the people, and in the same way false teachers will appear among you. They will bring in destructive, untrue doctrines, and will deny the Master who redeemed them, and so they will bring upon themselves sudden destruction. 2 Even so, many will follow their immoral ways; and because of what they do, others will speak evil of the Way of truth. 3 In their greed these false teachers will make a profit out of telling you made-up stories. For a long time now their Judge has been ready, and their Destroyer has been wide awake!

In these three verses Peter mentions the false teachers for the first time and describes their evil ways.

SECTION HEADING: the heading suggested by the Handbook outline for verses 1-3 may also be rendered "Peter warns Christians about false teachers" or "Warning about false teachers." The TEV section heading for the entire chapter, "False Teachers," may also be rendered as "Teachers who teach untrue doctrines (to the believers)," "Beware of those people who teach untrue doctrines," or "Peter warns his readers about people who teach false doctrines."

2.1   RSV   TEV

But false prophets also arose among the people, just as there will be false teachers among you, who will secretly bring in destructive heresies, even denying the Master who bought them, bringing upon themselves swift destruction.

False prophets appeared in the past among the people, and in the same way false teachers will appear among you. They will bring in destructive, untrue doctrines, and will deny the Master who redeemed them, and so they will bring upon themselves sudden destruction.

False prophets is a term used for people who claim to be sent by God to proclaim his message, when in fact God has not sent them at all. See, for example, Deut 18.22 (TEV), "If a prophet speaks in the name of the LORD and what he says does not come true, then it is not the LORD's message." The word "prophet" itself is sometimes used to refer to someone who predicts events in the future, but in most cases it refers to someone who is called and sent by God to proclaim a certain message. Therefore **prophets** may be effectively translated as "people who speak for God" or "people who proclaim God's message." **False prophets** can then be rendered as "fake (counterfeit) prophets," "people who pretend to speak God's message," or "people who pretend to speak on behalf of God." There were many false prophets who appeared among the Israelites at various times in their history. The punishment for false prophets was usually death: "But if any prophet dares to speak a message in my name when I did not command him to do so, he must die for it" (Deut 18.20, TEV; and see also Jer 14.15; 23.15; 28.16-17).

Arose translates the past tense of the verb "to be" and indicates that this refers to an event or events "in the past" (TEV), that is, in the history of Israel. Other ways of rendering "in the past" are "in olden times," "long ago," "years that are gone," or "many generations ago." **People** here refers to the Israelites as God's chosen people. To make this clear it is possible to translate **people** as "God's people."

Just as: in many languages translators will need to begin the verse with these words; for example, "Just as false prophets . . . so also false teachers . . . ."

The equivalent of **false prophets** in the present is **false teachers**. The focus here is not so much that these people claim to be sent by God when in fact they are not, or that they lay claim to the office of teacher to which they have no right, but that they have been teaching ideas and doctrines that are wrong. Their teachings are based not on any revelation from God but on their own ingenious inventions. This is made clear by the statement that these false teachers will secretly bring in destructive opinions. **False teachers** may be translated using the same sort of expressions as those used for **false prophets**. In certain languages **false teachers** can be expressed idiomatically; for example, "Teachers who weave lies with their mouths."

Secretly bring in translates a Greek verb that appears only here in the New Testament and that means either to **bring in** without indicating how it is done, or "to bring in under false pretenses." In this context secrecy is perhaps intended; they will introduce these teachings without anyone noticing it. Another word that fits this context is "unobtrusively." In some languages translators will be able to find an idiomatic expression like "slip in"; for example, "slipped in destructive opinions" (see Gal 2.4, where Paul uses the same Greek word but in a different context).

Heresies: in Greek thought the term "heresy" was used to refer to a particular school of thought or the teachings of such a group. This positive sense was later lost, and the negative sense of "faction" (as in 1 Cor 11.19) or "false teaching" became its primary meaning. In the present context **heresies** refers to teachings or doctrines that are false and against accepted Christian teaching (as in TEV "untrue doctrines"). These heresies taught by the false teachers are also described as **destructive**. It is possible, as some commentators suggest, that there were some **heresies** that were positive and useful, and that the addition of the term **destructive** indicates that these particular teachings were not useful. It is more likely, though, that **destructive** here refers not to the teachings themselves but to the bad effects of these teachings on the members of the Christian community. They are destructive because those who follow them become immoral and are therefore subject to judgment. And so **destructive** can also be rendered as "cause people to go astray" or "cause people to come under judgment." Some commentators notice irony here: the false teachers taught that there would be no final judgment; but in reality their teaching had the effect of leading people to experience the judgment that these teachers themselves had denied.

One part of these false doctrines is now mentioned: **denying the Master who bought them**. The Greek word translated **deny** can also mean "disown" or "renounce." Here the focus is on their not acknowledging the Master. **Master** can be used for either God or Christ, but in the present context it clearly refers to Christ. The Greek word translated **Master** is the general term for "owner." **Bought** strengthens the idea of ownership and gives the sense that, since Christ has bought them, he now owns them and they belong to him. (For further discussion, please see Jude 4.) In certain languages it will be necessary to include the name "Christ" in this context and say "who do not acknowledge Christ as their Master," or "who do not recognize Christ as their Lord," or even "who say that they no longer belong to Christ."

The word translated **bought** is the general word for buying anything, including slaves; here it is used with the extended sense of "ransom" or "redeem." The terms "ransom" and "redeem" include the component of paying a price and therefore raise the problem of who paid what to whom. This theological problem is at least avoided by stressing that we are here dealing with figurative language: by dying on the cross Christ gave his life as a "payment" for us, enabling us to be free from the power of sin and to belong to Christ, who now owns us. So we may translate the phrase **who bought them** as "who set them free," "who set them free from the power of sin," or even "who ransomed (or, paid for) them and set them free (from sin)."

The results of the activities of these false teachers are now mentioned. They will first of all bring **swift destruction** upon themselves. That this is a result is made clear in TEV by the use of "and so." The word **swift** can also be translated "fast," "speedy," "sudden" (TEV), "quick." The focus here is twofold: the suddenness with which destructive forces come upon the false teachers, and the quickness with which the teachers are destroyed. **Destruction** translates the same word translated **destructive** in **destructive heresies** earlier in this verse; perhaps a play on words is intended: in much the same way that these false teachers introduce teachings that destroy people's faith, so also these false teachers will be destroyed. Other ways of saying this are "and so they will cause themselves to suddenly receive destruction" or "Because they do this, God will destroy them suddenly."

An alternative translation model for this verse is:

> Just as people who pretended to speak God's message appeared long ago, so false teachers will appear among you. They will slip in untrue teachings that will cause people to stop believing in Christ (or, people's beliefs to be destroyed). These false teachers will even refuse to acknowledge Christ as their Master who owns them and freed them from the power of sin. In this way they will cause themselves to be destroyed suddenly.

2.2	RSV	TEV
	And many will follow their licentiousness, and because of them the way of truth will be reviled.	Even so, many will follow their immoral ways; and because of what they do, others will speak evil of the Way of truth.

This verse speaks of the effects the false teachers have in the Christian community. The first effect is that **many will follow their licentiousness**. The Greek word translated **licentiousness** is a general term for immorality (as in TEV "immoral ways"), with special emphasis on sexual excesses, hence "sensuality," "indecency." We should, however, avoid using a term for a particular kind of sexual sin in translating this word. Two other ways of rendering the expression **licentiousness** are "evil sexual practices" or "indecent conduct."

It should be noted that in Jude 4 **licentiousness** is related to the perversion of God's grace; such a statement is absent in 2 Peter.

Many may refer either to people in general, or more likely to some members of the Christian community. If this second alternative is chosen, then it can be made clear in the translation; for example, "many Christians" or "many of God's people."

The word translated **follow** is used only in this letter (here and in 1.16; 2.15) and nowhere else in the New Testament. It means doing the same thing, acting in the same manner, imitating someone.

A second effect of the activities of the false teachers is expressed in the second half of the verse: the Christian way of life will be open to ridicule from those outside the Christian community. **Them** is ambiguous, since it can refer either to the false teachers or to the **many** who follow them. Many translations keep the ambiguity, but most commentaries interpret **them** as referring to the false teachers. If this interpretation is correct, translators in some languages will need to expand TEV's rendering slightly and say "and because of what these teachers do."

The way of truth is a Hebrew expression that means "the true way" or "the right way" (see Gen 24.48). In the book of Acts the Christian faith is known as "the Way" (meaning "path" or "road"; see for example Acts 9.2; 19.9), "the way of salvation" (Acts 16.17), and "the way of the Lord" (Acts 18.25). It is in this light that we can take **the way of truth** as a technical term for the Christian way of life. Other ways of expressing it are "the true way," "the true path," "the way that leads to God" (where "truth" is interpreted as having the meaning "God.") In addition to **the way of truth**, 2 Peter also uses "the way of righteousness" (2.21) and "the right way" (2.15). All three of these expressions are used to refer to the Christian way of life with its moral and ethical demands.

Reviled translates a Greek word that is literally translated "blaspheme," and means here "speak against," "speak evil of" (TEV), "slander," "insult," "ridicule." The text does not say who will do the blaspheming, but it is clear that non-Christians are meant. As a result of Christians imitating the false teachers, the Christian community as a whole receives a bad name from non-Christians. **Reviled** may also be rendered as "say evil things about" or "speak bad about (against)."

An alternative translation model of this verse is:

> Even so, many of God's people will imitate the evil practices of these teachers, and because of the things that they do, people will say bad things about the True Way (or, the Way that leads to God).

2.3   RSV   TEV

And in their greed they will exploit you with false words; from of old their condemnation has not been idle, and their destruction has not been asleep. | In their greed these false teachers will make a profit out of telling you made-up stories. For a long time now their Judge has been ready, and their Destroyer has been wide awake!

Peter now turns to his immediate readers. He warns them of the false teachers' **greed**, that is, their desire to acquire more and more things for themselves and for their own exclusive benefit. The object of their greed is not mentioned, but perhaps NEB is correct in identifying it as "greed for money." If this interpretation is correct, the phrase **in their greed** may be rendered as "Because they are greedy," "Because these false teachers are greedy," or "Because these false teachers want a lot of money." This **greed** leads them to **exploit** Christians, that is, to "make a profit" (TEV) from the members of the

Christian community, or possibly, to "take advantage of" the Christians. One way they will do this is **with false words**. The Greek word translated **false** primarily means "invented," "fabricated," or "made up" (as in TEV "made-up stories"). **False words** therefore are stories or accounts or teachings that have no factual basis but are simply the result of the clever imaginations of the false teachers. This of course is related to 1.16, "cleverly devised myths," and the meaning is essentially the same, although Peter uses a different Greek word. What is being asserted here is that it is not the apostles and Christian teachers, but the false teachers, who are depending on concocted fairy tales.

The second half of the verse speaks of the judgment and destruction of the false teachers. **Condemnation** and **destruction** may be taken as having the same meaning, in which case the two clauses can be taken as parallel to each other. On the other hand **condemnation** may refer more specifically to the process of judgment in order to assess just punishment. **Destruction** can then be taken as the result of punishment: they will be punished to such an extent that they will be utterly destroyed. Here both **condemnation** and **destruction** are personified, that is, they are spoken of as if they are persons who are able to act. TEV has shifted the focus from the personified action to the doer of the action; hence "For a long time now their Judge has been ready, and their Destroyer has been wide awake!" It is clearly understood in the text that the agent in the judgment and destruction of the false teachers is God himself, and if necessary this information can be included in the translation; for example, "God, who judges them, is the one who will destroy them."

From of old refers to a time in the distant past, although the text does not indicate when or where their condemnation was pronounced. Among the possibilities suggested by commentators are:
1. The condemnation of false prophets in the Old Testament already included the condemnation of false teachers, and that condemnation shows how the false teachers will be judged and punished.
2. The examples in the following verses (verses 4-9) are pictures of the coming judgment, which means that the false teachers will be judged in a similar manner. For further discussion, see comments on Jude 4.

Has not been idle and **has not been asleep** are parallel expressions, stressing certainty and nearness of both judgment and destruction. It is possible that the time of punishment is associated with the end of the age, which will be signaled by the Parousia. There are in fact some references in the New Testament to the effect that the last days before the end will be characterized by the appearance of false prophets and false teachers (as in Matt 24.24; 1 Tim 4.1). In certain languages the order of the two verb phrases may be reversed; for example, "has been wide awake and ready to punish them."

An alternative translation model for this verse is:

Because these false teachers want a lot of money, they will take advantage of you by telling you made-up stories. For a long time now, God their Judge and Destroyer has been ready and wide awake to punish them.

Old Testament examples to show that God punishes the wicked and rewards those who are faithful to him
2.4-10a

RSV	TEV
4 For if God did not spare the angels when they sinned, but cast them into hell and committed them to pits of nether gloom to be kept until the judgment; 5 if he did not spare the ancient world, but preserved Noah, a herald of righteousness, with seven other persons, when he brought a flood upon the world of the ungodly; 6 if by turning the cities of Sodom and Gomorrah to ashes he condemned them to extinction and made them an example to those who were to be ungodly; 7 and if he rescued righteous Lot, greatly distressed by the licentiousness of the wicked 8 (for by what that righteous man saw and heard as he lived among them, he was vexed in his righteous soul day after day with their lawless deeds), 9 then the Lord knows how to rescue the godly from trial, and to keep the unrighteous under punishment until the day of judgment, 10 and especially those who indulge in the lust of defiling passion and despise authority.	4 God did not spare the angels who sinned, but threw them into hell, where they are kept chained in darkness, waiting for the Day of Judgment. 5 God did not spare the ancient world, but brought the flood on the world of godless people; the only ones he saved were Noah, who preached righteousness, and seven other people. 6 God condemned the cities of Sodom and Gomorrah, destroying them with fire, and made them an example of what will happen to the godless. 7 He rescued Lot, a good man, who was distressed by the immoral conduct of lawless people. 8 That good man lived among them, and day after day he suffered agony as he saw and heard their evil actions. 9 And so the Lord knows how to rescue godly people from their trials and how to keep the wicked under punishment for the Day of Judgment, 10 especially those who follow their filthy bodily lusts and despise God's authority.

To prove his assertion that within a short time these false teachers are certainly going to receive their just punishment, Peter reviews a little bit of biblical history in order to show that God always acts to punish the wicked and to reward those who are faithful to him. For this purpose he cites three examples, two of which are the fallen angels and the two wicked cities, and these are borrowed from Jude 6-7. A third example, the Flood, is substituted for Jude's example regarding the murmurings of the Israelites in the desert. Peter does two other things with Jude's account: first, he rearranges the examples in proper chronological order as against Jude's jumbled and disorganized version; and second, he adds the theme of God being trusted to protect and rescue the righteous from destruction.

These changes have led some commentators to suggest that Peter has supplemented the Jude material with material from another source that contained accounts of how God punishes the guilty and rescues the righteous. It is more likely, however, that 2 Peter is simply being influenced by 1 Peter. The Flood story may have been included as a direct influence of 1 Peter 3.20; such influence from 1 Peter would explain the other differences as well.

The structure of this section is quite interesting. First of all, it is one long sentence in the Greek, and those translations that follow the form of the Greek usually have one sentence here also. Some other translations break this section into several sentences, thus making the translation sound more natural. An example of this can be found in TEV, which translators can study and use to their benefit.

Secondly, this section consists of several double clauses, the first part being conditional (starting with "if") and the second part adversative (starting with "but"). In the Greek text the "if" is stated only once, at the beginning of the section; but it is clear from the structure of the whole passage that "if" should be read at the beginning of every double clause—a fact that is made clear in RSV. The "if" here, while conditional in form, is, however, declarative or assertive in function; it states a fact rather than questions it. Such an "if" can be rendered as "since" or "because"; and it may even be omitted altogether, in which case the conditional clause is changed to a statement of fact, which is what TEV has done. In such a case the sentence can start with "You know that . . . ," or "You remember that . . . ," or other similar statements. In at least one translation rhetorical questions are employed together with the appropriate answers: "Did God . . . ? No he did not!"

Thirdly, the climax or main point of the section is in the last part, that is, in verses 9-10. After giving four examples from the past, the author then proceeds to draw a conclusion, namely, that God knows how to rescue the godly and how to punish the ungodly. It is therefore very important to make sure that the translation of verses 4-8 builds up to verses 9-10. In some languages it may be even more natural to put the main point at the beginning of the section. But this should only be done if it is really required by the structure of the language.

SECTION HEADING: the Heading suggested by the outline may also be "Old Testament examples of how God deals with the wicked and the righteous," or else in shorter form, "How God deals with the wicked and the righteous."

2.4	RSV	TEV

For if God did not spare the angels when they sinned, but cast them into hell[f] and committed them to pits of nether gloom to be kept until the judgment;

[f] Greek *Tartarus*

God did not spare the angels who sinned, but threw them into hell, where they are kept chained in darkness,[c] waiting for the Day of Judgment.

[c] chained in darkness; *some manuscripts have* in dark pits.

Did not spare means in this context "did not refrain from punishing" or "God punished the angels who sinned. He threw them into . . . ."

The **angels** are mentioned in Jude 6. The most likely background for this account is Gen 6.1-4, in which case the angels are identified with the heavenly beings ("sons of God") who came down to earth and married mortal women. Later writings built on the Genesis account, telling of the sins of these heavenly beings and their subsequent punishment. The account in Jude 6 is based on these writings, and the present passage in turn is based on the Jude account (see Jude 6).

Cast (literally "hand over," "deliver") can also be "threw" (TEV), "banished," "consigned," or "hurled." **Hell** is the Greek word *Tartarus*, which in classical Greek mythology was an abyss under the earth reserved for the punishment of rebellious gods and human beings. There is a Greek legend to the effect that the Titans, ancient giants, were imprisoned in Tartarus by Uranus, who was known as the god of heaven and whose wife Sonia was known as the goddess of the earth. Uranus' own son Kronos, the youngest Titan, overthrew his father and set the Titans free. Kronos, however, was overthrown by his son Zeus, who again imprisoned the Titans in Tartarus.

This legend forms the background for the reference in Enoch regarding fallen angels taking human wives and thus giving birth to evil giants.

It is possible that the term "Tartarus" was used as a substitute for the Hebrew term *Sheol,* since both terms have common components of meaning. At any rate, the term "Tartarus" came into use in Judaism also and is present in some writings of that time (for instance, 1 Enoch 20.2, and the Septuagint translation of Job 40.20b "he causes joy to the quadrupeds of *the deep*"; Job 41.31 [Greek 41.24] "the lowest part of *the deep*"; Pro 30.16). In some languages the closest natural equivalent of Tartarus is "the place of fire." The danger of this rendering is that those who live in cold places may actually want to go there! Where a natural equivalent does not exist, it is possible to render the expression in a general way; for example, "a very very bad place" or "a place of punishment." The phrase **cast them into hell** in many languages will need a directional word that is the equivalent of the English "down"; for example, "cast them down into hell" or "hurled them down into hell."

The expression **pits of nether gloom** is taken from Jude 6 but with some modification. **Nether gloom** is marked as a place in Jude, "the nether gloom," whereas in 2 Peter the same word can be understood as a quality of the **pits**. Another difference is that 2 Peter uses **pits** here, which Jude 6 uses "chains." There is also a textual problem in 2 Peter, as indicated by the footnote in TEV. Some manuscripts have "chains of nether gloom," although the word for "chains" is different in Greek from the word used in Jude. It is difficult to understand **nether gloom** as describing "chains," and some manuscripts have **pits** (Greek *sirois*) rather than "chains" (Greek *seirais*), thus making possible the translation **pits of nether gloom**, "dark dungeons" (AT), or "gloomy dungeons" (NIV). Translations based on the manuscripts that have "chains" here are "chains of deepest darkness" (NRSV) and "chained in darkness" (TEV). The textual evidence is evenly balanced between the two alternatives, but the UBS Greek New Testament has adopted *seirais* "chains," and translators are advised to do the same. For a translation of "chains" see Jude 6.

The word for **nether gloom** is literally "darkness," or "gloom," and is used by the Greeks to describe the underworld or the world of the dead. If translators understand **nether gloom** to be a quality of "chains," then in many languages it will be necessary to restructure this phrase; for example, "deepest darkness that surrounded them like chains," "deepest darkness that imprisoned them like chains." The word "eternal" that is in Jude does not appear in 2 Peter. It is clear from the text that here the state is temporary; these angels are to be chained **until the judgment**, which refers to the final judgment at the end of the world and which will be ushered in by the return of Christ. **Judgment** here should not be understood as determining whether these angels are guilty or innocent, but rather as carrying out the punishment they deserve as a result of their evil deeds. It may be necessary therefore to make this clear, and translate **judgment** as "punishment" or "doom" (AT): "until the Day of Judgment when they will receive the punishment they deserve."

Alternative translation models for this verse are:

(1) For if God did not refrain from punishing the angels when they sinned, but hurled them down into hell, where deepest (thick) darkness surrounded them like chains, as they waited for the Day of Judgment when he will punish them as they deserve, . . .

(2) God did not refrain from punishing the angels when they sinned, but hurled them down into hell where they are kept chained in darkness, waiting for the Day when he will judge them.

2.5 RSV	TEV
if he did not spare the ancient world, but preserved Noah, a herald of righteousness, with seven other persons, when he brought a flood upon the world of the ungodly;	God did not spare the ancient world, but brought the flood on the world of godless people; the only ones he saved were Noah, who preached righteousness, and seven other people.

Instead of the account of the murmurings of the Israelites in Egypt, which is found in Jude, Peter substitutes the story of the Flood, perhaps for the following reasons:

1. In various writings of that time, the Flood was closely connected with the fallen angels; in fact the flood was supposed to have been punishment that resulted from the activity of the fallen angels and their offspring.
2. It is likely that this choice was influenced by 1 Peter (see 3.20).
3. The Flood story has overtones of the last judgment, since it reminds people of the end of the world.
4. Finally, the Flood account serves as a good example of God's act of punishing sinners and rewarding the righteous, and is therefore appropriate to 2 Peter.

The **world** denotes not only the world of human beings but also the universe as a whole. The Flood is understood to have a universal scope and thus is an appropriate reminder of the coming judgment that will also affect the whole world. However, for practical purposes in languages that do not have words or expressions that can refer to both the world of humans and the universe at the same time, translators should use a word that applies to the "world" of humans (**world of the ungodly** in the final sentence). The world before the flood is characterized as **ancient**. Peter seems to divide history into three stages: the ancient world, the present world, and the new world that will come about as a result of the day of the Lord. **Ancient** may be rendered as "a long time ago" or "many generations ago."

The world of the ungodly means the same as the ancient world and echoes Gen 6.5-7,12-13. The word for **ungodly** is used in other parts of this letter and is a favorite word also in Jude (see Jude 4 and the discussion there). In Jewish tradition the people who lived at the time of the flood committed the same sins as the people of Sodom and Gomorrah. **Ungodly** may also be expressed as "people who disobey God," "people who do not worship God," "people who have no use for God," or "people who are not faithful to God."

Noah, however, was saved from the Flood. In the Genesis account Noah is described as a good man with no faults (Gen 6.9-10; 7.1). He is held up by Jewish tradition as an example of moral excellence. Noah then stands for those faithful Christians who will be saved from the judgment that is coming.

Noah is described as **a herald of righteousness** (TEV "who preached righteousness"). While the Old Testament does not contain any account of Noah as a preacher, there are many references in Jewish (and Christian) tradition regarding his preaching to the people of the Flood generation. For example, the Jewish historian Josephus writes that Noah was "displeased" at the behavior of the people and tried to persuade them "to change their dispositions and their acts for the better" ("The Antiquities of the Jews" 1.3.1, in *The Works of Josephus*). In another publication known as "The Sibylline Oracles," a long sermon of Noah is recorded. **Righteousness** here is an ethical term, with the meaning of upright moral behavior, or in its wider sense, living according to God's will and purpose. **A herald of righteousness** will need to be radically restructured in many languages; for example, "who proclaimed (taught, announced, said) that people should live good lives according to God's will and purpose."

The word for **preserved** can also be "saved," "protected," "kept safe," or even "protected from death." In addition to Noah, the seven others saved were his wife, his three sons, and their wives (Gen 8.18). It is worth noting that the Greek is literally "Noah the eighth person," which is an idiomatic way of saying "Noah with seven other people." At any rate, the number of people saved in the Flood is eight, and many commentaries find this number significant. It is noted, for instance, that the eighth day is associated with the new creation, since the old creation was accomplished in seven days. Christians have associated the eighth day with Jesus' resurrection, which in turn is linked with the new creation. It is not certain, however, whether Peter had all of this in mind, although it should be noted that the number eight also appears in relation to Noah and the flood in 1 Peter 3.20. What is important for the translator is that, if the number eight is regarded as significant, then it should at least be retained in the translation; for example, "but protected the eighth person Noah, who preached righteousness, and seven other people from death, when he brought . . . ," or "but protected Noah and seven other people from death, when he brought . . . Noah, who was the eighth person, preached that people should live good lives following the will and purpose of God," or even "but protected Noah the eighth person, who was the one who preached that people . . . . He and seven others did not drown when God caused the Flood to cover the world of people who did not worship him."

One other thing needs to be noted. RSV follows the ordering of the Greek text. It is clear, however, from the grammar of the text that the note about Noah is an embedded clause, and that **when he brought . . .** connects directly with **the ancient world.** TEV has restructured the verse so that the embedded clause is put at the end of the verse. In many languages a similar restructuring needs to be done in order to insure that the translation is clear and conforms to the rules of naturalness in these languages. The clause **when he brought a flood upon the world of the ungodly** can be restructured as "when he caused a flood to cover the world where people who disobeyed him lived" or "when he caused water to entirely cover the world where people who disobeyed him lived."

2.6 RSV	TEV
if by turning the cities of Sodom and Gomorrah to ashes he condemned them to extinction and made them an example to those who were to be ungodly;	God condemned the cities of Sodom and Gomorrah, destroying them with fire, and made them an example of what will happen to the godless.

A third example is now given: after judgment by water, there is judgment by fire. The case of Sodom and Gomorrah is also found in Jude 7, but the differences are so significant that it is perhaps best to discuss the present passage separately.

The account of Sodom and Gomorrah is found in Gen 19.1-29. In that account God rained burning sulphur on the two cities, and they were burned to the ground. In the present passage the focus seems to be the state of the cities after the burning is over; they were turned to ashes. The term for **ashes** appears only here in the New Testament and can be literally translated as "covering of ashes," as in a volcanic eruption. Here again there are similarities with Jewish tradition. For example, this very term is used in some writings to describe Sodom and Gomorrah, and the region around the Dead Sea is known as "the land of ashes." Fire and the source of the fire (from heaven, from God) are implicit in the Greek and may need to be made explicit in the translation, otherwise, people may assume that it is a natural fire; for example, "by causing fire to burn the cities . . . until they were ashes."

He condemned them to extinction is interpreted by some as "condemned them with an overthrow" (the King James Version [KJV]), with "overthrow" referring to an earthquake that presumably followed the fire and resulted in the sinking of the cities and in the formation of the Dead Sea. This, however, is neither biblical nor historical but is part of the legends that came into being to explain why the Dead Sea was the way it was. Most modern translations, however, understand the text in the same way as RSV (for instance NEB "condemned them to total destruction," Phps "sentenced them to destruction," JB "he condemned . . . he destroyed them completely"). The meaning seems to be that God completely destroyed the cities and made it impossible for them to be rebuilt.

God did this to make these cities an **example** of what will happen to the **ungodly** if they do not repent. The word for **example** can be either positive (as in James 5.10) or somewhat negative, hence a "warning" (AT; NEB "object-lesson"). **Made them an example** can also be rendered "used them as a warning." For **ungodly** see verse 5 above. There is a textual problem here, as many manuscripts contain the variant reading followed by RSV, **to those who were to be ungodly**. This is reflected in some translations; for example, NEB "godless men in future days," JB "anybody lacking reverence in the future," Knox "the godless of a later time." With this in mind, possible alternative translation models for this verse are:

(1) If God condemned the cities of Sodom and Gomorrah and destroyed them completely by causing fire to burn them until they were ashes, and made them a warning of what will happen to those people who disobey him . . . .

(2) God condemned the cities of Sodom and Gomorrah, causing them to burn until they were ashes. He made them a warning to people of what will happen to those who disobey him.

2.7	RSV	TEV
	and if he rescued righteous Lot, greatly distressed by the licentiousness of the wicked	He rescued Lot, a good man, who was distressed by the immoral conduct of lawless people.

In this verse and the next, Lot is singled out to show that God does make a distinction between righteous and wicked people, and that he does rescue the righteous from danger. The story of Lot is found in Gen 19.1-29.

Rescued can also mean "delivered," "saved," "preserved a person from someone or something," "set free." It is not the same word as "preserved" in verse 5.

Lot is here described as **righteous,** a word with many meanings but which in this context means "good" (TEV), "upright," or perhaps "doing God's will." Lot himself is not described as a good man in the Genesis account; in fact the actions recounted there show Lot not as righteous but as a person of questionable character. There are, however, references in some literature, both Jewish and Christian, that refer to Lot as righteous. The best-known passage is Wisdom of Solomon 10.6: "Wisdom rescued a righteous man when the ungodly were perishing; he escaped the fire that descended on the Five Cities." The phrase **righteous Lot** (TEV "Lot, a good man") may be rendered in certain languages as "the good man Lot."

Lot's attitude toward the conditions of his environment is now described: he was **greatly distressed by the licentiousness of the wicked**. This can be treated simply as a description of Lot or as a reason for Lot being regarded as righteous: he deserves to be called **righteous** because of his attitude toward evil; this latter possibility relates this verse to verse 8, which has further descriptions of Lot as a righteous man.

The expression **greatly distressed** is the passive form of a verb that means "subdue," "torment," "wear out," "oppress," "wear down." In some languages this idea can be expressed idiomatically. Examples are "had a tormented heart or liver," "his heart or liver was very heavy," or "press hard upon his heart or liver."

Licentiousness is the same word found in verse 2. See comments there for discussion.

The wicked translates a term that can mean "unprincipled," "lawless" (TEV), "morally corrupt," and is used of people who disregarded divine and human laws and ordinances. This term is only used here and in 3.17 ("lawless"), and nowhere else in the New Testament.

Alternative translation models for this verse are:

(1) And if God rescued the good man Lot, whose heart (or, liver) was tormented by the indecent conduct of lawless men . . . .

(2) God rescued the good man Lot, whose heart (or, liver) was very heavy when he saw the indecent actions of morally corrupt men.

(3) God rescued Lot, who, because he was good, had a very heavy heart (or, liver) when he saw . . . .

2.8   RSV   TEV

(for by what that righteous man saw   That good man lived among them, and
and heard as he lived among them, he   day after day he suffered agony as he
was vexed in his righteous soul day   saw and heard their evil actions.
after day with their lawless deeds),

As indicated in RSV, this verse is a sort of a parenthetical statement. Its purpose is to further describe Lot's attitude toward the evil people in Sodom. As in the previous verses, TEV has converted this verse into a complete sentence.

That righteous man refers of course to Lot. For **righteous,** see verse 7 above.

The verse mentions three events with Lot as the doer or agent:
1. **He lived among them**, with **them** referring to the wicked people. This seems to be a general statement of setting.
2. He **saw and heard** what at the end of the verse is described as **their lawless deeds**. This describes Lot's daily experience. **Lawless deeds** (TEV "evil actions") may also be expressed as "criminal behavior," or "bad behavior."

3. As a result of what he saw and heard, **he was vexed in his righteous soul**. This is actually an expansion of "greatly distressed" in verse 7. The verb for **vexed** can also mean "tormented," "disturbed," or "tortured," either in a physical or in a mental sense. Here it focuses on the latter, since Lot did not suffer physically but mentally as a result of the wickedness of the people around him. **Righteous soul** has the same meaning as **righteous man**, and therefore in translation these can be combined, as TEV has done under "That good man." **Righteous soul** refers to the person himself, or to the person's inner self, hence "his good heart," "that good man's heart" (NEB), "a good man suffering spiritual agonies" (Phps).

This verse has the only occurrence of the phrase **day after day** in the New Testament. In some languages translators will find idiomatic expressions like the English, but in others it may be necessary to use an expression like "day and night."

A model for this is as follows:

> While this good man lived among them, day after day (or, day and night) he was tormented in his heart because of their evil actions.

2.9

RSV	TEV
then the Lord knows how to rescue the godly from trial, and to keep the unrighteous under punishment until the day of judgment,	And so the Lord knows how to rescue godly people from their trials and how to keep the wicked under punishment for the Day of Judgment,

The long sentence that began in verse 4 now reaches its conclusion in verses 9-10a. The three examples that are cited from the Old Testament are meant to lead to the conclusion that the Lord rescues the godly but punishes the ungodly. RSV's pattern of dependent clauses, all prefaced by the English word "if" from verse 4 on, was noted in the introductory comments to verses 4-10a. Translators who have been following this pattern should introduce the main clause in verse 9 with a connecting word such as "therefore"; for example, "Therefore the Lord knows how . . . ." However, it is also possible to show the connection between the dependent clauses and the main clause in verse 9 even more clearly by saying "Since the Lord has done all these things, he knows . . ." or "Because of these things, the Lord knows . . . ."

The Lord here is not identified, but it seems more likely that God is meant, and not Jesus Christ as in verse 1.

The expression **knows how** includes the meaning of "understands how," "can," "is well able" (NEB), "does not find it difficult."

For **rescue** see comments on verse 7, where the same word is used to describe Lot's deliverance from the difficulties he experienced in Sodom. **Trial** here is taken by some to mean "temptation to sin." But in fact it seems to be connected with the experiences of Noah and Lot, who were not primarily being tempted to commit sin but who were in fact fighting against sin. There are also some who take the **trials** here as eschatological, that is, referring to the final testing of Christians as the day of Judgment approaches. This is possible, considering the overall tone of the letter. However, it is more likely that **trials** here refer to the day-to-day experiences (sufferings, afflictions, persecutions, and so on) of the Christians in the midst of a non-Christian or even anti-Christian environment.

The word for **godly** is related to the word "godliness" that is used in 1.3. The godly person is the opposite of the "ungodly" in verse 6 and the **unrighteous** in the next part of this verse.

The clause **the Lord knows how . . . trial** may also be rendered as "the Lord understands the way to rescue good people from suffering."

But if the Lord knows how to protect the godly, he also knows how to punish the **unrighteous**. There is some disagreement on the expression translated in RSV **to keep the unrighteous under punishment**. The problem can be summarized as a question: "Does this mean that the unrighteous will only be judged and punished in the final day of Judgment, or that the unrighteous are now being punished and will continue to undergo punishment until the final Day of Judgment?" Some translations favor the first of these alternatives, as for example, Phps "to reserve his punishment for the wicked until his day comes," or JB "hold the wicked for their punishment until the day of Judgment." This is justified on the following grounds:

1. The Greek present participle for "being punished" can be interpreted as having the future sense; there are other examples of this usage in the New Testament (for example Luke 1.35; John 17.20).
2. In verse 4 the angels are being held awaiting judgment at the last day, and this is perhaps the sense here with regard to the ungodly.
3. The words for "judge" or "punish" in this verse are used elsewhere with reference to the last judgment.

Most translations, however, take the interpretation of RSV and TEV, and this is the preferred view. The grammatical form is regarded as decisive here: the expression "to keep under punishment" translates a present participle and a present infinitive, with the sense of a punishment that goes on until the day of judgment. That means that the false teachers are already suffering punishment because of their sins, although the full measure of their punishment will be inflicted later at the final day. Therefore we may translate this phrase as "punish wicked people continually until . . . ."

The day of judgment is of course the final day, referred to in the Old Testament as the day of the Lord, during which time God will judge all nations and bring punishment on the wicked. It is likely that to the readers of 2 Peter this is equivalent to the second coming of Jesus Christ, which in Christian circles was understood to bring joy to the godly and suffering to the ungodly. See the discussion on "the judgment" in verse 4.

An alternative translation model for this verse is:

Since the Lord has done all these things, this shows that he knows how to rescue good people from their sufferings, and to continually punish evil people until the Day of Judgment.

2.10a   RSV   TEV

and especially those who indulge in the lust of defiling passion and despise authority.	especially those who follow their filthy bodily lusts and despise God's authority.

In the previous verse Peter mentioned the unrighteous, a general term for sinners. In the present verse he moves on from the general statement and identifies two kinds of acts that will meet with the most severe punishment: sexual immorality and defiance of authority.

Especially translates an adverb in the superlative degree. Here it indicates that the Lord will mark the sinners mentioned here as deserving punishment more than any other sinners. Translators may have to use other ways of saying this, such as "and he will punish more than anyone else those who . . . ," or "most of all, punishment will fall upon those who . . . ," or changing to a superlative adjective phrase, "and the most evil will be those who . . . ."

Indulge in the lust of defiling passion is literally "go (or walk) after the flesh in desire (or, lust) of defilement (or, pollution). **Indulge**, or "walk," has the extended meaning of "order one's life," "conduct oneself," "follow a certain course of action." "Flesh" here is used in the ethical or moral sense, "totally depraved human nature," and is related to corrupt and unlawful sexual acts. "To walk after the flesh" therefore means, in this context, habitually engaging in sinful sexual practices. "Desire" is here used in the bad or derogatory sense of **lust**. **Defiling** translates a word that can literally mean "spot" or "stain" and is often used to describe a state of being ritually unclean. In this context, however, it is used in a moral sense referring primarily to impurity as a result of evil actions. The whole expression **lust of defiling passion** then means lust that is corrupt, "filthy bodily lusts" (TEV), "lust that makes people impure," or "lust that pollutes people." The first clause may also be expressed as "habitually engage in sinful (sexual) practices that make them morally impure."

Despise authority is related to a similar expression in Jude 8. However, there are some differences in meaning and emphasis. Whereas in Jude it is possible to interpret **authority** as referring to angelic beings or even to human authority in general, here the meaning is more likely to be the authority of God or the authority of Christ. And since **Lord** in verse 9 most probably refers to God, then the authority spoken of here is probably God's more than Christ's. If, however, the present verse is related to 2.1, then it is Christ's authority that is in focus. In any case, the former seems to be the most likely interpretation in this context. Other ways to say this are "refuse to obey God when he commands them" or "consider that God has no right to rule over them."

A further description of the false teachers
(2.10b-22)

The sins of the false teachers
2.10b-16

RSV	TEV
Bold and wilful, they are not afraid to revile the glorious ones, 11 whereas angels, though greater in might and power, do not pronounce a reviling judgment upon them before the Lord. 12 But these, like irrational animals, creatures of instinct, born to be caught and killed, reviling in matters of which they are ignorant, will be destroyed in the same destruction with them, 13 suffering wrong for their wrongdoing. They count it pleasure to revel in the daytime. They are blots and blemishes, reveling in their dissipation, carousing with you. 14 They have eyes full of adultery, insatiable for sin. They entice unsteady souls. They have hearts trained in greed. Accursed children! 15 Forsaking the right way they have gone astray; they have followed the way of Balaam, the son of Beor, who loved gain from wrongdoing, 16 but was rebuked for his own transgression; a dumb ass spoke with human voice and restrained the prophet's madness.	These false teachers are bold and arrogant, and show no respect for the glorious beings above; instead, they insult them. 11 Even the angels, who are so much stronger and mightier than these false teachers, do not accuse them with insults in the presence of the Lord. 12 But these men act by instinct, like wild animals born to be captured and killed; they attack with insults anything they do not understand. They will be destroyed like wild animals, 13 and they will be paid with suffering for the suffering they have caused. Pleasure for them is to do anything in broad daylight that will satisfy their bodily appetites; they are a shame and a disgrace as they join you in your meals, all the while enjoying their deceitful ways! 14 They want to look at nothing but immoral women; their appetite for sin is never satisfied. They lead weak people into a trap. Their hearts are trained to be greedy. They are under God's curse! 15 They have left the straight path and have lost their way; they have followed the path taken by Balaam son of Beor, who loved the money he would get for doing wrong 16 and was rebuked for his sin. His donkey spoke with a human voice and stopped the prophet's insane action.

After giving Old Testament examples and defining what these mean for his readers, Peter now speaks directly about the false teachers in the same way as he did in verses 1-3. This is the reason why most translations start with a new paragraph here, and some, like TEV, identify the false teachers as the subject.

Like the previous section, the rest of the chapter is related in many ways to the letter of Jude. Verses 10b-18 contain much information that is found in Jude 8-13 and 16. These relationships will be pointed out in the discussion, and in many cases a reference will be made to the discussion in Jude's letter. Here again it is to the translator's advantage to have Jude's letter alongside 2 Peter as a help in the translation process, since the translator can then take note of the similarities as well as the differences between the two letters.

Since this section contains indictments against the false teachers that are somewhat disconnected, it is quite difficult to decide where to mark the paragraph breaks. The model followed by this Handbook is that of the UBS Greek New Testament, which makes a new paragraph at verse 17; this is followed by many translations, including RSV and TEV. It may be useful to have section headings for verses 10b-16 and for verses 17-22. If this is desired, then the section heading for verses 10b-16 can be "The sins of the false teachers." However, this is not required, and it may be that the section heading at the beginning of the chapter will be sufficient.

SECTION HEADING: the major heading suggested by the Handbook outline for verses 10b-22, "A further description of the false teachers," may also be "Peter gives additional descriptions of the false teachers." The subheading that applies to verses 10b-16, "The sins of the false teachers," may also be "The false teachers have done these sins" or ". . . the following sins."

2.10b   RSV   TEV

Bold and wilful, they are not afraid   These false teachers are bold and
to revile the glorious ones,   arrogant, and show no respect for the
                                                glorious beings above; instead, they
                                                insult them.

The false teachers are first described as **bold and wilful** and **not afraid to revile the glorious ones**. The word for **Bold** can also mean "daring" or "audacious," but here it is used in a negative sense, "reckless," "brazen," "presumptuous" (for which see Jude 9 "did not presume," TEV "did not dare"). The word for **wilful** can mean "stubborn," "arrogant," "headstrong," "self-willed," "obstinate," and is a fitting description of people who feel sufficient to themselves and who always want to have their own way regardless of the consequences. In certain languages **wilful** may be expressed idiomatically. Examples are "having a high heart or liver" or "having a rising heart or liver," but used in a negative, uncomplimentary, contemptuous, or unflattering manner.

The false teachers show their recklessness and obstinacy in their attitude toward the **glorious ones.** This is the same term found in Jude 8, where it is interpreted to mean angels, particularly good ones. Here, however, since **the glorious ones** are compared to angels in verse 11, it is rather difficult to say that in this context they are the same as the "glorious ones" in Jude. Some of the suggestions as to the identity of the "glorious ones" are as follows:
1. They are human authorities, either ecclesiastical or civil. But this is unlikely, since the term "glorious ones" is usually used of celestial beings.
2. They are heavenly beings other than angels. In ancient times there was a prevalent belief in the existence of spiritual beings other than God or angels (for example, demons). These spiritual beings were not necessarily bad. In the New Testament, however, these beings were regarded as evil and as being under the leadership of Satan (the Devil).
3. They are bad angels, perhaps the fallen angels mentioned in verse 4. "Angels" in verse 11 then refers to good angels, and "them" in that verse refers to the bad angels. The sense of the verse would be that, while the

false teachers dare to insult the devil and his angels, the good angels themselves do not dare do this (that is, insult the devil and his angels).
4. The glorious ones are the same angels mentioned in verse 11. In this case "them" in verse 11 refers to the false teachers, giving the sense that, while the false teachers dare to insult angels, these same angels do not even say bad things about the false teachers. This, however, goes against the most natural reading of the Greek text, which seems to make a distinction between "glorious ones" in verse 10 and "angels" in verse 11.

Many translations render **glorious ones** literally and therefore avoid the problem of identifying who they are. TEV "the glorious beings above" follows the second of these possibilities. In some languages there are special expressions reserved for beings such as these; for example, "the Sacred Beings."

Revile translates the verb "blaspheme," which is the same word translated "reviled" in verse 2 and has the general meaning of "speak evil of," "insult," "show irreverence to." **Afraid** is literally "tremble, quiver," but it is used figuratively here to mean "be afraid" or "respect." The relation between **not afraid** and **revile** is interpreted in two different ways by RSV and TEV. In RSV **not afraid** goes with **revile**, hence, "they are not afraid to revile the glorious ones." In TEV, however, "not afraid" and "insult" are two parallel terms both describing the false teachers' attitude toward the glorious ones, so "they show no respect for the glorious beings above; instead, they insult them." This Handbook recommends TEV's interpretation as the more likely one for this context.

2.11   RSV   TEV

whereas angels, though greater in might and power, do not pronounce a reviling judgment upon them before the Lord.

Even the angels, who are so much stronger and mightier than these false teachers, do not accuse them with insults in the presence of the Lord.

This verse has some similarities with Jude 9. However, Peter omits any reference to the story of Michael and the body of Moses, and instead comes up with a general statement. Could it be that he could assume a knowledge of Jude among his readers? A more probable reason is that this is in keeping with his tendency to reduce if not eliminate altogether quotations from and allusions to literature outside the Old Testament. (See, for example, comments on his treatment of Jude 6 in 2.4, and on Jude 7 in 2.6).

The verse starts with **whereas**, which marks the contrast of what follows to the previous statement. In some languages it will be quite natural to express this contrast as follows: "Consider the angels (or, God's messengers)! They are so . . . ."

The angels are described as **greater in might and power**. **Might and power** are words of similar meaning. Their being mentioned together may be either a hendiadys (two expressions for a single idea), with **might** describing **power**, hence "mighty power," or a way of marking intensification, hence "having so much more power." A third possibility may be mentioned, and that is to interpret **might** as emphasizing outward physical strength, and **power** as emphasizing inward, spiritual virtue. It should be noted, however, that **power** can also be used to describe physical strength, and it is clearly understood as spiritual strength when properly marked as such by the context. Therefore the phrase **angels, though greater in might and power than** may also be rendered as "angels, though they are much more powerful physically and spiritually (in their hearts) than" or "angels, who are so much more powerful than . . . ."

The Greek text does not make clear who the angels are being compared with. Are they being compared with the false teachers or with the "glorious ones" in verse 10? Either alternative seems to be acceptable, depending on how **them** (in **do not pronounce . . . upon them**) is interpreted. The verse then can be saying one of the following:

1. The false teachers insult the glorious ones, but in contrast the angels, who are much more powerful than the false teachers, do not even do this (that is, insult the glorious ones). Here **them** refers to the false teachers, and the ones that the angels do not insult are the glorious ones.
2. The false teachers insult the glorious ones, but in contrast the angels, who are even more powerful than the glorious ones, do not even do this (that is, insult the glorious ones.) Here **them** is interpreted as referring to the glorious ones rather than to the false teachers.
3. The false teachers insult the glorious ones, but in contrast the angels, who are even more powerful than the false teachers, do not insult the false teachers. Here **them** refers to the false teachers, who are also the ones the angels do not insult.
4. The false teachers insult the glorious ones, but in contrast the angels, who are more powerful than the glorious ones, do not insult the false teachers.

TEV takes the first of these interpretations, except that it is not very clear who are the ones that the angels do not insult. It seems clear in NIV that the angels do not insult the glorious ones, but it is not clear with whom the angels are being compared. AT follows the second of these alternatives: "even angels far superior to these beings in strength and power bring no abusive charge before the Lord." Most other translations leave all these ambiguities alone.

It is best to resolve the above ambiguities in translation. For the purposes of this Handbook, the first two alternatives seem preferable, and of these two the second is slightly favored.

Reviling judgment is similar to the expression found in Jude 9, and we may refer to the discussion there. As the NRSV footnote indicates, there is a textual problem connected with **before the Lord**: "Other ancient authorities read *before the Lord*; others lack the phrase." Some very important manuscripts have the reading "from the Lord," whereas some other manuscripts omit the phrase altogether. The difference in Greek between "from the Lord" and "before the Lord" is a matter of a suffix only: *para kuriou* (genitive case) as against *para kuriō* (dative). Most modern translations follow the reading "before the Lord," which means "in the presence of the Lord" (TEV), who functions as judge. "Lord" here most probably refers to God. The picture is that of a heavenly court, where the "glorious ones" are on trial, and the angels are witnesses, but they refrain from harsh and insulting words in their testimony. The phrase **before the Lord** may also be expressed as "when they were before the Lord (God)," "when they were in the presence of God," or in certain languages it will be necessary to say "when they were standing before God." If "from the Lord" is the accepted reading, then the Lord will not be judge but accuser, and the angels are the Lord's messengers, who, however, do not use slanderous words in presenting the Lord's accusations before the court, because of their respect for these celestial beings. The omission of the words **before the Lord** in some manuscripts can be explained as an influence of the text of Jude 9.

An alternative translation model for this verse is:

> Consider the angels (or, God's messengers)! They are much more powerful than the false teachers. But they do not use insulting language when they accuse these teachers in the presence of God.

2.12   RSV   TEV

But these, like irrational animals, creatures of instinct, born to be caught and killed, reviling in matters of which they are ignorant, will be destroyed in the same destruction with them,	But these men act by instinct, like wild animals born to be captured and killed; they attack with insults anything they do not understand. They will be destroyed like wild animals,

Peter continues to describe the false teachers, contrasting their attitude with those of the angels in verse 11. This verse is very much influenced by Jude 10 but rearranged and restructured to fit Peter's style and purpose.

These, of course, refers to the false teachers and may be translated thus. These false teachers are compared with animals. This fact alone, together with the descriptions that follow, shows how Peter is angry and furious with the false teachers. This emotional aspect needs to be clearly shown in translation. The false teachers are first of all compared to animals that are **irrational,** or without any reasoning power. For a further discussion of this, see Jude 10.

Secondly, these animals are **creatures of instinct**, which is similar to the expression "they know by instinct" in Jude 10. The phrase **creatures of instinct** is sometimes related to what follows, namely **born to be caught and killed** (as, for example, NEB "These men are like brute beasts, born in the course of nature to be caught and killed"; Brc "They are no better than brute beasts, born by nature to be caught and killed"). While this is possible, it is more likely that **creatures of instinct** is related to **irrational** (as in TEV "wild animals"), since instinct by definition is action without the use of reason. On how this is related to the false teachers, see discussion on Jude 10.

Thirdly, these animals are **born to be caught and killed** (literally, "born to be caught and destroyed in the same destruction"). This accents the uselessness of these animals, especially the wild, irrational ones. The thought

123

that is expressed here is that, since these animals are not beneficial but rather harmful to society, then it is better for them to be captured and killed. The word for **caught** is the word used in reference to capturing or catching animals for food. The word for **killed** can also mean "destroyed," "ruined," but here primarily "slaughtered." Understood in this manner, what is being emphasized is not the wanton irresponsible destruction of these wild animals but capturing them for consumption. There is a play on words here, since the same word for **killed** is also used twice at the end of the verse (literally, **destroyed in the same destruction**.) In some languages translators must translate this clause in the active; for example, "born for people to catch and slaughter."

It should be noted that TEV takes **creatures of instinct** not as a description of the animals but of the false teachers themselves: "these men act by instinct."

Peter now abandons figurative language and directly describes the false teachers, describing them as people **reviling in matters of which they are ignorant**. This is similar to "revile whatever they do not understand" in Jude 10, for which see the discussion there. Here **of which they are ignorant** states positively what is stated negatively in Jude 10, "whatever they do not understand."

The last part of the verse can mean that the false teachers will be destroyed at the same time as the animals, which is what RSV seems to say. However, it is more likely that the destruction of the false teachers will be similar to the destruction of the animals. This may refer to the way the destruction is brought about, that is, violently and unexpectedly. Or it may refer to the actual destruction itself, that is, in much the same way in which animals are killed when they are captured, so also these false teachers will be punished when they receive their final judgment on the last day.

An alternative translation model for this verse is:

> But these false teachers act by instinct (irrationally) like animals
> of the jungle, which are born for people to capture and slaughter;
> they say bad things about matters they do not understand. God
> will destroy them just as people slaughter animals of the jungle.

One final note: All this discussion about the uselessness of wild and irrational animals may be disturbing to many people today who see such animals not as a nuisance, but as important parts of nature that need to be protected. While it is obvious that translators cannot change the text, they can at least make justifiable adjustments in order to deemphasize the negative message of the text, especially with regard to animals. Several ways of doing this have already been suggested in the analysis of the text. One other way needs to be mentioned, and that is to get rid of the figurative language altogether and translate the meaning directly. It should be noted, however, that every time this is done, there is a corresponding loss of emotive aspects which then need to be compensated through the addition of appropriate rhetorical features (for example, exaggeration, use of exclamation marks, and so forth).

2.13   RSV   TEV

suffering wrong for their wrongdoing.
They count it pleasure to revel in the
daytime. They are blots and blemishes,
reveling in their dissipation,^g carousing
with you.

^g Other ancient authorities read *love
feasts*

and they will be paid with suffering for
the suffering they have caused. Pleasure
for them is to do anything in broad
daylight that will satisfy their bodily
appetites; they are a shame and a disgrace as they join you in your meals, all
the while enjoying their deceitful ways!

The first part of this verse is still a part of the sentence that began in
verse 12, and explains why the suffering of these false teachers is justified:
they suffer as a result of their wrongdoings. In the last part their evil acts
have an adverse effect not only on themselves but also and primarily on others.

There is a play on words here on **suffering wrong** and **wrongdoing** (Greek
adikoumenoi and *adikias*; the whole expression translated literally is "being
treated wrongly as a reward for doing wrong"). Some translations have tried
to retain this play on words; for example, Brc "Injury they inflicted, and injury
they will receive in return," and NEB "suffering hurt for the hurt they have
inflicted." Another way to restructure this clause is as follows: "As they have
hurt other people, so they also will suffer hurt." It may not be possible, of
course, to retain or even to compensate for these wordplays in another
language. But it is still good to be aware of this rhetorical feature in order to
do justice to it whenever possible.

In verses 13b-15 Peter further describes the wickedness of the false
teachers. Of special interest to translators is the fact that this subsection
consists of only one sentence, a form that is difficult and sometimes impossible
to retain in translation. Furthermore it consists of a series of participial
clauses, with the only finite verb occurring in verse 15 ("have gone astray").
Normally participial clauses are dependent on a finite verb, but here every
participial clause seems to stand alone and is complete in itself. This helps in
splitting the long sentence into shorter sentences, since every participial clause
can be translated easily as one complete sentence.

It is also possible to start a new paragraph here, since there is a natural
break at the end of verse 13a. However, if these verses are understood as
describing "wrongdoing" in 13a, then a new paragraph is not necessary.

The word for **count** is literally "consider," "regard," "think." Many
translations omit this by restructuring the verse, as in TEV "Pleasure for them
is . . . ," and in NEB "To carouse . . . is their idea of pleasure." We can also say
"They get their pleasure from" or "They gain pleasure from." **Pleasure** can also
be "enjoyment," but the term is used only in a negative sense in the New
Testament. **To revel** translates a Greek noun that primarily means "luxury,"
but in the present context it means excessive self-indulgence in eating and
perhaps in sexual activity. The purpose of such activity is of course their own
self-satisfaction. In certain languages "reveling" can be expressed with words
for particular activities, sometimes idiomatically; for example, "partying-

licentiously-uproariously (Thai)." **In the daytime** is literally "in the day," but this is contrasted with night, hence TEV "in broad daylight." We may also say "while the sun is shining." If excessive partying is done at all, it is usually during the night. This does not mean that self-indulgence at night time is acceptable, but that the dark of night helps people keep shameful deeds from the view of others. In this case the very fact that these people can engage in this activity in broad daylight shows how wicked and immoral they really are.

These people are further described as **blots and blemishes. Blots** translates a word that is very similar to a word used by Jude (verse 12), one which can mean "reefs" or "half-submerged rocks." (In Greek, *spilas* is "blot," while *spilos* is "reef.") A blot or a spot dirties and spoils a clean garment. **Blemishes,** on the other hand, translates a word that means "defects," understood physically or morally, hence "disgrace" (TEV), "causing shame." **Blots and blemishes** may also be rendered as "they are like dirty spots and blemishes (physical defects) and cause you shame and disgrace" or "they are like . . . causing you to lose face greatly." It is interesting to note that later Peter admonishes the Christians to be "without spot or blemish," using the negative forms of the above words (3.14). So the idea here may be that these false teachers, by being "spots and blemishes" within the church, are preventing the church from being what it should be.

As the RSV footnote shows, there is a textual problem here: some manuscripts have "love feasts" (which appears in Jude 12) rather than **dissipation**. The two words look very similar in Greek (*agapai* for "love feasts" and *apatai* for **dissipation**.) Since "love feasts" is used in Jude, and since scholarly consensus holds that 2 Peter used Jude as a primary source, it can be concluded that the original text of 2 Peter probably had **dissipation** deliberately rather than "love feasts." A further question is why Peter changed Jude here, and what **dissipation** in fact means. **Dissipation** translates a word that can mean "pleasure" but in this context should most probably be taken with the more usual meaning "deceit" or "deception." Some scholars suggest that Peter was still referring to "love feasts" here but made a deliberate change of the Greek word to stress the fact that the love feasts have become "deceptions" because of the behavior of the false teachers. It is more likely, however, that Peter is actually referring to the behavior of these false teachers and their attitude during the common meals of the Christian community. In this case there are two possible ways of interpreting Peter's intention. First, the false teachers took advantage of their erroneous ideas to justify their actions during the common meals, thus using these meals as occasions for self-indulgence and not for real fellowship. Secondly, while they join the Christian community in their common meals, they nevertheless continue in their erroneous ways, thus deceiving the church. This seems to be the position reflected in TEV and some other translations (for instance, NEB "while they sit with you at table they are an ugly blot on your company, because they revel in their own deceptions").

Carousing translates a Greek word that simply means "eat with someone," without any negative sense (TEV "as they join you in your meals"). This seems to provide the context of all of verse 13b. This means that it is when Christians get together for a common meal that the false teachers indulge in their debauchery and deceptions. Whether these meals are religious meals or simply social meals is not made clear in the text, although the parallel passage in Jude 12 makes it clear that what is meant are the "love feasts," that is, common meals that included the celebration of the Lord's Supper or holy communion. It is not necessary, however, to bring this into the present passage, since the meaning is the same, whether the meals are religious or social in nature.

An alternative translation model for the second part of this verse is:

> Because they enjoy their deceitful ways, they get their pleasure from eating and drinking in an immoral fashion in broad daylight (while the sun is shining); they are like spots and blemishes that cause you to lose face greatly every time they eat food with you.

2.14 RSV TEV

They have eyes full of adultery, insatiable for sin. They entice unsteady souls. They have hearts trained in greed. Accursed children!

They want to look at nothing but immoral women; their appetite for sin is never satisfied. They lead weak people into a trap. Their hearts are trained to be greedy. They are under God's curse!

The letter now moves from the common meals to the day-to-day behavior of the false teachers.

They have eyes full of adultery is literally "having eyes full of an adulteress," with "adulteress" understood in a general way as referring either to the act of adultery or to adulterous women (TEV "immoral women"). The inclusion of the word **full** indicates that they are entirely engrossed and preoccupied with what they are doing. The whole expression can then be understood in two ways:
1. Every time they look at a woman, they think of committing adultery with her, or negatively, they cannot look at a woman without thinking of themselves as being in bed with her.
2. They are always engrossed in looking for immoral women so that they can have illicit sexual relations with them.

While the first of these alternatives makes more sense, the second takes seriously the fact that the text says "adulteress," not "adultery"; in other words it focuses on desire for the person rather than on desire for the act. Languages have varying ways to translate "immoral women." Examples are "easy women" or "women with easy hearts."

Insatiable means "unceasing," "restless," "unsatisfied." In the Greek text **insatiable for sin** is connected with the previous statement and directly related to **eyes**, which means that not only are their eyes always looking for women with whom they can commit adultery, but they are also looking for other

127

opportunities to commit sin. **Eyes** is used figuratively here to refer to the whole person, and the translator may need to express the meaning in plain terms, especially if this figurative usage of "eyes" is not natural in the language of the translation; for example, "they are never happy unless they are sinning," or "they never stop wanting to do sinful things."

Not only are they preoccupied with adultery and other sexual perversions, but the false teachers also **entice unsteady souls**. **Entice** comes from the world of fishing and hunting; it means "to lure with a bait," hence TEV "lead . . . into a trap." In certain languages this idea is rendered idiomatically; for example, "lure the hearts of" or "seduce the hearts of." **Souls** here means people, and these people are described as **unsteady**. This translates a word that occurs only here and in 3.16 in the whole Bible; it means "weak" (TEV), "unstable," "wavering" (Knox). The "unstable" people are those whose foundation in the Christian faith is rather weak, and who therefore can be led astray very easily, not only in their understanding of the Christian message, but also in their actions. Some identify these people as new converts in the Christian faith. Other ways of expressing this are "weak-hearted people," "people who have little faith," or "people who are not sure of what they believe." The sentence may be rendered "They entice people who are not sure of what they believe to commit sin."

In contrast to the unsteadiness of their victims, the false teachers **have hearts trained**, but their training is in **greed**. The heart is the center of emotion, will, and affection; it can be used figuratively to mean the whole person. **Trained** translates a participle of a verb that comes from athletics; it means "to exercise" and is used of an athlete exercising in the gymnasium and preparing to participate in athletic contests. Here it is the opposite of "unsteady," which was used to describe the victims of the false teachers. Unfortunately, however, they are well trained not for good but for ill. The term **greed** is related to the earlier term **insatiable**; it means "avarice," "covetousness," and is an apt description of a person who is never satisfied and always desires to have more. **Trained** is a perfect participle, which means that greediness has already become a habit for these false teachers; they have become experts in taking advantage of others in order to acquire for themselves the things for which they crave. Other ways of expressing this clause are "They train their hearts or minds to be greedy," "They train their hearts or minds to continually want what other people have," or "They are experts in acquiring whatever they want."

Having described the false teachers in this very disapproving manner, it is no surprise that Peter now pronounces a curse on them. The expression **accursed children** is literally "children of a curse," which is an idiom based on a Hebrew way of speaking. To be a child of something is to be included in something and share in its characteristics, as for example "children of iniquity" (Hos 10.9, KJV), which RSV translates as "wayward people" (positioning it in verse 10 of that chapter). Therefore to be "children of a curse" means that these people share the characteristics of being accursed. A literal translation may give the wrong meaning, for it may give the idea that these people are real children when in fact they are adults.

A curse is something that one person can pronounce on another but in fact cannot bring it to pass, for a curse is always addressed to a higher power, calling on that higher power to do something bad to the person upon whom the curse is pronounced. So here the higher power invoked is most probably God (as in TEV "They are under God's curse!"), and the statement means that God is sure to punish them because of all the bad things that they have done. The expression here means the same thing as "Woe to them" in Jude 11.

An alternative translation model for this verse is:

> They are continually looking for easy women; they never stop wanting to do evil things. They seduce to commit sin the hearts of people who believe in Jesus weakly. They themselves are experts in acquiring whatever their hearts desire. Because of all the evil things they do, God will punish them.

2.15 RSV	TEV
Forsaking the right way they have gone astray; they have followed the way of Balaam, the son of Beor, who loved gain from wrongdoing,	They have left the straight path and have lost their way; they have followed the path taken by Balaam son of Beor, who loved the money he would get for doing wrong

This verse has a great deal of similarity with Jude 11.

Forsaking the right way they have gone astray is related to "Balaam's error" in Jude 11. **Right** is used here in the sense of "correct," "right," "true." **Way** is literally a road, but it is also used metaphorically to mean "a course of conduct," "a way of doing things." In the Bible "straight path" (TEV) is used to describe proper and upright conduct (see 1 Sam 12.23; Hos 14.9; Acts 13.10). Some have taken **the right way** here as equivalent in meaning to "the way of truth" in verse 2 (for which see discussion there.) Other ways of expressing **the right way** are "behave in a just or righteous way," "have good conduct," or "walk good lives."

Forsaking can also be "They have abandoned" (NEB). It is a present participle in the Greek, but most modern translations understand it to function as a perfect tense, "having forsaken." It may be simply translated as a perfect verb, which is what RSV and TEV (and most translations) have done. **Forsaking the right way** may also be expressed as "They have left the way of righteousness," "They have stopped doing good," "Their conduct has become evil," or "They no longer walk good lives."

The result of all this is that the false teachers **have gone astray,** a most logical conclusion. This expression is used figuratively here to mean they have been corrupted both spiritually and morally; they have accepted and followed doctrines and disciplines of life that led them to reject God rather than trust in him. In some languages this may be translated as "their hearts have become corrupt (or, evil)," or "they do evil things."

So, instead of following the right way, they follow **the way of Balaam, son of Beor**. Balaam is also mentioned in Jude 11. In the Old Testament Balaam's father is named "Beor" (see Num 22.5; 24.3, 15), which explains why "Beor" is the form in many of the Greek manuscripts. It is very likely, however, that the variant form "Bosor" is the original in the Greek. In any case, rendering "Bosor" as "Beor" is justified here on the principle of using only the more common name when someone or something is known by two or more names. The clause **they have followed the way of Balaam** may be expressed as "They have done exactly what Balaam . . . did," "They have imitated Balaam . . . ," or "They have followed the example of Balaam . . . ."

The **way of Balaam** is not explained any further; there are three suggested possible points of comparison: greed, leading people to sin, and claiming to be God's prophet or teacher. Perhaps the first of these, namely "greed," is the most probable point of comparison, since it is mentioned in verse 14. This also fits what follows, since Balaam is described as one **who loved gain from wrongdoing**. We are told in the Old Testament that it was love of money that caused Balaam to lead Israel to sin (see Num 22–24; 31.16, and especially Jude 11 for further discussion of Balaam). In certain languages **gain** will need to be rendered as "the money he would be paid," or in the active as "the money they would pay him."

An alternative translation model for this verse is:

> They have stopped doing good and turned to evil ways (their hearts have become corrupt). They have followed the example of Balaam, who loved the money people would pay him for doing evil.

2.16

RSV	TEV
but was rebuked for his own transgression; a dumb ass spoke with human voice and restrained the prophet's madness.	and was rebuked for his sin. His donkey spoke with a human voice and stopped the prophet's insane action.

Balaam, however, did not get away with his wickedness; in fact, he **was rebuked for his own transgression**.

Rebuked may also be rendered as "scolded." Instead of the passive form **was rebuked**, some languages will employ an expression using the equivalent of the English word "suffer" and say "But he suffered scolding for his sins"; but in other languages it will be necessary to use the active and say "But God scolded him for his sins" or "But God scolded him for the evil he had done." **Transgression** translates a word that means "lawlessness," "evil act" (TEV "sin"), and refers to a particular action, perhaps Balaam's readiness to accept a bribe, or even his readiness to curse Israel.

The reference to the **dumb ass** speaking to Balaam is found in Num 22.21-35. The word for **ass** (TEV "donkey") is a term that is literally "under the yoke"; that is, it means a beast of burden, or an animal that is used to carry things—a fitting description for a donkey. **Dumb** here means "unable to speak," not "unable to think." This dumb donkey, however, **spoke with a human voice**, that is, it used human language to communicate with Balaam. The account in Numbers mentions an angel who spoke after the donkey spoke, but Peter is apparently not intending to be thorough at this point. It is not the details that he is interested in but the result of such an unusual event: it **restrained the prophet's madness**. Balaam is here called a **prophet**, that is, he was a person who spoke for God and who proclaimed the message that God revealed to him. (For further discussion of **prophet** see 2.1.) Here **prophet** stands in sharp contrast to **dumb ass**. See comments on verse 1 for ways to translate "prophet." **Restrained** translates a verb that means "hinder," "prevent," "forbid," "stop." **Madness** on the other hand means "insanity" (as in TEV), "senselessness." Balaam is therefore described as someone who was not in his right mind in agreeing to curse Israel for the sake of material gain. However, his stupidity was stopped by the human voice of a dumb ass. The whole expression is translated by Knox as "to bring a prophet to his senses." The final clause **restrained the prophet's madness** may also be rendered "stopped the prophet from doing an insane thing" or "stopped the prophet from acting irrationally."

There is humor here as well as irony. In verse 12 the false teachers were compared to "irrational animals." Here they are compared to a stupid and insane prophet, who is rebuked by a dumb donkey.

An alternative translation model for this verse is:

> But God scolded him for the evil that he had done. His donkey spoke using human language and stopped the prophet from acting irrationally.

The punishment of the false teachers
2.17-22

RSV

TEV

17 These are waterless springs and mists driven by a storm; for them the nether gloom of darkness has been reserved. 18 For, uttering loud boasts of folly, they entice with licentious passions of the flesh men who have barely escaped from those who live in error. 19 They promise them freedom, but they themselves are slaves of corruption; for whatever overcomes a man, to that he is enslaved. 20 For if, after they have escaped the defilements of the world through the knowledge of our Lord and Savior Jesus Christ, they are again entangled in them and overpowered, the last state has become worse for them than the first. 21 For it would have been better for them never to have known the way of righteousness than after

17 These men are like dried-up springs, like clouds blown along by a storm; God has reserved a place for them in the deepest darkness. 18 They make proud and stupid statements, and use immoral bodily lusts to trap those who are just beginning to escape from among people who live in error. 19 They promise them freedom while they themselves are slaves of destructive habits—for a person is a slave of anything that has conquered him. 20 If people have escaped from the corrupting forces of the world through their knowledge of our Lord and Savior Jesus Christ, and then are again caught and conquered by them, such people are in worse condition at the end than they were at the beginning. 21 It would have

knowing it to turn back from the holy commandment delivered to them. 22 It has happened to them according to the true proverb,
The dog turns back to his own vomit, and the
sow is washed only to wallow in the mire.

been much better for them never to have
known the way of righteousness than to know
it and then turn away from the sacred command that was given them. 22 What happened
to them shows that the proverbs are true: "A
dog goes back to what it has vomited" and "A
pig that has been washed goes back to roll in
the mud."

Translators should note the introductory comments on verses 10b-16,
which apply to this section as well.

SECTION HEADING: if translators are using the Handbook outline to
determine section headings, the subheading for verses 17-22 can also be "The
punishment that the false teachers will receive" or "False teachers are
doomed."

2.17   RSV   TEV

These are waterless springs and
mists driven by a storm; for them the
nether gloom of darkness has been
reserved.

These men are like dried-up
springs, like clouds blown along by a
storm; God has reserved a place for
them in the deepest darkness.

Verses 17-22 further describe the foolish teachers and stress their
inevitable doom.

These is emphatic and refers to the false teachers, and this information
can be included in translation (for example, TEV "These men"). This verse has
similarities with Jude 12-13; however, instead of "waterless clouds carried
along by winds" (see Jude 12), Peter compares the false teachers to **waterless
springs and mists driven by a storm**. This actually consists of two metaphors
from nature, but each with the same message: there is a great difference
between expectation and fulfillment. The word for "spring" includes "water" as
one component of its meaning and refers to a living fountain. Many languages
have words for a "spring," but in some it will be necessary to describe it and
say, for example, "a place where water pours out of the ground or rock."
Waterless indicates the actual state of the spring, which is contrary to what
is really expected. So **waterless springs** may be expressed as "springs have no
water" or "places where water should pour forth, but it doesn't."

The same is the case with the **mists**. There are several possible grounds
of comparison that may be intended here.

1. Some have suggested that it is the ease with which the mists are blown
   away by the storm, indicating how easily the false teachers will be
   destroyed.
2. Another suggestion is that the focus here is the quality of darkness that
   characterizes the mist, and which therefore indicates obscurity and
   instability.

3. A further suggestion is that the focus here is on the function of mists: they are supposed to refresh the ground, especially during the dry seasons; but here instead they are **driven** (away) **by a storm** and therefore never get a chance to provide moisture. The word for **storm** indicates a whirlwind or a hurricane (or typhoon), characterized by violent winds.

This third possibility seems preferable, since it connects the second metaphor with the first. Both figures therefore indicate the uselessness and worthlessness of the false teachers, together with their teaching, despite all the promises that they have made. In certain languages **mists driven by a storm** may be translated as "clouds that suffer storm blow along," "clouds that the storm or hurricane or typhoon drives along," or "clouds that violent winds drive away."

It should be noted that RSV retains the metaphor form, that is, **These are waterless springs** . . . . It may be advisable and even necessary to change the metaphor into a simile (that is, "These . . . are like . . .") as TEV has done; it is important, however, to make sure that the impact of the passage is not lost if this is done.

Due to the wickedness of the false teachers, their punishment is certain. **The nether gloom of darkness** is a description of Sheol, the world of the dead. (For a further discussion of this term, see comments on Jude 13). As in Jude 13, the passive construction here is a divine passive, with God as the unnamed agent, a fact made clear in TEV. "Sheol" of course refers to a place below the earth; this may be relevant in some languages. However, in languages where this information is difficult to include, the element of "deep darkness" may be sufficient to describe the place where the false teachers are destined to go. Therefore **for them the nether gloom of darkness has been reserved** may also be rendered as "God has prepared a place for them in deepest darkness," "God has prepared for them a place that is completely covered by thick darkness," ". . . a place of darkness where there is no light at all," or "the world of the dead which is covered by thick darkness."

2.18	RSV	TEV
	For, uttering loud boasts of folly, they entice with licentious passions of the flesh men who have barely escaped from those who live in error.	They make proud and stupid statements, and use immoral bodily lusts to trap those who are just beginning to escape from among people who live in error.

This verse, together with verse 19, describes the teaching of the false teachers and the effect of such teaching both on themselves and others, especially new converts to the Christian faith.

What they say is characterized as "bombastic nonsense" (NRSV), literally, **uttering loud boasts of folly**. The expression **loud boasts** is also found in Jude 16 and translates a Greek word that means "boastful," "haughty," "bombastic," "high sounding," in other words, something that sounds much more impressive than it really is. **Folly** on the other hand translates a word that means "worthlessness," "emptiness," "futility," or "purposelessness." What it means, then, is that the false teachers make impressive, high sounding, and boastful speeches that are in fact worthless and devoid of any value whatsoever.

The effect of such teaching is that **they entice with licentious passions of the flesh** new converts to the faith. For **entice** see comments on verse 14; for **licentious** see comments on verse 2; and for **passions** see comments on verse 10, where the word is translated "lust." The whole expression **licentious passions of the flesh** refers to sexual desires that are characterized by lust and that lead people to indulge in excessive and uncontrolled immorality. How do the false teachers use this to entice people? It seems that through their teaching they have justified indulgence in immoral acts by presenting these sexual acts as legitimate expressions of Christian freedom. And since this kind of life characterizes those who belong to pagan religions, those who are most easily affected by this attitude are the new converts. These new converts are described as people **who have barely escaped from those who live in error.** The word **barely** may mean "to a small extent," which indicates that these people are not yet completely free of pagan influences. In favor of this view is the fact that **escaped** is a present participle, which can be rendered "in the process of escaping." These people, then, were in the process of making a complete break with pagan society as a whole. More probably, however, **barely** means "for a short time" or "newly," which indicates that these people are new converts who are not yet firmly established in the Christian faith and are therefore easily swayed by non-Christian influences.

Those who live in error are most probably non-Christians or pagans (as in JB "who have only just escaped from paganism"). This use of **error** for pagan living is in accordance with New Testament usage (see for instance Rom 1.27; Titus 3.3 "led astray"). **Live** translates a verb that means "act," "behave," or "conduct oneself." **Error** is literally "wandering," but it is used figuratively for straying from truth, hence "deceit," "deception," when the wandering is caused by others. This final clause **who have just escaped from those who live in error** should not be understood to mean that these people are literally running away from other people (pagans) who stray from the truth. What it means is that they have just begun to stop believing like those people who live their lives according to wrong ideas.

2.19	RSV	TEV
	They promise them freedom, but they themselves are slaves of corruption; for whatever overcomes a man, to that he is enslaved.	They promise them freedom while they themselves are slaves of destructive habits—for a person is a slave of anything that has conquered him.

They refers to the false teachers, and **them** to the new converts referred to in the previous verse. The **freedom** that is promised is not political but spiritual freedom. Many suggestions have been made as to what this freedom refers to, among which are the following:

1. It is freedom from fear of punishment at the end of the world. As verse 3 and chapter 3 indicate, the false teachers seem to have become skeptical regarding judgment in general and about the second coming of Christ in particular. In view of this they no longer believe in the idea of a final judgment.
2. It is freedom from corruption or perishability. This means that the false teachers taught that they and their followers are already beyond the bounds of human mortality. This also connects the idea of freedom with what follows in the verse, where the false teachers are described as "slaves of corruption."
3. If the false teachers are Gnostics, then the freedom that they are talking about is freedom from the enslavement of powers in the universe that are inferior to God, with the result that people feel they are completely free. However, there is no agreement among scholars that these false teachers are Gnostics.
4. It may be freedom from the law, that is, freedom from any rules and regulations that govern the Christian life. This results in a life completely free of any moral restraints. This relates "freedom" to the attitude of the false teachers, who considered themselves completely free from the law and therefore able to do anything they please, including immorality and debauchery.

Although alternative 4 is the most likely interpretation, translators should, if possible, use a general word for freedom. However, in the case of languages that require an object of freedom, we will need to say, for example, "freedom from rules and regulations."

These people who promise freedom to others are themselves **slaves of corruption**. This again is a Hebrew idiom; to be a slave of something is to be so controlled and overcome by that thing that you become helpless and hopeless in the face of it. **Corruption** is one of the key words in 2 Peter; it is used also in 1.4 and 2.12 ("destruction"). It can mean moral depravity, and certainly this was true of the false teachers with their moral laxness and their indulgence in immoral acts. But more probably **corruption** here puts emphasis not so much on moral character as on final and ultimate destruction as a result of sin. Thus TEV "destructive habits" is closer to the meaning than **slaves of corruption**. Other ways of rendering this are "completely controlled by destructive habits" or "completely controlled by habits that will destroy them." **They themselves** is emphatic in the Greek.

Peter reinforces his argument with a popular proverb. **Whatever** (TEV "anything") translates a dative form that can be taken as masculine, "to whom," thus "to whomever one becomes subject." This fits the origin of the proverb, which stemmed from the practice of slave trading; the slaves are first overcome before they are sold. The masculine also fits the context, since the main subject of the discussion is the false teachers. However, it is perhaps more likely that what we have here is a generic neuter, **whatever** referring to any force, whether personal or impersonal; thus "to whatever one becomes subject." **Overcomes** means "defeats" or "overpowers." **Enslaved** translates a passive verb that brings out the idea of taking upon oneself the characteristics

135

of slaves, among which are complete ownership by someone, absence of any rights, absolute obedience and loyalty to owners, and helplessness in overcoming such a degrading condition. The final part of this verse may also be rendered "for a person is completely under the control of anything that has conquered him (defeated him)."

2.20   RSV   TEV

For if, after they have escaped the defilements of the world through the knowledge of our Lord and Savior Jesus Christ, they are again entangled in them and overpowered, the last state has become worse for them than the first.	**If people have escaped from the corrupting forces of the world through their knowledge of our Lord and Savior Jesus Christ, and then are again caught and conquered by them, such people are in worse condition at the end than they were at the beginning.**

The subject of this verse (**they**) can be either the recent converts mentioned in verse 18 or the false teachers. An argument in favor of the former position (recent converts) is the fact that the verb "escape" is used in both verses, and since it is clear that in verse 18 this verb refers to the escape of recent converts, it is likely that it is used here in the same way. On the other hand the proverbs in verse 22 are rather harsh if applied to recent converts but are appropriate for the false teachers. This is probably the reason why some translations interpret **they** as referring to people in general; for example, TEV "If people . . . ." Considering the three verses together (verses 20-22) makes it appear more likely that these refer to the false teachers rather than to recent converts who have gone back to their former heathen ways. In many languages it will be helpful to make this clear and say, for example, "If these false teachers . . ." or "If these new converts . . . ." It is also possible to render this in a general way, referring to everyone: "If people . . ." (TEV) or "If anyone . . ." (similarly Phps, JB).

For connects this verse with the previous verses, probably going back to the whole idea of their being under corruption, or perhaps to the idea of "escape" in verse 18. If this connection is already clear in the translation, then **For** doesn't have to be translated, as can be seen in many translations (for instance, TEV, NIV, NEB, Phps) The word **if** is used here not to mark a condition that is contrary to fact, but rather to mark a conditional statement that is true. In other words Peter is not questioning or doubting the initial faith of the false teachers (or, recent converts) but is asserting the fact that they had at one time left their heathen loyalties and become members of the Christian community. It will be helpful in certain languages to place the word **if** before the second sentence rather than the first and say "These false teachers (or, recent converts) have escaped . . . . So, if they are caught . . . ."

As in 1.4, conversion to Christianity is defined as escaping **the defilements of the world**. The word for **defilements** is a word similar in meaning to that used in 1.4, "corruption," and it is used figuratively here to mean moral corruption through evil acts. The **world** can be understood generally here as all of creation, but perhaps as referring in particular to society which is viewed as evil because it is corrupted by pagan practices. The whole expression **the defilements of the world** is similar in meaning to "licentious passions of the flesh" in verse 18. The way of escaping the pollutions of the world, that is, of becoming a Christian, is **through the knowledge of our Lord and Savior Jesus Christ**. For **Lord** see comments on 1.2; for **Savior** and **Jesus Christ** see comments on 1.1. **Our** is of course inclusive, referring to all Christians. **Knowledge** is a key term in this letter, having been used in 1.2,3, and 8; see comments there for further discussion. This clause may also be rendered as "by coming to know our Lord . . . ," "through coming to know our Lord . . . ," or "through believing in our Lord . . . ."

Leaving the Christian faith and returning to heathen practices is described as being **again entangled** and **overpowered** by these forces. **In them** goes back to **the defilements of the world**. **Entangled** is "to be mixed up with," "to be implicated," or "to be involved in." This pictures people who have renounced their pagan religion, but who now again involve themselves in pagan practices. However, these people do not only get entangled in these practices; they are **overpowered** as well, that is, they are defeated and become slaves to these evil forces from which they have been delivered in the past. The clause **they are again entangled in them and overpowered** may also be expressed as "So if they are trapped again by the powers of these worldly lusts . . ." or "So if they are trapped again by the power of this evil worldly system . . . ." And since this is the case, then **the last state has become worse for them than the first**. **The last state** refers to their state of having been mixed up with and defeated by immoral pagan practices. **The first** refers to their state before they became Christians, that is, before they came to know Jesus Christ as Lord and Savior.

Alternative translation models for this verse are:

(1) If people (or, these false teachers, or, recent converts), through their coming to know our Lord and Savior Jesus Christ, have escaped from the forces of the world that cause peoples' hearts to become dirty, and if they are again trapped by the power of this evil worldly system, they are in a worse condition at the end than before they came to know Jesus Christ (believed in Jesus Christ).

(2) People (or, These false teachers, or, Recent converts) have escaped from the evil and licentious forces of the world through their knowing our Lord and Savior Jesus Christ. But if they are again caught and conquered by these forces, they are in a worse condition . . . .

2.21   RSV   TEV

For it would have been better for them never to have known the way of righteousness than after knowing it to turn back from the holy commandment delivered to them.	It would have been much better for them never to have known the way of righteousness than to know it and then turn away from the sacred command that was given them.

This verse expands on the previous verse, asserting that it would have been much better for these people to remain heathen, rather than to become Christians and then to turn their backs on the Christian way of life. The connection of this verse to the verse before it is expressed by the connective **For**, which has the sense of "Because" or "It is a fact."

It would have been better (literally, "it was better" or "it were better") expresses a judgment on a present state that is considered unsatisfactory, and a preference for a previous state that does not now exist. The present state that is regarded as unsatisfactory is **to have known the way of righteousness** only to be unfaithful to it; whereas the previous state, which is preferred, is **never to have known the way of righteousness**. Peter uses the word "know" again here, for which see comments on "knowledge" in the discussion of 1.2.

The way of righteousness is a new term introduced by Peter at this point. **Righteousness** is one of those words in the New Testament that has a variety of meanings. Some understand **the way of righteousness** to be equivalent to the Christian faith or the Gospel, and to mean the same as "the way of truth" in verse 2. However, the emphasis here may be on its moral aspects: right conduct, a godly life, a life lived according to the will of God, the Christian way of life. **Way** is a term used to refer to the Christian life and has already been discussed in verse 2.

The expression translated **turn back** indicates a change of mind, or a change in a course of action, either for better or for worse. Here, of course, it is for the worse, for these people turn back **from the holy commandment**. Here again Peter introduces a new technical term. **Holy commandment** seems to be parallel to **the way of righteousness** in the first part of the verse; here it probably refers to Christian teaching as a whole, with emphasis on its ethical and moral demands. This **commandment** is described as **holy** because it originates from God and is sustained by God. This source is the significance of the term **delivered**, which is the same term used in Jude 3; see comments there for further discussion. The unnamed agent is perhaps Jesus Christ, but he acts through the apostles, who are given the responsibility of instructing new converts to the faith. In many languages the phrase **holy commandment delivered to them** may be expressed as "the sacred command that they received," or the translator may use an impersonal pronoun to avoid the passive and say "the sacred command that they (agents not named) have given to them."

138

2.22   RSV   TEV

It has happened to them according to   What happened to them shows that the
the true proverb, The dog turns back to   proverbs are true: "A dog goes back to
his own vomit, and the sow is washed   what it has vomited" and "A pig that
only to wallow in the mire.   has been washed goes back to roll in the
                                               mud."

Peter ends his indictment of the false teachers by applying to them two
proverbs that were obviously popular during that time. These proverbs
appropriately explain what really happened to the false teachers. While there
are two proverbs mentioned, Peter simply describes these as **the true proverb**;
it may be better in translation to talk of two proverbs rather than one.

A proverb is a popular saying drawn from the world of nature, or of
animals, or of ordinary human relationships, and which is used to express a
certain truth demonstrated in the life of people, both individually and in their
relation with others. In Hebrew the proverb is usually a doublet; that is, it
consists of two lines, with the second line reinforcing the first, either as a
parallel or in contrast to it. The important thing for translators at this point
is to recognize the literary form of the proverb in their own language, together
with its function, and then to translate these proverbs according to the
demands of their language. For example, if a proverb is usually poetic in form
in a language, then these two sayings should, as far as possible, be translated
according to that poetic form. If a proverb usually has two lines, then these
proverbs should also consist of two lines in the translation.

The first proverb deals with a **dog** and his **vomit**. The quotation here is
from Pro 26.11, although there are some variations. The point of the saying is
that a dog may get rid of its filth (represented by the vomit) but cannot resist
going back to it, to sniff at it or even to eat it. The second proverb is about a
pig and mud. The message seems to be that no matter how clean a pig
becomes, it always goes back to dirty itself in the mud, because part of the
pig's nature is to wallow in mud to keep cool. This second proverb is not found
in the Bible, but there are similar proverbs that are common both in Greek
and Rabbinic literature. Both proverbs use animals that were considered by
Jews as dirty and ritually unclean. This reminds the readers of Peter's
description of the false teachers as "irrational animals" in verse 12 (and see
also verse 16), which is now made worse by their being compared to unclean
dirty animals. The message of both proverbs is clear: the false teachers had
once become clean through the forgiveness of their sins, but they have now
gone back to wallow in the immorality and wickedness that characterized their
pagan past. See the similar statement in 1.9.

Chapter 3

A discussion on the Parousia
(3.1-18)

The previous chapter dealt primarily with the false teachers, their way of life, arrogance, and impending doom. This chapter deals with the Parousia, that is, the teaching about the second coming of Christ, a doctrine that was apparently scorned by the false teachers.

The chapter starts with an introductory statement reminding the readers of a former letter and of the earlier parts of the present one. It then goes on to deal with the Parousia, mentioning objections to the doctrine (verses 3-7), reasons for its delay (verses 8-10), and what this delay means for Christian living (verses 11-15a). The arguments are strengthened by mentioning the support of the apostle Paul (verses 15b-16). The chapter ends with a closing charge and doxology (verses 17-18).

Introductory statement about a former letter
3.1-2

RSV

1 This is now the second letter that I have written to you, beloved, and in both of them I have aroused your sincere mind by way of reminder; 2 that you should remember the predictions of the holy prophets and the commandment of the Lord and Savior through your apostles.

TEV

The Promise of the Lord's Coming

1 My dear friends, this is now the second letter I have written you. In both letters I have tried to arouse pure thoughts in your minds by reminding you of these things. 2 I want you to remember the words that were spoken long ago by the holy prophets, and the command from the Lord and Savior which was given you by your apostles.

SECTION HEADING: the major heading suggested by the Handbook outline covers the entire chapter, as does the TEV section heading, and translators may follow either pattern. The TEV heading may also be rendered as "The Lord's return," "The Lord is coming again," "Jesus will come again," or "Peter writes about the problems of Christ's return." Similar are alternatives for the outline heading, "The problem of the Lord's return" or "Peter discusses the problem of the Lord's return."

The subheading of the outline covers verses 1-2, "Introduction statement about a former letter." This may also be "Peter refers to a former letter," or simply "A former letter."

3.1   RSV   TEV

    This is now the second letter that I have written to you, beloved, and in both of them I have aroused your sincere mind by way of reminder;

    My dear friends, this is now the second letter I have written you. In both letters I have tried to arouse pure thoughts in your minds by reminding you of these things.

For **beloved** see comments on Jude verse 3.

Now is emphatic; its function is to emphasize that it is not one letter but two that have been written. This may stress Peter's deep concern for his readers, or the importance of the subject matters he is dealing with in the letters.

Referring to this letter as **the second letter** almost certainly implies that the earlier one is *The First Letter from Peter.* Both letters serve as "reminders." This reminds us of 1.13, where the same Greek word is used, and where it is established that the present letter is a testament. The testament form of writing, however, has been abandoned for the whole of chapter 2, so that here, at the beginning of chapter 3, it is Peter's intention to go back to it. If the first of the two letters referred to is indeed 1 Peter, this suggests that both letters are intended to be testaments. The use of the word **reminder** also suggests that the readers already know what they are being reminded of. **Them** clearly refers to the two letters, hence TEV "both letters."

Aroused can also be "stimulated," "awakened," or "stirred up." **Sincere** translates an adjective found only here and in Phil 1.10, and which can be translated literally "examined by the sun's light and found to be genuine," and hence "pure," "without blemish," "free from falsehoods." In the present context it points to moral and ethical purity, uncontaminated by sensual passion and the other vices of the false teachers. **Sincere mind** can therefore be translated as "pure thoughts" (TEV), "wholesome thinking" (NIV), "true understanding" (JB), "minds uncontaminated by error" (Phps). It should be noted that RSV can be interpreted to mean that the minds are already sincere, and all that is needed is for these sincere minds to be aroused. The meaning of the Greek text is reflected more accurately in TEV, where it is clear that the purpose of the two letters is to stir up pure thoughts in the readers' minds. The clause **I have aroused your sincere mind by way of reminder** may therefore be rendered as "I have reminded you of these things in order to stimulate your minds to think pure (clean) thoughts" or "I have . . . in order to stir up your minds to think pure . . . ."

3.2   RSV   TEV

that you should remember the predictions of the holy prophets and the com-

I want you to remember the words that were spoken long ago by the holy mandment of the Lord and Savior through your apostles.

prophets, and the command from the Lord and Savior which was given you by your apostles.

This verse is related to Jude 17, with the difference that Jude refers only to Jesus Christ and the apostles, whereas here the prophets are mentioned as well. Furthermore Jude mentions only one warning, whereas here every prophecy and teaching seems to be included as long as it has a bearing on the second coming of Christ.

Remember is an infinitive in the Greek and is related to "reminder" in verse 1. In many translations **remember** is treated as the main verb of a complete sentence, as in NEB "Remember the predictions . . . ," and TEV also restructures to a complete sentence, "I want you to remember . . ."; it may also be expressed as "I want you to bring to your mind." This results in sentences that are not only shorter but also much easier to understand. What the readers are to remember are **the predictions** (TEV "the words") spoken in the past by the **holy prophets** as well as the **commandment** of the **Lord and Savior** that came to them through the **apostles.**

Predictions of the holy prophets recalls 1.21. **Predictions** is the same word as in Jude 17, where it is translated by TEV as "what you were told." **Prophets** are people who proclaim a message that they receive from God; the prophets referred to here are most likely Old Testament prophets rather than Christian prophets. See also the comments on 2.1. **Holy** in this context does not refer to moral or ethical virtue but to the relationship of the prophets to God, that is, their dedication to him and their consecration as people who speak for God (note NEB "God's own prophets"). In certain languages this phrase will be rendered as "devoted people who spoke God's message," or "God's special people who spoke his message," or even "God's specially appointed spokesmen." **Predictions** is literally "words spoken before," and this refers back to the time of the Old Testament, hence TEV "long ago." In the present context **predictions** refers to Old Testament prophecies and predictions about false teachings and godless actions, although no particular Old Testament reference is pointed out.

Commandment is singular and may refer to one command; it is more likely, however, that it is intended here to refer generally to the teachings of the Lord as a whole, with emphasis on their ethical and moral aspects. For further discussion see comments on 2.21 above. **Lord** and **Savior** clearly refer to Jesus Christ, and if necessary this information can be included in the translation. For **Lord** and **Savior** see 1.1,2,11.

The phrase **through your apostles** presents some problems. The Greek text is in the genitive case and can be translated literally as "of your apostles." This understanding is reflected in KJV "the commandment of us the apostles of the Lord and Saviour." Most modern translations, however, take the genitive here to mean "through," in which case the apostles are understood as the instruments and vehicles of the Lord's message. The use of the pronoun **your** may be a way of speaking of the apostles as a group actively functioning when the letter was written, since at that time they were recognized as the ones mainly responsible for transmitting the Christian message to various parts of the world. It is more likely, however, that what is meant here is the messengers who at a much earlier time first brought the Christian message to the communities the letter is addressed to, and who founded the churches there. Included in this list is the apostle Paul (verse 15). For **apostle** see comments on 1.1.

An alternative translation model for this verse is:

> I want to bring to your mind the words that God's own prophets spoke long ago, and the command of our Lord and Savior that he caused your apostles to speak.

If translators wish to follow RSV and join verses 1 and 2 together, we may translate:

> 1 My dear Friends! This is now the second letter I have written to you. In both letters I have tried to cause you to think pure thoughts, 2 by bringing to your minds what God's own prophets spoke long ago and the commandment of our Lord and Savior that he caused your apostles to speak.

The Parousia and reasons for its delay
3.3-10

RSV

3 First of all you must understand this, that scoffers will come in the last days with scoffing, following their own passions 4 and saying, "Where is the promise of his coming? For ever since the fathers fell asleep, all things have continued as they were from the beginning of creation." 5 They deliberately ignore this fact, that by the word of God heavens existed long ago, and an earth formed out of water and by means of water, 6 through which the world that then existed was deluged with water and perished. 7 But by the same word the heavens and earth that now exist have been stored up for fire, being kept until the day of judgment and destruction of ungodly men.

8 But do not ignore this one fact, beloved, that with the Lord one day is as a thousand years, and a thousand years as one day. 9 The Lord is not slow about his promise as some count slowness, but is forbearing toward you, not wishing that any should perish, but that all should reach repentance. 10 But the day of the Lord will come like a thief, and then the heavens will pass away with a loud noise, and the elements will be dissolved with fire, and the earth and the works that are upon it will be burned up.

TEV

3 First of all, you must understand that in the last days some people will appear whose lives are controlled by their own lusts. They will make fun of you 4 and will ask, "He promised to come, didn't he? Where is he? Our fathers have already died, but everything is still the same as it was since the creation of the world!" 5 They purposely ignore the fact that long ago God gave a command, and the heavens and earth were created. The earth was formed out of water and by water, 6 and it was also by water, the water of the flood, that the old world was destroyed. 7 But the heavens and the earth that now exist are being preserved by the same command of God, in order to be destroyed by fire. They are being kept for the day when godless people will be judged and destroyed.

8 But do not forget one thing, my dear friends! There is no difference in the Lord's sight between one day and a thousand years; to him the two are the same. 9 The Lord is not slow to do what he has promised, as some think. Instead, he is patient with you, because he does not want anyone to be destroyed, but wants all to turn away from their sins.

10 But the Day of the Lord will come like

a thief. On that Day the heavens will disappear with a shrill noise, the heavenly bodies
will burn up and be destroyed, and the earth
with everything in it will vanish.

This passage states some allegations of the false teachers regarding the
Parousia, as well as Peter's answer to these allegations. The Parousia is
certain to occur, but it is delayed for a purpose: to allow for people to repent
and thus be saved from judgment.

The whole passage, which runs from verse 3 to verse 10, follows a chiastic
structure as follows:

> A — denial of the Parousia (verses 3-4a)
>   B — universal stability as a reason for denying the Parousia (verse
>   4b)
>   B′ — reply to B (verses 5-7)
> A′ — reply to A (verses 8-10)

SECTION HEADING: the subheading suggested by the Handbook outline for
verses 3-10 may also be "Why the Lord's return is delayed."

3.3	RSV	TEV
	First of all you must understand this, that scoffers will come in the last days with scoffing, following their own passions	First of all, you must understand that in the last days some people will appear whose lives are controlled by their own lusts. They will make fun of you

This verse goes back to the subject of the second coming of Christ, which
was first mentioned in 1.16 but which has been interrupted by the lengthy
discussion regarding the false teachers.

First of all is a way of expressing priority and importance, hence "above
all." The use of **first** may present a problem in translation, especially in
languages that require a second point if a first point is mentioned. In such
cases a natural way of expressing priority should be used without necessarily
mentioning a number. See comments on 1.20, where the same phrase occurs,
for other translation models.

For **you must understand this**, see comments on 1.20. It is not clear in the
Greek text if what follows is intended to be part of the prophetic message and
of the Lord's teachings, all of which the readers have just been told to
remember; however, the context seems to indicate that this is the case. **In the
last days** is equivalent to **in the last time** in Jude 18, for which see discussion
there. The expression **in the last days** is actually the more familiar one and is
used frequently in the Greek translation of the Old Testament, the Septuagint
(see Gen 49.1; Jer 30.24 [37.24 in the Septuagint]; Dan 2.28; Hos 3.5; Micah
4.1) and in many writings during the period after the apostles.

One of the features of the last days is the appearance of people who make fun of God's message. For **scoffers** see also comments on Jude 18. The two verses are very similar, with these differences: Jude has only "scoffers following," while 2 Peter has **scoffers will come . . . with scoffing, following . . .**; and 2 Peter has **passions** while Jude has "ungodly passions." The emphasis of both statements is that the scoffers are following their own will and not God's. It is not clear whether these **scoffers** are the same people as the false teachers in chapter 2, but it makes sense to understand the two groups as one and the same. **Scoffing** is the action that scoffers do; its double use here, **scoffers . . . with scoffing**, is perhaps a form of Hebrew idiom signifying intensity or emphasis. In some cases the two terms can be combined into one to produce a more natural translation; for example, "they will mock you," or TEV "they will make fun of you," and NEB "men who scoff at religion." Other ways to translate **scoffing** are "making jokes about" or "laughing at." The mocking statements are found in verse 4, and for this reason it is desirable to put "mock" right before that verse.

An alternative translation model for this verse is:

> The most important thing is that you understand that in the days just before the end time, some people will appear whose lives are controlled by their own lusts (evil desires). They will mock you by saying . . . .

3.4   RSV   TEV

and saying, "Where is the promise of his coming? For ever since the fathers fell asleep, all things have continued as they were from the beginning of creation."	and will ask, "He promised to come, didn't he? Where is he? Our fathers have already died, but everything is still the same as it was since the creation of the world!"

For **coming** see comments on 1.16. The second coming of Jesus Christ as judge is a very important part of apostolic teaching and is echoed in some words of Jesus recorded in the Gospels (for instance, Matt 24.3; Mark 9.1). The delay of this event created tremendous problems for the early church, as can be seen in some of Paul's letters, such as his letters to the Thessalonians. This same problem is a major concern of the readers of 2 Peter. Apparently some people (most probably the false teachers mentioned in chapter 2) have been raising questions about this doctrine, or even denying its truth, and making fun of those who still hold on to it. So these people ask **Where is the promise of his coming?** In the Old Testament, doubts or denials are frequently expressed in the form of a rhetorical question with the same structure as above, as in Mal 2.17, "Where is the God who is supposed to be just?" (TEV) or Jer 17.15, "Where are those threats the Lord made against us? Let him carry them out now!" (TEV; see also Psa 42.3; Jer 17.15; Luke 8.25). So this rhetorical question form is very appropriate to express the cynical attitude of those who reject the Parousia because of its delay. **Promise** here refers to statements regarding the Parousia; these may be Old Testament prophecies, or teachings of the apostles, or even the very words of Jesus himself in which he spoke of his imminent return. **Where is the promise** seems to ask for the location of the promise, but in fact this is an idiomatic expression that means "Where is the fulfillment of the promise?" The aim of the question is not to find out where these promises are, but to express doubt and skepticism regarding them. TEV offers a model for restructuring: "He promised to come, didn't he? Where is he?" Another way is to put this in the passive: "Hasn't it been promised that he would come? What happened to that promise?" (See also Knox: "What has become of the promise that he would appear?") Another possibility is to change the rhetorical question into statements such as "His promise to come is not true! He is not coming at all!" Or even "He lied when he said, 'I am coming again.' Actually he is not coming at all." In restructuring rhetorical questions, translators must make sure that the impact of the text is retained in the translation, namely, that this is an emphatic statement.

Some commentators take **fathers** to refer to important people in the Old Testament, since the word was used with this meaning in the literature of that time. In the present context, however, it makes more sense to take it as referring to the first generation of Christians, that is, the first Christian disciples who were given the promise of the early return of Christ, and in whose lifetime this event was expected to happen. "Died" is literally **fell asleep**, a euphemism or indirect way of referring to dying. **Ever since** marks the beginning of the period that concerns the doubters: the period from the death of the first-generation Christians to the time of the writing of the letter. The sense of the Greek is captured in TEV: "Our fathers have already died, but . . . ." (See also NEB "Our fathers have been laid to their rest, but still . . . .")

All things have continued as they were: the Lord's return has been proclaimed as coming with upheavals of various kinds in the world. The mockers contend that all things are exactly the same, and in fact things have been this way ever since the **beginning of creation**. The regularity of the world and the stability of existence are used as arguments against the Parousia. **Creation** refers to "the creation of the world" (TEV, also NEB "since the world began"), with God as the agent, hence we can also say "from the time God created the world." The statement **all things have continued as they were from the beginning of creation** is of course an exaggeration, but this should be clearly marked in the translation. One way of doing it is show in TEV, where an exclamation point is used at the end of the statement. Similar rhetorical devices may be employed as far as they are appropriate in the receptor language.

3.5	RSV	TEV

They deliberately ignore this fact, that by the word of God heavens existed

They purposely ignore the fact that long ago God gave a command, and the long ago, and an earth formed out of water and by means of water, | heavens and earth were created. The earth was formed out of water and by water,

They deliberately ignore this fact can also be translated as "In taking this view they lose sight of the fact" or "they are inclined to forget . . . ." This second alternative is arrived at by translating the Greek text as "They can assert this (4b) only because they have overlooked (or have forgotten) that . . . ." The first alternative translates the Greek text as "They can assert this (verse 4b) because they willfully ignore . . . ." The choice then is between deliberate ignoring and involuntary forgetting. Both are possible, and it is difficult to say which is more correct; most modern translations, however, prefer the first interpretation. **Ignore** may be expressed as "choose to overlook" or "choose to not notice."

By the word of God recalls Gen 1.3; Psa 33.6,9, and other Old Testament verses that stress the creative power of God's word. In Hebrew thought a person's word can act on behalf of that person, since it embodies both spirit and personality. God's word, then, is God's agent in creation. In the Greek text this comes at the end of the verse, and there are three ways of relating it to the rest of the verse:

1. It could relate only to the heavens. This is a possible reading of the text, but it goes against the biblical evidence that both heaven and earth came about as a result of God's word.
2. It could relate to both heaven and earth. This is the most natural interpretation and is made clear in TEV. (See also NEB: "there were heavens and earth long ago, created by God's word . . . .")
3. It could relate only to earth. Some translations take this position (for instance Knox ". . . earth which God's word had made . . . .")

It may be difficult in some languages to translate this literally, in which case a restructuring similar to TEV will be appropriate, with **word** being translated as a verb: "God spoke, and . . . ."

Heavens refers not to the place where God dwells, but to the dome-like structure that is above the earth and shields the earth from the water that is above the dome. In languages where there is a distinction between these two kinds of "heaven," the word for the dome-like structure should be used here. **Heavens** is plural in form but singular in meaning; its plural form is influenced by Hebrew usage, where the word for "heaven" is always plural. Many translations retain the plural here; however, it may be more natural to speak of "heaven" in the singular, as indeed many other translations have done.

Long ago goes back to the beginning of creation and emphasizes the vast age of the created order. The Greek text connects this grammatically with **heavens** (so RSV and many other translations); it is possible, however, to connect **long ago** with both earth and the heavens (so TEV, Knox, AT). For ways to translate **long ago**, see the comments on Jude 4; 2 Peter 2.3.

An earth formed out of water and by means of water is literally "earth standing out of water and through water." The background of this expression

147

includes the many creation stories in the Near East, in which the sky and the earth arose out of an ocean of water (see Pro 8.27-29; Psa 136.6). But it primarily recalls Gen 1.1-10, which tells of how the earth, initially engulfed by a chaotic ocean, was formed by creating the sky to divide the stormy water into two (above and below the sky), and finally by gathering the water below the sky into one place. **Out of water** expresses this idea, namely, that the earth emerged out of the water, and not, as some commentaries hold, that water was the original or basic element from which all other things were made. **By means of water** may express the idea that God used water as the element in creating the earth; some translations in fact can be read with this meaning (such as NEB "with water"). It is more likely, however, that what is being emphasized here is that water is the instrument of creation in the sense that it was by doing something to the water (dividing and gathering it) that God gave the earth its existence. Thus we may translate "By his word he separated the earth from the ancient waters and brought the dry land out through the water."

For languages that do not use the passive, an alternative translation model for this verse is the following:

> They deliberately ignore the fact that many many generations ago God spoke and the heavens came into being. By his word he separated the earth from the ancient waters and brought the dry land out through the water.

3.6   RSV   TEV

RSV	TEV
through which the world that then existed was deluged with water and perished.	and it was also by water, the water of the flood, that the old world was destroyed.

Through translates the same preposition rendered "by means of" in verse 5. **Which** is a plural relative pronoun and can be interpreted in many ways, three of which are worth mentioning:
1. It goes back to "word" in verse 5. This makes verses 5, 6, and 7 structurally parallel: heaven and earth were created, the world was destroyed by water, and all creation will be destroyed by fire, all by means of God's word. However, the plural form of the Greek for **which** argues against this position.
2. It refers to both "word" and "water." These three verses will then be structurally connected thus: word and water (verse 5), word and water (verse 6), word and fire (verse 7).
3. It refers to "water." The plural form can either refer to the two types of water (water above and water below the heavens) from which the flood had come (Gen 7.11), or be taken as a Hebrew idiom, since in Hebrew, water, like heaven, is usually plural in form.

This third possibility is the choice of by far the most translations. There is a need, however, to restructure the verse because of the mention of **water** in the second half (**through which** [water] **the world . . . was deluged with water and perished**), which makes the sentence somewhat awkward. A possible way of resolving this problem is to identify "water" in the first part of the verse with "water" in the second part, which is what TEV has done ("and it was also by water, the water of the flood, that the old world was destroyed." We may also translate "and God also used water, the water of the flood, to destroy the old world."

World translates the Greek word *kosmos*, the world of order and harmony, as contrasted with the pre-creation state of chaos and disorder. **The world that then existed** (TEV "the old world") is taken by many commentaries as referring to the whole universe, which includes both heaven and earth; this stresses the cosmic scope of the great flood, affecting not only earth but heaven as well. It is more likely, however, that in the present context **world** refers only to the inhabited earth and human beings in particular. Since the earth is formed by means of water, it can also be destroyed in the same way. In certain languages the RSV rendering **world that then existed** (NRSV "world of that time") will be preferable to that of TEV "the old world." However, we may also translate "that world long ago."

Deluged is literally "flooded"; the whole expression refers to the great flood recorded in Genesis 6–8. **Perished** is more naturally "was destroyed" (TEV), since the whole physical universe together with its inhabitants can be destroyed, whereas only living beings, and more especially human beings, can be described as perishing. The destruction here is primarily viewed in terms of being submerged in water, that is, the ordered universe (the *kosmos*) goes back to its original chaotic state (see Gen 1.1-2).

It should be noted that in the Genesis account of the flood (chapters 6–8) it is not the earth that was destroyed but human beings and other living things. Here the focus is on the whole earth and not simply human beings and other living things. It is true, of course, that the destruction of living things has the effect of putting the earth into a very chaotic state. However, translators should translate the picture here rather than going back to the Genesis account.

3.7 RSV	TEV
But by the same word the heavens and earth that now exist have been stored up for fire, being kept until the day of judgment and destruction of ungodly men.	But the heavens and the earth that now exist are being preserved by the same command of God, in order to be destroyed by fire. They are being kept for the day when godless people will be judged and destroyed.

By the same word recalls the first part of verse 5, hence TEV "by the same command of God." As noted in the discussion of verse 6 above, the three verses

(5,6,7) may have God's word as the common element. If, however, verse 6 is made to refer only to water, then the three verses will be related in a different way: word . . . water . . . word, which is what is called a chiastic pattern. The idea seems to be that, since God's word has been proven as powerful and trustworthy in the act of creation, this same word can also be trusted when it proclaims that in the future the universe will be destroyed by fire.

The heavens and earth that now exist refers to the universe as it is at present, with **now** denoting the time of writing the letter. In the Bible **heavens and earth** can sometimes be taken as an idiom meaning "everything," "the whole universe," "all creation."

Stored up for fire is unusual, since the word translated **stored up** is usually used for storing goods, treasures, and other valuable things, which are for use at a future time. **For** can also be interpreted as instrumental, "by means of" or "with"; but it is much more likely that **for** here defines purpose: the universe is being kept from destruction now (TEV "preserved"), so that in the future it can be destroyed by means of fire. (See NEB "kept in store for burning," and TNT "have been saved up . . . they will be burnt.")

The idea of destruction by fire is found only in this passage and nowhere else in the New Testament. This has led some scholars to trace the background of this idea from nonbiblical literature (Iranian or Stoic). However, the Old Testament does contain references to judgment by fire, not to destroy the universe but to punish the wicked (see, for example, Deut 32.22; Psa 97.3; Isa 30.30; 66.15-16; Mal 4.1 [3.19 in the Hebrew]). This is echoed in many parts of the Gospels (for instance, Matt 3.11; 5.22). In Jewish literature of the apocalyptic type, the Old Testament idea of judgment by fire has been developed into a picture of universal conflagration that will usher in the end of the world.

The two ideas of the punishment of the **ungodly** and the destruction of the world by fire are combined in the present verse. **The day** refers to the final day of judgment. The purpose of **judgment** is not to determine whether the **ungodly** are guilty or not, but rather to carry out the punishment that they deserve. For comments on **judgment** see Jude 15. **Destruction** is the result of such judgment: people will be punished to such an extent that they will be completely destroyed. For comments on **destruction** see 2.1,3. For comments on **ungodly** see 2.5 and Jude 4.

An alternative model for this verse for languages that do not favor the passive is the following:

> But God is keeping (preserving) by that same command the
> heavens and earth that now exist, in order to destroy them with
> fire. He is keeping them for the day when he will judge and
> destroy people who don't obey (honor) him.

3.8   RSV   TEV

But do not ignore this one fact, beloved, that with the Lord one day is as a thousand years, and a thousand years as one day.

But do not forget one thing, my dear friends! There is no difference in the Lord's sight between one day and a thousand years; to him the two are the same.

For **beloved** see comments on Jude verse 3.

But do not ignore this one fact recalls verse 5 and deliberately contrasts the attitude of the false teachers with the attitude that the readers of this letter should have. **Ignore** translates the same word in both verses: in verse 5 the false teachers are accused of deliberate ignorance or neglect; in verse 8 the readers are urged not to do this. Furthermore, in the Greek the plural pronoun "you" is used in verse 8 and placed in the emphatic position, "don't *you* ignore," thus contrasting it with "they" in verse 5; the sense is something like "you yourselves must not do what these false teachers deliberately do."

Since **ignore** translates the same word found in verse 5, the interpretation of this word in verse 5 will affect the way it is interpreted in verse 8. It may therefore be advisable to use the same word in both verses in order to reflect this relationship. This is in fact done in many translations: RSV **ignore**, JB "forget," NEB "lose sight of."

With the Lord may be rendered as "the way that the Lord thinks" or "the way that the Lord reckons things."

With the Lord one day is as a thousand years . . . ; the delay of the Parousia can be explained by the fact that the Lord's way of reckoning time is different from human reckoning and does not conform to human ways of thinking. The statement in this verse is based on Psa 90.4, "A thousand years to you are like one day" (TEV). Most commentaries take the statement to mean that what may seem long to us as people may in fact be short to God, and what may seem short to us may in fact be long to him.

And a thousand years as one day: the repetition of the statement (but in reverse) needs to be noted. Some commentaries and translations take this repetition to be simply stylistic and regard the two parts as parallel to each other. This is the position reflected in TEV "There is no difference in the Lord's sight between one day and a thousand years; to him the two are the same." Others take this as emphasizing that on the one hand God is able to act quickly to fulfill his promises (as in verse 10), while on the other hand he gives sufficient time for people to repent (as in verse 9), although for the unrepentant the time is too brief. If this second position is taken, then the two parts of the statement need to be retained in translation. It seems likely, however, that the stylistic interpretation is to be preferred.

3.9   RSV   TEV

The Lord is not slow about his promise as some count slowness, but is forbearing toward you,[h] not wishing that any should perish, but that all should reach repentance.	The Lord is not slow to do what he has promised, as some think. Instead, he is patient with you, because he does not want anyone to be destroyed, but wants all to turn away from their sins.

[h] Other ancient authorities read *on your account*

The Lord may refer either to God or to Christ, but in the context of this whole passage it may be best to take **Lord** in these three verses as referring to God.

Slow comes from a verb that can mean "to delay," "to linger," "to be slack," "to be late," especially in reference to a designated or determined time. What is being denied here is the allegation of **some** people that God is **slow about his promise**, that is, he is negligent in fulfilling his promise at the appointed time. **Promise** ties this statement to the question in verse 4. Apparently the delay of the Parousia had been interpreted to mean that God was either indifferent or powerless to fulfill what he had promised. The phrase **not slow about his promise** may also be rendered as "not negligent (slow) in making what he promised to do happen." **As some count slowness** can be expanded in translation; for example, "as some people think . . ." or "as some people think slowness means."

Peter accepts that there is some delay, but he says that the delay has a positive purpose. It shows first of all that God is **forbearing**. This word, sometimes rendered as "longsuffering" or "patient," is that quality of God which allows him to be somewhat lenient with sinners, in the sense that he refrains from punishing them immediately, but instead gives then an opportunity to turn back from their sins and thus escape receiving the punishment they deserve. (See also how "God's patience waited" in 1 Peter 3.20.) God's patience is here made to relate directly to the readers of the letter: he is patient **toward you**. **Forbearing** is literally "long-souled" and may be translated idiomatically in some languages as "having a big heart" or "large-hearted."

As the RSV footnote shows, there is a textual problem here. Instead of the preposition **toward** (Greek *eis*), some manuscripts have "on account of" (Greek *dia*), which is reflected in some translations such as Mft "he is longsuffering for your sake." The meaning is not all that different, since both single out the readers as the object of God's patience, and both equally affirm that this is for their own benefit. Most modern translations follow the text reflected in RSV and TEV. **You** is strange in this context, since he has been speaking about others, especially scoffers; perhaps it is used here to indicate God's great concern for the readers of the letter, but it is also possible that many of the readers have begun to succumb to the influence of the false teachers, and therefore would need sufficient time to renounce their heretical beliefs and ungodly practices. At any rate, the strangeness of **you** in this verse remains, and this has led to the change of **you** to "us" in some manuscripts, as the UBS Greek New Testament indicates (and see KJV "is longsuffering to us-ward"). It is clear, however, from the conclusions of textual scholars, that the primary reading here is not "us" but **you**.

Related to God's patience is his **not wishing that any should perish**. **Wishing** comes from a verb that means "to want," "to desire," "to will." **Perish** is "be lost" (NEB) or "be destroyed" (TEV) as a result of God's judgment. The phrase **not wishing that any should perish** may be rendered in some languages as "not wanting anyone to receive destruction" or "not wanting anyone to suffer destruction." **Any** emphasizes God's encompassing desire to save people from punishment; he doesn't want even one person to be destroyed. The last part of the verse expresses the same idea positively: as a patient God, he wants **all** to **reach repentance**, that is "to turn away from their sins" (TEV). The term **repentance** includes the negative element of turning away from evil and the positive element of doing God's will. Thus we may translate as "turn away from evil and follow God's will," or idiomatically as "change their hearts and return to God."

An alternative translation model for this verse is:

> The Lord is not slow in making (causing) what he promised to do happen, as some people think slowness means (is). Instead, he is big-hearted toward you, because he doesn't want anyone to suffer destruction, but wants all people to turn away from their sins and return to him.

3.10 RSV	TEV
But the day of the Lord will come like a thief, and then the heavens will pass away with a loud noise, and the elements will be dissolved with fire, and the earth and the works that are upon it will be burned up.	But the Day of the Lord will come like a thief. On that Day the heavens will disappear with a shrill noise, the heavenly bodies will burn up and be destroyed, and the earth with everything in it will vanish.[d]
	[d] vanish; *some manuscripts have* be found; *others have* be burned up; *one has* be found destroyed.

It should be noted that RSV and TEV are different here, in that TEV starts a new paragraph, whereas RSV treats this verse as part of the paragraph that started in verse 8. In view of the fact that verses 8-15a seem to form a single unit dealing with the reasons for the delay of the Parousia and how Christians should live during the period of the delay, it seems best to follow the RSV paragraphing at this point.

But connects this verse with the verse before it; it clears up any misunderstanding that may arise as a result of the assertion that the delay of the Parousia is due to God's patience and his desire for everyone to be saved from judgment. Despite all of this, it is certain that the Lord will return, and the day of judgment will come. This is made clear by the word order in the Greek, in which **will come** is placed first and therefore is emphatic.

The **day of the Lord** is a popular biblical expression used for the end time. In the Old Testament the Day of the Lord refers to any event where God's people (Israel) are victorious over God's enemies (other nations). The defeat of God's enemies is considered as God's judgment on those people. It was only later that this act of judgment was understood to apply to Israel as well. In the present passage, as in the rest of the New Testament, this expression is used primarily for the Parousia, that is, when Jesus Christ returns in victory to judge all peoples, both living and dead. This can be made clear in translation; for example, "the day of the Lord's coming," "the day of the Lord's return," or "the day when the Lord returns." The coming of the Lord is compared to the coming of a **thief**, which is unexpected or sudden, and this is brought out in many translations (for instance, Phps "suddenly and unexpectedly as a thief," NEB "unexpected as a thief"). Other possible translations are "The Lord will come as unexpectedly as a thief does in the night," or even "The Lord will come when no one expects him, just as a thief comes when no one is expecting him." It is also possible to remove the figure of **thief** and simply translate the basis or ground of the comparison: "the day of the Lord will come suddenly and unexpectedly" or "The Lord will come suddenly at a time when he is not expected." It is also suggested that the use of the picture of the **thief** carries with it an element of threat, especially for those who continue in their unrepentant ways. The use of this picture as a figurative expression for the end that is coming is common in the teachings of Jesus (see for example Matt 24.43-44; Luke 12.39-40), and in other parts of the New Testament (1 Thes 5.2; Rev 3.3; 16.15). It is important here to indicate clearly the ground or basis of comparison with a thief (unexpectedly, suddenly), in order to avoid the interpretation that the Lord is himself a thief.

And then refers back to **day**, hence TEV "On that Day." For **heavens** see comments on verse 5 above. **Pass away** is "disappear" (TEV) or "vanish."

With a loud noise translates the Greek word *hroizēdon*, which is considered to be onomatopoeic, that is, a word that sounds like the thing it names. In this case *hroizēdon* is used of hissing, crackling, and rushing sounds, sounds that are made by a snake, a fire, or an arrow. Here the sound being described is that of fire, referring to the roaring and crackling sounds of the sky as it burns down. Some translations try to do justice to this feature: TEV "a shrill noise," NEB "a great rushing sound," Phps "a terrific tearing blast," TNT "a roaring sound," Mft "a crackling roar." In languages that use ideophones, translators should consider using one here.

What are the **elements** that are going to be **dissolved with fire**? There are at least four possible interpretations:
1. They are the rudiments of knowledge. This is based on the historical origin of the Greek word *stoicheia*, which can be literally rendered "things

arranged in a row," as, for instance, the letters of the alphabet. This meaning is reflected in Heb 5.12, where *stoicheia* is translated "first principles," TEV "first lessons." This meaning, however, does not fit the present context.

2. They are the physical elements, namely earth, air, fire, and water. This was a common meaning of **elements** (Greek *stoicheia*). A prevalent idea among the Stoics was that, in the final conflagration, these four elements will be dissolved into the primary element, namely fire. Considering the Greek background of 2 Peter, this interpretation has some validity; it is, however, rather inappropriate in the present context, since **elements** comes right after the mention of heaven and before the mention of earth.

3. They are angelic or spiritual beings. In Paul's letters *stoicheia* is used in a similar manner, referring to spiritual powers (see for example Gal 4.3; Col 2.8,20).

4. They are the heavenly bodies: the sun, the moon, the stars, the planets. In other biblical references, these are also referred to as "the powers of the heavens" (see for example Isa 34.4; Matt 24.29). The use of *stoicheia* in this sense is attested in the literature of that time, both from Greek and Christian writers.

This last meaning is what most commentaries prefer, and consequently it is reflected in many translations, such as TEV "the heavenly bodies," and Mft "the stars." Taking this meaning relates this part of the verse with the first part, which talks of the sky, whereas this second part refers to things located in the sky. This also makes the first two parts parallel to the third part of the verse, which talks of the earth and everything in it. A literal translation of **elements** here allows for all four possibilities but sacrifices clarity in the process, and so should be avoided. As is often said, if it means everything, it does not mean anything.

Dissolved is literally "destroyed." **With fire** translates a Greek medical term for body temperature, particularly in connection with a high fever. So the expression can be rendered literally as "destroyed in the heat." The picture here is that the heat is so intense that the heavenly bodies begin to melt and eventually are reduced to nothing. Some translations try to reflect this meaning: TEV "burn up and be destroyed," JB "catch fire and fall apart," NEB "disintegrate in flames," Mft "be set ablaze and melt."

And the works that are upon it is literally "its works," which can mean all the results of both human and divine activity on earth, or in a wider sense, everything that is in the earth; hence TEV "with everything in it," JB "and all that it contains," NEB "with all that is in it."

As can be seen from the TEV text and footnote, there is a textual problem related to **will be burned up**. The UBS Greek New Testament has in its text "will be found," and this is reflected in the NRSV text "will be disclosed" and also NEB "will be laid bare." TNT follows the UBS Greek text but translates this part as a rhetorical question: "will the earth and everything in it remain?" with "No" as the unspoken answer. Another way of understanding "will be found" is to take it as a so-called "divine passive" and interpret it as meaning "will be found by God," that is, ready for God to examine. The picture that we have in the whole verse of the UBS Greek text is that, when heaven and all that is in it are destroyed, the earth will be laid bare, and all peoples will face the judgment of God. RSV and JB follow a variant found in a number of manuscripts. TEV translates another variant, namely "will vanish." Yet another variant is represented by AT, "will melt away." Two things should be noted here: first, that in the UBS Greek New Testament the rating given is "D," which means that there is a very high degree of uncertainty with regard to the reading selected for the text; and secondly, treating the statement as a rhetorical question (as IN TNT above) will result in a translation similar to TEV, with "will vanish" representing the unspoken answer to the rhetorical question. Since there is no clearly favored text, the translator may choose to follow any of the variant readings, with perhaps NRSV and TEV a slightly better choice. Or it may be wise to follow the choice of a translation in a related language that is known and widely used. In any case, translators should provide a footnote similar to that of TEV. In some languages we may translate TEV's "will vanish" as "will no longer exist."

Alternative translation models for this verse are:

> But the Lord will come when no one expects him, just as a thief does (comes when no one is expecting him). On that Day there will be a great roaring sound as the heavens (or, sky) disappear (or, vanish). The bodies in the sky will burn up and disintegrate, and the earth and everything that is in it will no longer exist (or, melt away).

Or for the final sentence:

> . . . and God will find the earth and all that is in it ready for him to judge . . . .

Or:

> . . . When all this happens, will the earth and everything in it still remain?

Ethical implications of the Parousia and the disaster connected with it
3.11-15a

RSV	TEV
11 Since all these things are thus to be dissolved, what sort of persons ought you to be in lives of holiness and godliness, 12 waiting for and hastening the coming of the day of God, because of which the heavens will be kindled and dissolved, and the elements will melt with fire! 13 But according to his promise we wait for new heavens and a new earth in which righteousness dwells.	11 Since all these things will be destroyed in this way, what kind of people should you be? Your lives should be holy and dedicated to God, 12 as you wait for the Day of God and do your best to make it come soon—the Day when the heavens will burn up and be destroyed, and the heavenly bodies will be melted by the heat. 13 But we wait for what God has promised: new heavens and a new earth, where

14 Therefore, beloved, since you wait for these, be zealous to be found by him without spot or blemish, and at peace. 15 And count the forbearance of our Lord as salvation.

righteousness will be at home.

14 And so, my friends, as you wait for that Day, do your best to be pure and faultless in God's sight and to be at peace with him. 15 Look on our Lord's patience as the opportunity he is giving you to be saved,

Peter concludes his letter in much the same way as other letters in the New Testament, namely with a section that defines for his readers how they should live as God's people in the world in the light of their faith. In particular this section of the letter spells out the moral and ethical requirements for believers in the light of the Day of the Lord that will soon come, and the disaster connected with it.

We have earlier identified 2 Peter as a "testament." Some commentaries note that such a testament usually concludes with an ethical section that contains overtones of the end time.

Translators following the section headings suggested by the Handbook outline may wish to say, for example, "How Christians should live as they wait for the Lord to return."

3.11   RSV   TEV

Since all these things are thus to be dissolved, what sort of persons ought you to be in lives of holiness and godliness,

Since all these things will be destroyed in this way, what kind of people should you be? Your lives should be holy and dedicated to God,

All these things refers both to the "heavens" and to the "elements" mentioned in verse 10. The phrase may or may not include the earth and everything in it, depending on which textual variant is chosen in verse 10.

Are . . . to be dissolved translates a present participle, which may give the sense that these things are even now in the process of being destroyed, thus stressing the extreme urgency of the situation. The present participle, however, can be taken with a future sense, as RSV and most translations have done (note TEV "will be destroyed"). **Thus**, or "in this way," refers back to verse 10; **dissolved** translates the same Greek word used there.

The words **what sort of persons ought you to be** may be interpreted in various ways:
1. As the beginning of a question that includes verse 12. This is the position represented by RSV.
2. As a question, with the answer following immediately. This is the position reflected in TEV (also NIV, and Phps "what sort of people ought you to be? Surely men of good and holy character . . . .")
3. With an imperative sense ("you ought to," "it is necessary for you"). Many translations take this position; for example, JB "you should be living holy and saintly lives," AT "what holy and pious lives you ought to lead," and

157

NEB "think what sort of people you ought to be, what devout and dedicated lives you should live!")

The Greek text allows for all three interpretations. However, in the UBS Greek New Testament, verses 11 and 12 are treated as one sentence and are punctuated not with a question mark but with a period. This seems to indicate that the second and third possibilities are closer to the meaning and intent of the Greek text. This also makes it possible for the long Greek sentence to be restructured into two or more sentences.

For **godliness** see comments on 1.3. **Holiness** (literally, "holy behavior") is used here in a moral sense, describing a life characterized by dedication to God, dislike of anything evil or sinful, and blameless moral conduct. In the Greek both **holiness** and **godliness** are plural, which perhaps indicate various forms of godly and holy conduct. The phrase **in lives of holiness and godliness** may also be rendered as "You should live lives that are pure and dedicated to God" or "You should walk your lives in a holy (blameless) way, dedicated to God."

3.12 RSV	TEV
waiting for and hastening[i] the coming of the day of God, because of which the heavens will be kindled and dissolved, and the elements will melt with fire!	as you wait for the Day of God and do your best to make it come soon—the Day when the heavens will burn up and be destroyed, and the heavenly bodies will be melted by the heat.

[i] Or *earnestly desiring*

Waiting can also be "looking for," "expecting"; it is used of expectation of the coming end time (see, for instance, Matt 11.3; Luke 7.19-20). For further discussion see comments on Jude 21, where the same word is used. **Hastening** can also be "earnestly desiring" (RSV footnote), "striving for," "looking for," "waiting for." This is so because the Greek participle here can be derived from a verb that means "to be eager" or "to be zealous" (hence, "desire earnestly"), or from another verb that means "to hasten," "to speed up." The main question here is whether Christians can cause the day of the Lord to come more quickly by their actions (in this case, by living godly and holy lives), or whether this is solely in the hands of God, and the only thing that Christians can do is to longingly expect it. The verb allows for either possibility; background literature, however, favors the interpretation **hastening**. In Rabbinic literature there are references attesting to the belief that repentance does bring in the end. A passage from 2 Clement (12.6) cites a statement from Jesus to the effect that when Christians live godly lives and refrain from sexual impurities, then the kingdom of God will come. Connected with this, of course, is the delay of the Parousia, which is motivated by God's desire for people to repent; in the light of this, repentance may be said to ultimately affect the eventual return of the Lord. Most translations prefer this second possibility; for example TEV "do your best to make it come soon," NIV "speed its coming," NEB "work to hasten it on." For the first alternative, see JB "long for the Day of God to come."

The expression **the coming of the day of God** is unusual in two ways:

1. The word for **coming** is usually used in connection with a person, such as Christ or the Son of Man, but not with a day or a time. It does seem that this usage was a later development.

2. **The day of God** is used nowhere else with the same Greek terms in the New Testament. Here it seems to be used as a parallel for "the day of the Lord" in verse 10. If this is the case, it is possible to translate the two expressions in the same way; and this is especially important for languages where the same word is used for both "Lord" and "God." However, the distinction can be maintained, in which case the focus of **the day of God** would be the function of God as judge, hence "the day when God will judge the world."

It is possible therefore to restructure the expression **the coming of the day of God** as "the day when God will come as judge" or "the day when God will come to judge the world." The sentence **waiting for and hastening the coming day of God** may be rendered as "as you wait for the day when God will come to judge the world, and do your best to make that day come soon." For ways to express "judge" see comments on "condemnation" and "judgment" in 2.3,4 and Jude 15.

Because of which (or "on account of which") expresses result or effect, which will follow on the coming of the day of God (see, for example, TNT "That Day will cause," NEB "that day will set . . . ."). In many cases this is simply stated as something that happens at that time: TEV "the Day when," Phps "This day will mean." What the expression seems to stress is that the calamities at that time will not be due to natural causes but to divine action. So in a real sense it is not the day that causes these things to happen, but God. This is important in view of contemporary Greek philosophy, which believed that nature acts by itself, and that events happen according to a natural pattern.

Kindled recalls "stored up for fire" in verse 7, although here it is the heavens that will be burned up. For **dissolved, elements,** and **fire,** see comments on verse 10. The word for **melt** appears only here in the New Testament; in the Old Testament Greek Septuagint it is used to describe the melting of the mountains on the day of the Lord (for example, Isa 63.19 [Septuagint; RSV 64.1]; Micah 1.4). See also comments on verse 10.

An alternative translation model for this verse is:

> . . . as you wait for the day when God will come to judge the world, and do your best to make that day come soon. That day is the one when fire will burn up and destroy the heavens, and heat will melt the heavenly bodies.

3.13   RSV   TEV

But according to his promise we wait | But we wait for what God has prom-
for new heavens and a new earth in | ised: new heavens and a new earth,
which righteousness dwells. | where righteousness will be at home.

The destruction of creation described in verses 10 and 12 pictures a return to chaos, disorder, and lifelessness. Verse 13, however, talks about a new creation to replace the old creation that will be destroyed. Whether this is an entirely new creation or a renewal of creation will depend on our interpretation of the previous verses, especially the last part of verse 10.

His refers to God. The **promise** referred to is probably Isa 65.17 or 66.22, or both. For **heavens** see comments on verses 5 and 10 above.

We includes the writer and all his readers. One possible translation is "we Christians."

Righteousness may be "justice" or "goodness," but it is probably better taken as living according to God's demands, doing God's will. **Righteousness** here is personified, that is, it is spoken of as acting like a person; this may not be natural in some languages, and therefore the clause may need to be restructured; for example, "people everywhere will live according to God's will." **Dwells** describes both constancy and naturalness, that is, it will be part of the nature of people to live righteously. Translations find different ways of capturing the intent of the idiom **righteousness dwells**; for example, NEB "the home of justice," AT "uprightness will prevail."

An alternative translation model for this verse is:

> But we Christians wait for the new heavens and new earth that God has promised (to bring into being), where people everywhere will live according to God's will (do what God wants them to do).

3.14   RSV   TEV

Therefore, beloved, since you wait | And so, my friends, as you wait for
for these, be zealous to be found by him | that Day, do your best to be pure and
without spot or blemish, and at peace. | faultless in God's sight and to be at
| peace with him.

Therefore connects this verse with the verses before it, primarily with the thought of the day of the Lord and the resulting end of the existing creation. For comments on **beloved** see Jude verse 3.

Since you wait for these translates a participial phrase that can be interpreted either in a temporal sense, as in TEV "as," or as expressing reason, **since**, as in RSV and NIV. Some translations can be understood in an ambiguous way, like NEB "With this to look forward to." For **wait** see comments on verse 12. **These** is translated "that Day" by TEV rather than as "these things."

Either interpretation is possible in this context. **These** things will happen on the day when God judges the world.

Be zealous is the same verb translated "hastening" in verse 12. It may also be "do your best" (TEV), "make every effort," "do your utmost," "make certain," "strive," "be diligent." The word speaks of intense effort. For further comment see 1.10.

To be found translates a verb which is the basis of "may be found" in verse 10. Some take this as an argument for regarding "may be found" as the preferred reading in that verse; however, this is not as decisive as it looks, since it is possible that the present verse may have been read back into verse 10. **To be found** may also be expressed as "that God may find you . . ." or "that God may see that you are . . . ."

By him may also be translated as "in him," "in his sight," or "with him." The phrase can refer to Christ, but more likely God is meant, as in TEV "in God's sight."

Without spot or blemish is taken from the vocabulary of the Jewish sacrificial system. These are the characteristics of animals that are acceptable as sacrifices. For **without spot**, see comments on Jude 24. This form of the word for **without . . . blemish** is used only here in the New Testament; in ordinary Greek it is used in an ethical sense, hence "morally blameless." The two terms taken together compare Christians to perfect sacrificial animals and characterize Christian life as morally faultless and ethically irreproachable.

Peace may be interpreted as a state characterized by serenity, tranquility, contentment and freedom from trouble, or right relationship with one another, or more likely, right relationship with God. The third interpretation is reflected in TEV (so also NEB, NIV).

The Greek words in this clause (literally, "strive to be spotless and blameless in him [or, by him] to be found in peace") can be put in different orders, depending on the meaning that the translator wants to bring out. Among the possibilities are the following:
1. "Strive to be found by him spotless and blameless and in peace." This is the meaning reflected in RSV.
2. "Strive to be found at peace with him, spotless and blameless in his sight." This is the meaning reflected in TEV.
3. "Strive to be spotless and blameless, so that you will be found by him to be at peace." This is the meaning reflected in JB, "do your best to live lives without spot or stain so that he will find you at peace."

Alternative translation models for this verse, following the three possible interpretations mentioned above, are:

(1) Therefore, my friends, as you wait for the day when God will judge the world, you must do your best to have him find you pure and faultless and with peaceful hearts.

(2) Therefore, my friends . . . you must do your best to have him find you pure and faultless and at peace with him.

(3) Therefore, my friends . . . you must do your best to be pure and faultless, so that God see that you are living at peace (with peaceful hearts) when he comes.

3.15a   RSV   TEV

And count the forbearance of our Lord   Look on our Lord's patience as the
as salvation.   opportunity he is giving you to be
                                               saved,

Count may be rendered as "think about" or "consider." "Look on" (TEV) is an idiom that may be too difficult, and translating it literally should not be attempted.

The forbearance of our Lord recalls verse 9. **Lord** is again ambiguous, referring either to God or to Christ; in the light of verse 9, perhaps God is meant here, but Christ is also possible. **Salvation** primarily refers to deliverance from judgment at the end of the age and the gift of blessedness as a result of fellowship with God. For further comment see 1.1 ("Savior") and 1.4 ("divine nature"). The whole expression defines the purpose of God's patience, that is, it gives people the opportunity to repent and to receive salvation. TEV makes this clear: "Look on our Lord's patience as the opportunity he is giving you to be saved." In certain languages **salvation** will require mentioning a specific danger from which one is saved; for example, "salvation from judgment." Or the whole expression may be restructured as follows: "as the way he is providing you to escape from the coming judgment."

A mention of Paul and his letters as supporting the above ideas
3.15b-16

RSV   TEV

15b So also our beloved brother Paul wrote to   15 just as our dear brother Paul wrote to you,
you according to the wisdom given him,   using the wisdom that God gave him. 16 This
16 speaking of this as he does in all his letters. is what he says in all his letters when he
There are some things in them hard to under-   writes on the subject. There are some difficult
stand, which the ignorant and unstable twist   things in his letters which ignorant and unsta-
to their own destruction, as they do the other   ble people explain falsely, as they do with
scriptures.   other passages of the Scriptures. So they bring
                                                   on their own destruction.

Translators using the Handbook outline as a guide for section headings may prefer to say something more simple, such as "The apostle Paul and his letters."

3.15b   RSV   TEV

So also our beloved brother Paul wrote   just as our dear brother Paul wrote to
to you according to the wisdom given   you, using the wisdom that God gave
him,   him.

The apostle Paul is now brought into the argument to give support to the ideas just expressed. It is not clear, however, what **So also** refers to. It can refer either to what comes immediately before, namely, the relation between the Lord's patience and salvation, or, less likely, to all of verses 14 and 15. Paul is described as **our beloved brother**, which is obviously a term of endearment; **brother** has the general meaning of "fellow believer" and the special meaning of "fellow worker," that is, a colleague in the Christian ministry. If the former is meant, then **our** has to be interpreted as inclusive, meaning "all of us Christians." However, if the special meaning "fellow worker" is intended, then **our** would be interpreted as exclusive, that is, "we the apostles." It is more likely that the inclusive sense is intended. Paul is further described as one who **wrote to you**, that is, to the readers of 2 Peter. **Wrote to you** may also be expressed as "wrote to you in a letter."

According to the wisdom given him is a divine passive, and God is certainly meant as the source of wisdom; this gives real importance to Paul's letters and raises them to the level of Scripture. In many languages this divine passive construction may have to be abandoned in favor of mentioning God as the source and giver of this wisdom; for example, "according to the wisdom that God has given him" or "according to the wisdom that he received from God." **Wisdom** is not simply knowledge; it includes the application of such knowledge to life. **Wisdom** as the gift to writers inspired by God is found in a few writings at that time. Which letter of Paul is referred to is not indicated; many suggestions have been put forward, such as 1 Thessalonians, which deals with the problem of the Parousia, or Romans, which deals with the new creation. Fortunately for translators, we don't have to be sure of this information in order to translate meaningfully, since it is not necessary to identify which letter of Paul is meant.

Alternative translation models for this verse are:

(1) Think about (consider) our Lord's patience as the way he is providing for you to escape from the coming judgment, just as Paul, our beloved fellow-believer, wrote in a letter to you, using the wisdom that God gives him.

(2) Think about how our Lord shows patience . . . This is what Paul our beloved colleague wrote about in a . . . .

3.16   RSV   TEV

speaking of this as he does in all his letters. There are some things in them hard to understand, which the ignorant and unstable twist to their own destruction, as they do the other scriptures.	This is what he says in all his letters when he writes on the subject. There are some difficult things in his letters which ignorant and unstable people explain falsely, as they do with other passages of the Scriptures. So they bring on their own destruction.

The meaning of **this** is dependent on how we take "So also" in the previous verse. **All his letters** seems to suggest that Peter knew several of Paul's letters; it may even indicate that at that time there was already in existence a collection of Paul's letters. Paul of course wrote to particular Christian communities and to individuals; later on his letters were collected and bound together and were made available to the Christian communities at that time. Another possible rendering is "This is what he talks about in all his letters."

The description of Paul's letters as difficult is definitely borne out by the collection of them that we have. Not that all of his letters are of this nature, but **some things in them** are **hard to understand.** This expression translates a rare Greek word used of writings that are difficult to interpret. This characteristic of Paul's letters is mentioned with a purpose: it explains how they can be misused by people. Here the **ignorant** and the **unstable** are singled out as "twisting" the contents of Paul's letters. **Ignorant** translates a word used nowhere else in the New Testament. It means not simply ignorant but "unlearned," "uneducated," "uninstructed," and is used primarily of people who have not received sufficient instruction in the interpretation of scripture, and who are therefore prone to error. **Unstable** on the other hand describes those who are not firmly rooted in the teachings of the Christian faith and are therefore easily misled. The same word is used in 2.14, where it is translated as "unsteady" (TEV "weak"). Whether it is the false teachers who are being referred to here or believers who have been misled by these false teachers is not at all clear. In 2.14 it is those who are ensnared by the false teachers who are described as "unsteady." So perhaps it is also these same people who are referred to in this verse. However, it may be more natural to speak of the false teachers as "twisting" Paul's ideas. The word used here is literally "to twist," "to torture," "to dislocate" (as in dislocating the limbs of a person on a rack), and is an appropriate word to describe the act of distorting or misinterpreting the Scriptures through faulty methods of interpretation. There are various ways of translating this term; for example, NEB "misinterpret," JB "distort," TEV "explain falsely," TNT "pervert." Whether the followers of the false teachers are capable of deliberately perverting the meaning of Paul's ideas is debatable.

This act of distortion is not limited to Paul's letters but includes **the other scriptures. Scriptures** is literally "writings," but in this context as well as in other contexts, the term is used to describe writings that are accepted as authoritative by the believing community and suitable for various functions within the community, including worship, proclamation, nurture, and apologetics or defense of the faith. **Other** marks the letters of Paul as part of this collection of authoritative writings. It is very likely that the whole Old Testament is also included in this category. However, it is difficult to be sure as to what else is being described as **scriptures**. It must be kept in mind that at that time a definitive list of authoritative books had not yet been fixed but was in the process of formation. Many writings that are now excluded from the present list of biblical books were at one time or another regarded as authoritative by the Christian community. It was only very much later that a definitive list of twenty-seven books for the New Testament was fixed. In view of all this it probably is not possible to determine the actual content of the authoritative writings that Peter is referring to; this, however, does not reduce the importance of the phrase, since it shows that an authoritative collection started to evolve very early in the history of the Christian church. **Scriptures** may also be expressed as "holy writings." The phrase **as they do with the other scriptures** can be expressed in many languages as "as they do with other parts of the holy writings."

The result of all this misinterpretation is the **destruction** of those who are involved in such distortions. **Destruction** here should be understood not in a physical but in a spiritual sense, and includes loss of salvation and subjection to God's punishment. **To their own destruction** may also be expressed as "and so cause themselves to be destroyed" or "and so cause themselves to suffer (receive) destruction."

It should be noted that in RSV **to their own destruction** is placed immediately after **twist**, whereas in TEV it is placed at the end of the verse and is marked clearly as a result of distortion of scripture.

Closing doxology
3.17-18

RSV	TEV
17 You therefore, beloved, knowing this beforehand, beware lest you be carried away with the error of lawless men and lose your own stability. 18 But grow in the grace and knowledge of our Lord and Savior Jesus Christ. To him be the glory both now and to the day of eternity. Amen.	17 But you, my friends, already know this. Be on your guard, then, so that you will not be led away by the errors of lawless people and fall from your safe position. 18 But continue to grow in the grace and knowledge of our Lord and Savior Jesus Christ. To him be the glory, now and forever! Amen.

Translators who use the Handbook outline for providing section headings may say "Closing doxology," or else "Praise to God," or more fully, "Peter praises God for helping the Christians."

3.17	RSV	TEV
	You therefore, beloved, knowing this beforehand, beware lest you be carried	But you, my friends, already know this. Be on your guard, then, so that

away with the error of lawless men and
lose your own stability.

you will not be led away by the errors
of lawless people and fall from your
safe position.

Here again Peter addresses his readers directly, spelling out for them the consequences of what he has just said regarding the distortion and misinterpretation of scripture. Once again he addresses his readers with the intimate term **beloved**. RSV retains the Greek form here and begins the verse with **You therefore**. It is clear from the context, however, that Peter is contrasting the attitude of the people he mentions in verse 16 with that of his own readers; therefore beginning the verse as TEV does ("But you") is much more appropriate.

Knowing this beforehand may also be expressed as "know in advance," hence TEV "you . . . already know this." It is possible that what is meant by **this** is the content of the present letter; it is more likely, however, this **this** refers to what has been mentioned in the last part of verse 16, namely, that people destroy themselves by misinterpreting scripture.

Beware is literally "to guard" and is a term that has its origin in the military. It includes a sense of being on guard, watching out, being very careful, taking extra precaution. **Carried away** is literally "led away" in a negative sense; in this context it can be rendered as "to be overwhelmed," "to be seduced," "to succumb," "to be lured." **Lest** is no longer used very much in contemporary English; it is an expression that introduces a negative purpose. So **Lest you** (RSV) is equivalent to "so that you will not" (TEV). **Lest you be carried away** may also be expressed as "so that lawless people do not lead you astray."

Error recalls the previous verse, particularly the misinterpretation of the meaning of Paul's ideas and the consequences of such distortions. **Lawless** was used to describe the people of Sodom in 2.7; here it gives a picture of the false teachers and their followers going beyond the restraints and limits of Christian moral and ethical teaching, hence "unprincipled" (Phps).

Lose is literally "fall" (TEV) with the idea of losing or being separated from something. **Stability** is the opposite of the term "unstable" in the previous verse. The Greek word describes not an abstract state or quality ("steadfastness") but a firm, stable position, as that of a mountain or a large rock, for example. So JB has "the firm ground that you are standing on," and Phps "your proper foothold."

An alternative translation model for this verse is:

> But you, friends, are already aware of this. Be very careful then, that lawless people will not lead you astray with their false teachings and you fall from your present stable condition.

166

3.18   RSV   TEV

But grow in the grace and knowledge of our Lord and Savior Jesus Christ. To him be the glory both now and to the day of eternity. Amen.	But continue to grow in the grace and knowledge of our Lord and Savior Jesus Christ. To him be the glory, now and forever! Amen.

The letter ends very appropriately with a doxology, or expression of praise. The first part (**grow in the grace and knowledge of our Lord and Savior Jesus Christ)** recalls previous parts of the letter: **grace** recalls 1.2; **knowledge** recalls 1.5 and 1.8; **our Lord and Savior Jesus Christ** recalls 1.1, 1.8, and 1.11. **Grace** of course originates from and is given by Jesus Christ; **knowledge** may also be taken as knowledge imparted by Jesus Christ, although it is much more likely that this refers to the deeper understanding of the believers as they continue to study and meditate on the Good News of Jesus Christ. **Grow** is significant; it emphasizes the fact that it is not enough to refrain from being carried away or from losing your firm footing. More important than not falling is making a steady progress in your faith. The verb here is a present imperative, giving the sense of continuous action, as in TEV "continue to grow." Another translation model for the first part of this verse is "But you should continue to experience more and more of the love and mercy of our Lord and Savior Jesus Christ, and grow in your understanding of him."

The concluding expression of praise is unusual in that it is addressed to Jesus Christ, whereas usually such praises are addressed to God. It should be noted, however, that in this letter God and Jesus Christ are given the same titles and attributes, such as "Savior" (1.1,11; 2.20; 3.2,15), "divine" (1.3,4). **Glory** can be honor or greatness, but in the context of this doxology is better taken as "praise." **The day of eternity** is also unique in the New Testament, where the usual expression would be "forever." Perhaps this is a reference to the day of the Parousia, which is thought of as lasting forever. The actual phrase **day of eternity** occurs in Sirach 18.10: "Like a drop of water from the sea and a grain of sand, so are a few years among the days of eternity" (NRSV).

For **Amen** see comments on Jude verse 25.

It has been noted by some scholars that this concluding verse of 2 Peter blends beautifully Greek, Jewish, and Christian ideas and expressions. It is therefore a fitting conclusion to the letter, which as we have seen uses Greek and Jewish ideas and transforms them into appropriate vehicles of the Christian message. In this way this letter presents Christians of later generations, even today, with a model of how the wealth of various cultures can be appropriated for the Christian faith without sacrificing or compromising its truths and its demands.

Selected Bibliography

Texts

The Greek New Testament. 3rd edition (corrected), 1983. K. Aland, M. Black, C.M. Martini, B.M. Metzger, and A. Wikgren, editors. Stuttgart: United Bible Societies.

Novum Testamentum Graece. 26th edition, 1979; corrected, 1981. Erwin Nestle and Kurt Aland, editors. Stuttgart: Deutsche Bibelgesellschaft.

Versions

Die Bibel in heutigem Deutsch: Die Gute Nachricht des Alten und Neuen Testaments. 1982. Stuttgart: Deutsche Bibelgesellschaft. (Cited as German common language version, GECL.)

The Bible: A New Translation. 1925. Translated by James Moffatt. New York: Harper and Brothers; London: Hodder and Stoughton. (Cited as Mft.)

La Bible en français courant. 1982. Paris: Alliance Biblique Universelle. (Cited as French common language version, FRCL.)

Bible for Today's Family: New Testament. Contemporary English Version. 1991. New York: American Bible Society. (Cited as CEV.)

The Complete Bible: An American Translation. 1923. Translated by J.M. Powis Smith and Edgar Goodspeed. Chicago: University of Chicago Press. (Cited as AT.)

Dios Habla Hoy: La Biblia con Deuterocanonicos. Version Popular. 1979. New York: Sociedades Biblicas Unidas. (Cited as Spanish common language version, SPCL.)

Good News Bible: The Bible in Today's English Version. 1976, 1979. New York: American Bible Society. (Cited as TEV.)

The Holy Bible (Authorized or King James Version). 1611. (Cited as KJV.)

Holy Bible: A Translation from the Latin Vulgate in Light of the Hebrew and Greek Originals. 1950. Translated by Ronald Knox. New York: Sheed and Ward. (Cited as Knox.)

The Holy Bible: New International Version. 1978. Grand Rapids, Michigan: Zondervan Bible Publishers; and London: Hodder and Stoughton. (Cited as NIV.)

The Holy Bible: New Revised Standard Version. 1989. New York: Division of Christian Education of the National Council of the Churches of Christ in the United States of America. (Cited as NRSV.)

The Holy Bible: Revised Standard Version. 1952, 1971, 1973. New York: Division of Christian Education of the National Council of the Churches of Christ in the United States of America. (Cited as RSV.)

The Jerusalem Bible. 1966. London: Darton, Longman & Todd. (Cited as JB.)

The Living Bible. 1971. Translated by Kenneth Taylor. Wheaton, Illinois: Tyndale House.

The New American Bible. 1970. Camden, New Jersey: Thomas Nelson. (Cited as NAB.)

The New American Bible: Revised New Testament. 1988. Northport, New York: Costello; and Grand Rapids, Michigan: Eerdmans.

The New English Bible. Second edition, 1970. London: Oxford University Press and Cambridge University Press. (Cited as NEB.)

The New Jerusalem Bible. 1985. Garden City, New York: Doubleday.

The New Testament: A New Translation. Volume 2: The Letters and the Revelation. 1968. Translated by William Barclay. London and New York: Collins. (Cited as Brc.)

The New Testament in Modern English. 1972. Translated by J.B. Phillips. New York: Macmillan. (Cited as Phps.)

The Translator's New Testament. 1973. London: British and Foreign Bible Society. (Cited as TNT.)

Lexicons

Arndt, William F., and F. Wilbur Gingrich. Second edition, 1979. *A Greek-English Lexicon of the New Testament and Other Early Christian*

Literature. Revised and augmented by F. Wilbur Gingrich and Frederick W. Danker. Chicago and London: University of Chicago Press.

Louw, Johannes P., and Eugene A. Nida. 1988. *Greek-English Lexicon of the New Testament: Based on Semantic Domains.* 2 volumes. New York: United Bible Societies.

An invaluable tool for determining the meaning of words and their relationship with other words that have related meanings.

Commentaries

Barnett, A.E., and E.G. Homrighausen. 1957. "The Second Epistle of Peter" and "The Epistle of Jude." In *The Interpreter's Bible,* volume 12, pages 161-206, 315-343. New York: Abingdon.

Good brief commentary and exposition. No knowledge of Greek required.

Bauckham, Richard J. 1983. *Jude, 2 Peter* (Word Biblical Commentary 50). Waco, Texas: Word Books.

A very good commentary. But translators may have to search through a lot of material to find what they want. Knowledge of Greek is necessary.

Bigg, Charles. Second edition, 1902. *An Exegetical and Critical Commentary on the Epistles of St. Peter and St. Jude* (International Critical Commentary). Edinburgh: T. & T. Clark.

A complete exegetical and expository commentary. Very technical. Knowledge of Greek required.

Bratcher, Robert G. 1984. *A Translator's Guide to the Letters from James, Peter, and Jude* (Helps for Translators). London, New York, Stuttgart: United Bible Societies.

Brief relevant comments for translators. Good model translations. Knowledge of Greek is not required.

Elliott, John H. 1982. *1–2 Peter/Jude* (Augsburg Commentary on the New Testament). Minneapolis, Minnesota: Augsburg.

Based on the translation of Moffatt. Commentary is good but somewhat brief. No knowledge of Greek is required.

Mayor, J.B. 1961. "The General Epistle of Jude." In *The Expositor's Greek New Testament,* volume 5, pages 209-278. Grand Rapids, Michigan: Eerdmans.

> Commentary on the Greek Text. Some notes quite useful. Knowledge of Greek is required.

Sidebottom, E.M. 1967. *James, Jude, 2 Peter* (The New Century Bible Commentary). Grand Rapids, Michigan: Eerdmans; and London: Marshal, Morgan and Scott.

> RSV text included. Comments are concise but good. Knowledge of Greek is not required.

Strachen, R.H., and J.B. Mayor. 1961. "The Second Epistle General of Peter." In *The Expositor's Greek New Testament,* volume 5, pages 81-148. Grand Rapids, Michigan: Eerdmans.

> Commentary on the Greek Text. Some notes quite useful. Knowledge of Greek is required.

Other Works

Charlesworth, James H., editor. 1986. *Old Testament Pseudepigrapha.* Two volumes. Garden City, New York: Doubleday.

> In this volume may be found many of the writings said to be prepared, for example, by patriarchs or prophets, but written many years after the supposed author had died. Included, for example, are the Testament of Levi (and testaments of the other sons of Jacob) and 1 Enoch.

Goodspeed, Edgar J., translator. 1950. *The Apostolic Fathers: An American Translation.* New York: Harper & Brothers.

> The first and second letters of Clement of Rome are included here, as well as other writings of early Christian leaders who are said to have known the apostles personally and learned from them.

Josephus, Flavius. 1987. *The Works of Josephus: Complete and Unabridged.* New updated edition. Translated by William Whiston. Peabody, Mass.: Hendrickson.

Glossary

This Glossary contains terms that are technical from an exegetical or a linguistic viewpoint. Other terms not defined here may be referred to in a Bible dictionary.

ABSTRACT noun is one which refers to a quality or characteristic, such as "beauty" or "darkness."

ACTIVE. See **VOICE**.

ACTOR. See **AGENT**.

ADJECTIVE is a word which limits, describes, or qualifies a noun. In English, "red," "tall," "beautiful," and "important" are adjectives.

ADVERB is a word which limits, describes, or qualifies a verb, an adjective, or another adverb. In English, "quickly," "soon," "primarily," and "very" are adverbs.

ADVERSATIVE describes something opposed to or in contrast with something already stated. "But" and "however" are adversative conjunctions that introduce an adversative **CLAUSE**, for example.

AGENT is that which accomplishes the action in a sentence or clause, regardless of whether the grammatical construction is active or passive. In "John struck Bill" (active) and "Bill was struck by John" (passive), the agent in either case is John.

AMBIGUOUS (AMBIGUITY) describes a word or phrase which in a specific context may have two or more different meanings. For example, "Bill did not leave because John came" could mean either (1) "the coming of John prevented Bill from leaving" or (2) "the coming of John was not the cause of Bill's leaving." It is often the case that what is ambiguous in written form is not ambiguous when actually spoken, since features of intonation and slight pauses usually make clear which of two or more meanings is intended. Furthermore, even in written discourse, the entire context normally serves to indicate which meaning is intended by the writer.

GLOSSARY

AORIST refers to a set of forms in Greek verbs which denote an action completed without the implication of continuance or duration. Usually, but not always, the action is considered as completed in past time.

APPOSITION is the placing of two expressions together so that they both refer to the same object, event, or concept; for example, "my friend, Mr. Smith."

ARTICLE is a grammatical class of words, often obligatory, which indicate whether the following word is definite or indefinite. In English the **DEFINITE ARTICLE** is "the," and the **INDEFINITE ARTICLE** is "a" or "an."

CASE is the syntactical relation of a noun, pronoun, or adjective to other words in a sentence.

CAUSATIVE (**CAUSAL**) relates to events and indicates that someone or something caused something to happen, rather than that the person or thing did it directly. In "John ran the horse," the verb "ran" is a causative, since it was not John who ran, but rather it was John who caused the horse to run.

CHIASTIC describes a reversal of words or phrases in an otherwise parallel construction. For example: "I (1) / was shapen (2) / in iniquity (3) // in sin (3) / did my mother conceive (2) / me (1)."

CLAUSE is a grammatical construction, normally consisting of a subject and a predicate. An **INDEPENDENT CLAUSE** may stand alone. The **MAIN CLAUSE** is that clause in a sentence which could stand alone as a complete sentence, but which has one or more dependent or subordinate clauses related to it.

CLIMAX is the point in a discourse, such as a story or speech, which is the most important, or the turning point, or the point of decision.

COMMAND. See **IMPERATIVE**.

COMPARATIVE refers to the form of an adjective or adverb that indicates that the object or event described possesses a certain quality to a greater or lesser degree than does another object or event. "Richer" and "smaller" are adjectives in the comparative degree, while "sooner" and "more quickly" are adverbs in the comparative degree. See also **SUPERLATIVE**.

COMPLEX SENTENCE contains at least one modifying clause in addition to the main clause.

COMPONENTS are the parts or elements which go together to form the whole of an object. For example, the components of bread are flour, salt, shortening, yeast, and water. In a similar way, the phrases, words, and other elements in a sentence may be considered its components.

CONDITION is that which shows the circumstance under which something may be true. In English, a **CONDITIONAL** phrase or clause is usually introduced by "if."

CONNECTIVE is a word or phrase which connects other words, phrases, clauses, etc.

CONSTRUCTION. See **STRUCTURE**.

CONTEXT is that which precedes and/or follows any part of a discourse. For example, the context of a word or phrase in Scripture would be the other words and phrases associated with it in the sentence, paragraph, section, and even the entire book in which it occurs. The context of a term often affects its meaning, so that a word does not mean exactly the same thing in one context that it does in another context.

CULTURE (**CULTURAL**) is the sum total of the beliefs, patterns of behavior, and sets of interpersonal relations of any group of people. A culture is passed on from one generation to another, but undergoes development or gradual change.

DATIVE in Greek and certain other languages is the case which indicates the indirect or more remote object of the action or influence expressed by a verb, or the instrument used to perform the action of the verb, or the location where the action occurs. Dative is generally indicated in English by prepositions such as "to," "for," "with," "at," etc.

DECLARATIVE refers to forms of a verb or verb phrase which indicate statements assumed to be certain; for example, "prepared" in "She prepared a meal." Such a statement is, for example, declarative rather than imperative or interrogative.

DEFINITE ARTICLE. See **ARTICLE**.

DEPENDENT CLAUSE is a grammatical construction consisting normally of a subject and predicate, which is dependent upon or embedded within some other construction. For example, "if he comes" is a dependent clause in the sentence "If he comes, we'll have to leave." See **CLAUSE**.

DIRECT QUOTATION. See **DISCOURSE**.

DIVINE PASSIVE is the use of the passive form of a verb in order to avoid mentioning God or the name of God. For example, "You will be blessed" uses the passive "be blessed" but may be understood to mean "God will bless you." See also **VOICE, PASSIVE**.

DOXOLOGY is a hymn or other expression of praise to God, typically in a heightened or poetic literary form.

EMBEDDED CLAUSE is a dependent clause inserted within the structure of another clause, as in "The houses, many of which are old, needed repair."

EMOTIVE refers to one or more of the emotions (anger, joy, fear, gratitude, etc.). The emotive impact of a discourse is its effect on the emotions of the person(s) to whom it is addressed.

EMPHASIS (EMPHATIC) is the special importance given to an element in a discourse, sometimes indicated by the choice of words or by position in the sentence. For example, in "Never will I eat pork again," "Never" is given emphasis by placing it at the beginning of the sentence.

ESCHATOLOGICAL refers to the end of the world and the events connected with it. In this connection, the "world" is understood in various ways by various persons.

EUPHEMISM is a mild or indirect term used in the place of another term which is felt to be impolite, distasteful, or vulgar; for example, "to pass away" is a euphemism for "to die."

EVENT is a semantic category of meanings referring to actions, processes, etc., in which objects can participate. In English, most events are grammatically classified as verbs ("run," "grow" "think," etc.), but many nouns may also refer to events, as for example, "baptism," "song," "game," and "prayer."

EXAGGERATION is a figure of speech which states more than the speaker or writer intends to be understood. For example, "Everyone is doing it" may simply mean "Many people are doing it."

EXCLUSIVE first person plural excludes the person(s) addressed. That is, a speaker may use "we" to refer to himself and his companions, while specifically excluding the person(s) to whom he is speaking. See **INCLUSIVE**.

EXEGESIS (EXEGETICAL) is the process of determining the meaning of a text (or the result of this process), normally in terms of "who said what to whom under what circumstances and with what intent." A correct exegesis is indispensable before a passage can be translated correctly.

EXPLICIT refers to information which is expressed in the words of a discourse. This is in contrast to implicit information. See **IMPLICIT**.

FIGURE, FIGURATIVE EXPRESSION, or **FIGURE OF SPEECH** involves the use of words in other than their literal or ordinary sense, in order to bring out some aspect of meaning by means of comparison or association. For example, "raindrops dancing on the street," or "his speech was like thunder." **METAPHORS** and **SIMILES** are figures of speech.

FINITE VERB is any verb form which distinguishes person, number, tense, mode, or aspect. It is usually referred to in contrast to an **INFINITIVE** verb form, which indicates the action or state without specifying such things as agent or time. See **INFINITIVE**.

FIRST PERSON. See **PERSON**.

FOCUS is the center of attention in a discourse or in any part of a discourse.

FUTURE TENSE. See **TENSE**.

GENERAL. See **GENERIC**.

GENERIC has reference to a general class or kind of objects, events, or abstracts; it is the opposite of **PARTICULAR**. For example, the term "animal" is generic in relation to "dog," which is a particular kind of animal. However, "dog" is generic in relation to the more particular term "poodle."

GENITIVE case is a grammatical set of forms occurring in many languages, used primarily to indicate that a noun is the modifier of another noun. The genitive often indicates possession, but it may also indicate measure, origin, characteristic, as in "people of God," "pound of flour," "child's toy," or "Garden of Eden."

GRAMMATICAL refers to **GRAMMAR**, which includes the selection and arrangement of words in phrases, clauses, and sentences.

GREEKS, strictly speaking, were the inhabitants of Greece, corresponding to the Roman province of Achaia in New Testament times. In the New Testament, the term is used in a wider sense as referring to all those in the Roman Empire who spoke the Greek language and were strongly influenced by Greek culture. Frequently the term Greeks is used as synonymous with Gentiles.

HEBREW is the language in which the Old Testament was written. It belongs to the Semitic family of languages. By the time of Christ, many Jewish people no longer used Hebrew as their common language.

HENDIADYS is a figure in which a single complex idea is expressed by two words or structures, usually connected by a conjunction. For example, "weary and worn" may mean "very tired."

HYPERBOLE is a figure of speech that makes use of exaggeration. That is, a deliberate overstatement is made to create a special effect. For example, "John ate tons of rice for dinner."

IDIOM or **IDIOMATIC EXPRESSION** is a combination of terms whose meanings cannot be understood by adding up the meanings of the parts. "To hang one's head," "to have a green thumb," and "behind the eightball" are American English idioms. Idioms almost always lose their meaning or convey a wrong meaning when translated literally from one language to another.

IMPERATIVE refers to forms of a verb which indicate commands or requests. In "Go and do likewise," the verbs "Go" and "do" are imperatives. In most languages imperatives are confined to the grammatical second person; but some languages have corresponding forms for the first and third persons. These are usually expressed in English by the use of "must" or "let"; for example, "We must not swim here!" or "They must work harder!" or "Let them eat cake!"

IMPLICIT (IMPLIED) refers to information that is not formally represented in a discourse, since it is assumed that it is already known to the receptor, or evident from the meaning of the words in question. For example, the phrase "the other son" carries with it the implicit information that there is a son in addition to the one mentioned. This is in contrast to **EXPLICIT** information, which is expressly stated in a discourse. See **EXPLICIT**.

INCLUSIVE first person plural includes both the speaker and the one(s) to whom that person is speaking. See **EXCLUSIVE**.

INDEFINITE ARTICLE. See **ARTICLE**.

INFINITIVE is a verb form which indicates an action or state without specifying such factors as agent or time; for example, "to mark," "to sing," or "to go." It is in contrast to **FINITE VERB** form, which often distinguishes person, number, tense, mode, or aspect; for example "marked," "sung," or "will go."

INSTRUMENT (INSTRUMENTAL) is the object used in accomplishing an action. In the sentence "John opened the door with a key," the "key" is the instrument. See also **AGENT**.

INTERPRETATION of a text is the exegesis of it. See **EXEGESIS**.

IRONY is a sarcastic or humorous manner of discourse in which what is said is intended to express its opposite; for example, "That was a smart thing to do!" when intended to convey the meaning, "That was a stupid thing to do!"

LEVEL refers to the degree of difficulty characteristic of language usage by different constituencies or in different settings. A translation may, for example, be prepared for the level of elementary school children, for university students, for teen-agers, or for rural rather than urban people. Differences of level also are involved as to whether a particular discourse is formal, informal, casual, or intimate in nature.

LITERAL means the ordinary or primary meaning of a term or expression, in contrast with a figurative meaning. A **LITERAL TRANSLATION** is one which represents the exact words and word order of the source language; such a translation is frequently unnatural or awkward in the receptor language.

MAIN CLAUSE. See **CLAUSE**.

MANUSCRIPTS are books, documents, or letters written or copied by hand. Thousands of manuscript copies of various Old and New Testament books still exist, but none of the original manuscripts. **MANUSCRIPT EVIDENCE** is also called **TEXTUAL EVIDENCE**. See **TEXT, TEXTUAL**.

MARKERS (MARKING) are features of words or of a discourse which signal some special meaning or some particular structure. For example, words for speaking may mark the onset of direct discourse, a phrase such as "once upon a time" may mark the beginning of a fairy story, and certain features of parallelism are the dominant markers of poetry. The word "body" may require a marker to clarify whether a person, a group, or a corpse is meant.

METAPHOR is likening one object, event, or state to another by speaking of it as if it were the other; for example, "flowers dancing in the breeze" compares the movement of flowers with dancing. Metaphors are the most commonly used figures of speech and are often so subtle that a speaker or writer is not conscious of the fact that he or she is using figurative language. See **SIMILE**.

MOOD defines the psychological background of the action, and involves such categories as possibility, necessity, and desire. Some languages (for example, Greek) use specific verb forms to express mood.

NOUN is a word that names a person, place, thing, or idea, and often serves to specify a subject or topic of discussion.

NOUN PHRASE. See **PHRASE**.

OBJECT of a verb is the goal of an event or action specified by the verb. In "John hit the ball," the object of "hit" is "ball."

179

ONOMATOPOEIA (ONOMATOPOEIC) is the use or invention of words that imitate the sounds of what they refer to; for example, "swishing," "bang!" or "bubble."

OPTATIVE means expressing desire or choice, as in "May it not rain today!" This is indicated in some languages by certain verb forms.

PAPYRI (singular **PAPYRUS**) are, in the context of this Handbook, those texts of the Scriptures which were written originally on papyrus (an early form of paper) and which are representative of the earliest forms of the Greek text.

PARAGRAPH is a distinct segment of discourse dealing with a particular idea, and usually marked with an indentation on a new line.

PARALLEL generally refers to some similarity in the content and/or form of a construction; for example, "The man was blind, and he could not see." The structures that correspond to each other in the two statements are said to be parallel.

PARENTHETICAL STATEMENT is a statement that interrupts a discourse by departing from its main theme. It is frequently set off by marks of parenthesis ( ).

PARTICIPIAL indicates that the phrase, clause, construction, or other expression described is governed by a **PARTICIPLE**.

PARTICIPLE is a verbal adjective, that is, a word which retains some of the characteristics of a verb while functioning as an adjective. In "singing children" and "painted house," "singing" and "painted" are participles.

PARTICLE is a small word whose grammatical form does not change. In English the most common particles are prepositions and conjunctions.

PARTICULAR is the opposite of **GENERAL**. See **GENERIC**.

PASSAGE is the text of Scripture in a specific location. It is usually thought of as comprising more than one verse, but it can be a single verse or part of a verse.

PASSIVE. See **VOICE**.

PAST TENSE. See **TENSE**.

PERFECT tense is a set of verb forms which indicate an action already completed when another action occurs. The perfect tense in Greek also indicates that the action continues into the present.

PERSON, as a grammatical term, refers to the speaker, the person spoken to, or the person or thing spoken about. **FIRST PERSON** is the person(s) speaking (such as "I," "me," "my," "mine," "we," "us," "our," or "ours"). **SECOND PERSON** is the person(s) or thing(s) spoken to (such as "thou," "thee," "thy," "thine," "ye," "you," "your," or "yours"). **THIRD PERSON** is the person(s) or thing(s) spoken about (such as "he," "she," "it," "his," "her," "them," or "their"). The examples here given are all pronouns, but in many languages the verb forms have affixes which indicate first, second, or third person and also indicate whether they are **SINGULAR** or **PLURAL**.

PHRASE is a grammatical construction of two or more words, but less than a complete clause or a sentence. A phrase is usually given a name according to its function in a sentence, such as "noun phrase," "verb phrase," or "prepositional phrase."

PLAY ON WORDS in a discourse is the use of the similarity in the sounds of two words to produce a special effect.

PLURAL refers to the form of a word which indicates more than one. See **SINGULAR**.

POSSESSIVE PRONOUNS are pronouns such as "my," "our," "your," or "his," which indicate possession.

PREPOSITION is a word (usually a particle) whose function is to indicate the relation of a noun or pronoun to another noun, pronoun, verb, or adjective. Some English prepositions are "for," "from," "in," "to," and "with."

PRESENT TENSE. See **TENSE**.

PRONOUNS are words which are used in place of nouns, such as "he," "him," "his," "she," "we," "them," "who," "which," "this," or "these."

READ, READING, frequently refers to the interpretation of the written form of a text, especially under the following conditions: if the available text appears to be defective; or if differing versions of the same text are available; or if several alternative sets of vowels may be understood as correct in languages such as biblical Hebrew, in which only the consonants were written. See also **TEXT, TEXTUAL**.

RECEPTOR is the person(s) receiving a message. The **RECEPTOR LANGUAGE** is the language into which a translation is made. For example, in a translation from Hebrew into German, Hebrew is the source language and German is the receptor language.

RELATIVE PRONOUN is a pronoun which refers to a noun in another clause, and which serves to mark the subordination of its own clause to that noun; for example, in "This is the man who came to dinner," "who" is the relative pronoun referring to "the man" in the previous clause. The subordinated clause is also called a relative clause.

RENDER means translate or express in a language different from the original. **RENDERING** is the manner in which a specific passage is translated from one language to another.

RESTRUCTURE is to reconstruct or rearrange. See **STRUCTURE**.

RHETORICAL refers to forms of speech which are employed to highlight or make more attractive some aspect of a discourse. A **RHETORICAL QUESTION**, for example, is not a request for information but is a way of making an emphatic statement.

SARCASM is an ironical and frequently contemptuous manner of discourse in which what is said is intended to express its opposite; for example, "What a brilliant idea!" when intended to convey the meaning, "What a ridiculous idea!"

SECOND PERSON. See **PERSON**.

SENTENCE is a grammatical construction composed of one or more clauses and capable of standing alone.

SEPTUAGINT is a translation of the Hebrew Old Testament into Greek, begun some two hundred years before Christ. It is often abbreviated as LXX.

SIMILE (pronounced SIM-i-lee) is a **FIGURE OF SPEECH** which describes one event or object by comparing it to another, using "like," "as," or some other word to mark or signal the comparison. For example, "She runs like a deer," "He is as straight as an arrow." Similes are less subtle than metaphors in that metaphors do not mark the comparison with words such as "like" or "as." See **METAPHOR**.

SINGULAR refers to the form of a word which indicates one thing or person, in contrast to **PLURAL**, which indicates more than one. See **PLURAL**.

STRUCTURE is the systematic arrangement of the elements of language, including the ways in which words combine into phrases, phrases into clauses, clauses into sentences, and sentences into larger units of discourse. Because this process may be compared to the building of a house or bridge, such words as **STRUCTURE** and **CONSTRUCTION** are used in reference to it. To separate and rearrange the various components of a sentence or other unit of discourse in the translation process is to **RESTRUCTURE** it.

STYLE is a particular or a characteristic manner in discourse. Each language has certain distinctive **STYLISTIC** features which cannot be reproduced literally in another language. Within any language, certain groups of speakers may have their characteristic discourse styles, and among individual speakers and writers, each has his or her own style. Various stylistic devices are used for the purpose of achieving a more pleasing style. For example, synonyms are sometimes used to avoid the monotonous repetition of the same words, or the normal order of clauses and phrases may be altered for the sake of emphasis.

SUBJECT is one of the major divisions of a clause, the other being the predicate. In "The small boy walked to school," "The small boy" is the subject. Typically the subject is a noun phrase. It should not be confused with the semantic **AGENT**, or "actor."

SUFFIX is a letter or one or more syllables added to the end of a word, to modify the meaning in some manner. For example, "-s" suffixed to "tree" changes the word from singular to plural, "trees," while "-ing" suffixed to "sing" changes the verb to a participle, "singing."

SUPERLATIVE refers to the form of an adjective or adverb that indicates that the object or event described possesses a certain quality to a greater or lesser degree than does any other object or event implicitly or explicitly specified by the content. "Most happy" and "finest" are adjectives in the superlative degree. See also **COMPARATIVE**.

SYNONYMS are words which are different in form but similar in meaning, such as "boy" and "lad." Expressions which have essentially the same meaning are said to be **SYNONYMOUS**. No two words are completely synonymous.

TENSE is usually a form of a verb which indicates time relative to a discourse or some event in a discourse. The most common forms of tense are past, present, and future.

TEXTUAL refers to the various Greek manuscripts of the New Testament. A **TEXTUAL READING** is the form in which words occur in a particular manuscript (or group of manuscripts), especially where it differs from others. **TEXTUAL EVIDENCE** is the cumulative evidence for a particular reading. **TEXTUAL VARIANTS** are readings of the same passage that differ in one or more details.

THEME is the subject of a discourse.

THIRD PERSON. See **PERSON**.

TONE is the spirit, character, or emotional effect of a passage or discourse.

TRANSITION in discourse involves passing from one thought-section or group of related thought-sections to another.

TRANSLATION is the reproduction in a receptor language of the closest natural equivalent of a message in the source language, first, in terms of meaning, and second, in terms of style.

TRANSLATIONAL refers to translation. A translator may seem to be following an inferior textual reading (see **TEXTUAL**) when he is simply adjusting the rendering to the requirements of the receptor language, that is, for a **TRANSLATIONAL REASON**.

TRANSLITERATION is the representation in the receptor language of the approximate sounds or letters of words occurring in the source language, rather than translating their meaning; for example, "Amen" from the Hebrew, or the title "Christ" from the Greek.

VERBS are a grammatical class of words which express existence, action, or occurrence, such as "be," "become," "run," or "think."

VERBAL has two meanings. (1) It may refer to expressions consisting of words, sometimes in distinction to forms of communication which do not employ words ("sign language," for example). (2) It may refer to word forms which are derived from verbs. For example, "coming" and "engaged" may be called verbals, and participles are called verbal adjectives.

VERSIONS are translations. The ancient, or early, versions are translations of the Bible, or of portions of the Bible, made in early times; for example, the Greek Septuagint, the ancient Syriac, or the Ethiopic versions.

VOICE in grammar is the relation of the action expressed by a verb to the participants in the action. In English and many other languages, the **ACTIVE VOICE** indicates that the subject performs the action ("John hit the man"), while the **PASSIVE VOICE** indicates that the subject is being acted upon ("The man was hit").

VULGATE is the Latin version of the Bible translated and/or edited originally by Saint Jerome. It has been traditionally the official version of the Roman Catholic Church.

Index

This Index includes concepts, key words, and terms for which the Handbook contains a discussion useful for translators. Hebrew and Greek terms have been transliterated and occur in English alphabetical order.

PRINTED IN THE UNITED STATES OF AMERICA